Scott Gibbs

MICHEL FOUCAU

The

MICHEL FOUCAULT
The Will to Truth

◇

Alan Sheridan

TAVISTOCK PUBLICATIONS
London and New York

First published in 1980 by
Tavistock Publications Ltd
11 New Fetter Lane, London EC4P 4EE
Reprinted twice
Reprinted 1984

Published in the USA by
Tavistock Publications
in association with Methuen, Inc.
733 Third Avenue, New York, NY 10017

Printed in the United States of America

British Library Cataloguing in Publication Data

Sheridan, Alan
Michel Foucault.
1. *Foucault, Michel*
194   *B2430.F72*

ISBN 0–422–77350–6
ISBN 0–422–76570–8 *Pbk*

To Bruno Taddeo Sonzogni
baccalauro in gaya scienza

◇

Contents

◇

Author's Note

I refer to Foucault's works by their original French titles—I use
English titles only when referring to the translations as such. Each
quotation is followed by a note in brackets giving page references,
first to the French edition and, second, where available, to the English
translation. The titles are abbreviated to two or three capital letters.
Thus (HF, 21–2; MC, 10–12) refers the reader to pages 21–2 of *Histoire de
la folie* and to the corresponding passage in the translation, *Madness
and Civilization*. Full details of publication are provided in the
Bibliography. The following abbreviations of titles have been
adopted:

AK   *The Archaeology of Knowledge*
AS   *L'archéologie du savoir*
BC   *The Birth of the Clinic*
DP   *Discipline and Punish*
HF   *Histoire de la folie*
HJH *Hommage à Jean Hyppolite*
HS   *The History of Sexuality*, vol. 1, An Introduction
LCP *Language, Counter-Memory, Practice*
MC   *Les mots et les choses* (1st. ref.)
     Madness and Civilization (2nd. ref.)
MIP *Mental Illness and Psychology*
MMP *Maladie mentale et psychologie*
NC   *Naissance de la clinique*
OD   *L'ordre du discours*
OT   *The Order of Things*

Author's Note

PR   *Moi, Pierre Rivière . . .* (1st. ref.)
      I, Pierre Rivière . . . (2nd. ref.)
SP   *Surveiller et punir*
VS   *La volonté de savoir*

Interviews and articles quoted are preceded in the Bibliography by a number. This number is given in the bracketed note that follows the quotation itself, preceded by the letter 'B' (for Bibliography). Thus the reference B1, 751 refers to page 751 of the entry in the Bibliography preceded by the number 1.

I wish to thank Foucault's American and British publishers for permission to quote from the published translations. Excerpts from the following are reproduced by permission of Penguin Books Ltd: *Discipline and Punish: The Birth of the Prison*, © Editions Gallimard 1975, translation © Alan Sheridan; *La volonté de savoir*, translation in this volume, Alan Sheridan. Excerpts from the following are reproduced by permission of Pantheon Books, a Division of Random House, Inc.: *Madness and Civilization*, translation Richard Howard, © 1965 Random House, Inc.; *The Birth of the Clinic*, translation Alan Sheridan, © 1973 Tavistock Publications Ltd.; *The Archaeology of Knowledge and the Discourse on Language*, translation Alan Sheridan, © 1972 Tavistock Publications Ltd.; *Discipline and Punish: The Birth of the Prison*, translation Alan Sheridan, © 1977 Alan Sheridan; *The History of Sexuality*, Volume I, *An Introduction*, translation Robert Hurley, © 1978 Random House, Inc. I have taken the liberty, on occasion, of rewording the extracts quoted.

There is more ado to interpret the interpretations than to interpret the things, and there are more books upon books than upon any other subject. We do nothing but write glosses upon one another.

MICHEL DE MONTAIGNE

It may well be that we belong to an age of criticism whose lack of primary philosophy reminds us at every moment of its reign and its fatality: an age of intelligence that keeps us irremediably at a distance from an original language. . . We are doomed historically to history, to the patient construction of discourses about discourses, and to the task of hearing what has already been said.

MICHEL FOUCAULT

◇

Introduction

In an ideal world a book such as this would be unnecessary, indeed inconceivable; it would belong to the world of pale reflections. In the perfect world of Borges the only possible commentary would be the recopying by hand of the subject's collected works, but the conventions of our publishing industry forbid such an enterprise: an author is an altogether nobler thing than a scribe. And yet my aim is modest enough: to provide a guidebook, perhaps, profusely illustrated. Not so much, for guidebooks gain in usefulness. As the landscapes and monuments of which they speak alter and disappear, they attain by subtraction the additional status of fiction. Even the photographs say more with time. Like everything else, Foucault's books will no doubt change and finally disappear, but mine will not outlast them. Meanwhile, it must not take their place: rather it should create readers. I come not to bury beneath commentary, but to praise, as Erasmus praised Folly, by making room. In this, at least, my book will be original: few of his commentators allow him that. Even the favourably disposed seek the meaning *beneath* his gleaming words. But style is not an ornament: it cuts, to shape and to wound; it is a tool and a weapon—a stylus. So I make no apology for the length and frequency of my quotations and much of the rest is précis or disguised quotation. Even précis is a dangerous art: without quotation, it can be as lethal as commentary. It is not the letter that kills.

'Who is Foucault?' The question crops up less often than it used to. But people are still asking, with some justification, 'What is he?' If a thinker confines himself to a single, accepted discipline—as does a Lévi-Strauss to anthropology, a Lacan to psychoanalysis, an

1

Althusser to Marxist theory—one has at least a unified object, with recognizable limits and a recognizable history, against which one can assess his personal contribution. At the beginning of his career Foucault turned his back on two such disciplines, yet no one could say that he had founded a new one. 'Is he some kind of philosopher?' people ask. 'Well, yes, in a way,' one answers. 'He studied philosophy and has spent much of his adult life teaching it.' 'Then why does he write not about Plato, Descartes and Kant, but about the history of madness and medicine, prisons and sexuality?' 'Well, he is more of a historian than a philosopher, though his approach to his material is very different from that of a historian.' 'Ah, a historian of ideas!' 'Well, no. He has spent a lot of time and energy undermining the preconceptions and methods of the history of ideas. In fact, it was to distinguish what he was doing from the history of ideas that he coined the term "archaeology of knowledge".' 'The what?' . . . Foucault has occupied chairs of philosophy at a number of universities, but it was not until his election to the Collège de France in 1970 that he was able for the first time to provide his own description: he became 'Professor of the History of Systems of Thought'. One senses the effort that went into the exact choice and placing of the words. It sounds like a compromise solution arrived at by a committee, rather than the proud device of a great prose stylist.

'Do not ask who I am and do not ask me to remain the same,' he remarks in *L'archéologie du savoir*. 'Leave it to our bureaucrats and our police to see that our papers are in order' (AS, 28; AK, 17). At the risk of invading privacy, I offer a few, possibly irrelevant, details. Michel Foucault was born at Poitier in 1926. He was educated in local state schools until his father, a surgeon, dissatisfied with his son's progress, transferred him to a Catholic school, where he passed his *baccalauréat* with distinction. In a conversation, Foucault described his experience of the French educational system as a form of initiation in which the secret knowledge promised was always postponed to a later date. In the primary school he learned that the really important things would be revealed when he went to the *lycée*; at the *lycée* he found that he would have to wait until the *'classe de philo'* (the final year). There he was told that the secret of secrets was indeed to be found in the study of philosophy, but that this would only be revealed at the university stage, that the best place to find it was at the Sorbonne and that the holy of holies was the École Normale

2

Supérieure. So the end of the war in 1945 found Foucault in Paris, a boarder at the Lycée Henri IV, preparing the entrance examination for the holy of holies. The ENS is one of a number of *'grandes écoles'* where France trains its intellectual élite. Entry is by open competition and the successful pursue their studies at the University of Paris, while enjoying the additional privileges of board and special tuition. The role of the ENS is to produce teachers, and, in addition to their university *licence* (degree), its students prepare for the *agrégation*, a competitive examination for those who wish to teach in secondary or higher education. Foucault became a *normalien* and took his *licence de philosophie* in 1948.

In his Preface to the first edition of *Histoire de la folie*, Foucault pays tribute to three men who, in different ways, contributed to his intellectual formation: Jean Hyppolite, Georges Canguilhem, and Georges Dumézil. A more extended homage of the same three men appeared in his inaugural lecture at the Collège de France. Hyppolite was Foucault's philosophy teacher at Henri IV and at the Sorbonne and was later to become the head of the École Normale. His main work had been on Hegel and, in addition to a commentary, he had produced a remarkable translation of the *Phenomenology of Mind*. Foucault represents Hyppolite's relations with Hegel as a life-long struggle conducted on our behalf. Hyppolite pushed Hegel's philosophy to the limit: he tried to use it as a means of understanding the present and to make modernity the test of Hegelianism. He used other great figures of modern philosophy to challenge Hegel's hegemony—'Marx with the question of history, Fichte with the problem of the absolute beginning of philosophy, Bergson with the theme of contact with the non-philosophical, Kierkegaard with the problem of repetition and truth, Husserl with the theme of philosophy as an endless task bound up with the history of our rationality' (OD, 79)—but Hegel remained all pervasive. For Hyppolite, it was a relationship that thrived on difficulties, but brooked no serious threat. For Foucault, however, the promise of meaning held out by the dialectical triad was not fulfilled. Yet he was aware of the price of rejection, 'the extent to which Hegel, insidiously perhaps, is close to us . . . to which our anti-Hegelianism is possibly one of his tricks directed against us, at the end of which he stands, motionless, waiting for us' (OD, 74–5). His rejection of Hegel took the form, therefore, not of confrontation—Marx, Fichte, Bergson, Kierkegaard,

Husserl—but of circumvention, in the manner of the one thinker whose name is conspicuously absent from that list, Nietzsche.

Phenomenology, too, held a promise of meaning: how is my experience to be meaningful, how and on what basis is meaning to be constituted? A few years earlier Sartre had published *L'être et le néant* *(Being and Nothingness)* and there was much of Husserl in Sartrean 'existentialism'. For the French philosophy students of the late forties, Sartre represented what Gilles Deleuze has called 'our Outside', a breath of fresh air. Inside the lecture-hall it was above all Maurice Merleau-Ponty who conveyed the pure message of phenomenology. Like Hyppolite, he was much concerned with the question of how philosophical inquiry could be related to action, to political choice. Yet, curiously, in an intellectual world so heavily charged with politics, the theoretical problems of Marxism received little attention. The Communist Party had its ideologists, of course, but they made little impact in the Latin Quarter. Existentialism and phenomenology, with their premise of the individual subject's freedom of choice and their rejection of materialism as well as idealism, had done much to undermine Marxism as a tenable philosophical position. It was to be some years before Louis Althusser, through his classes at the École Normale, brought the problems of historical materialism back into the centre of French intellectual concern. Meanwhile, in a world that had known horrors as a matter of daily experience, and learned of still greater horrors after the event, it was action, not words that counted—a perhaps naïve, but certainly understandable view. Accordingly, it was not so much Marxist theory as the Party, an organization dedicated to action, that dominated the minds of French intellectuals—the reverse of the situation today. Many whose knowledge of Marxism was too sketchy to warrant acceptance or rejection found it quite natural to join the Party. Among them, for a time, was Foucault. Others, like Sartre or Merleau-Ponty, whose understanding of Marxism precluded party membership, saw themselves nevertheless as loyal allies. Criticism, especially of the Soviet Union, could safely be left to their enemies. The Party was the Party of the Working Class; it alone would bring Socialism; Socialism existed only in the Soviet Union. Doubts and questionings were objectively counter-revolutionary. The choice was clear.

Foucault's philosophical quest was coming to an end. There was, after all, no secret knowledge. The prospect of spending the rest of his life teaching philosophy appalled him. His aversion to the subject even extended to its practitioners; his friends were painters, writers, musicians, not philosophers. It was the world of experience, of the *vécu*, that fascinated him. Phenomenology, it seemed, was a poor attempt, on the part of minds capable of nothing but philosophy, to deal as best they could with that world. Foucault had no talent for painting or music but he never had any desire to be a writer either. He had sought the real world in political commitment. He was still a Communist, though increasingly aware that such 'commitment' was an act of faith rather than meaningful action, that the access to reality it offered was mythical rather than effective, that, in fact, there was little to choose between a branch meeting of the Party and a philosopy class. At this point, a new possibility opened up. Perhaps science, in particular the science of human behaviour, provided the true access for an intellectual to the real world. Two years after his *licence* in philosophy he took his *licence* in psychology. This was followed in 1952 by a Diplôme de Psycho-Patho-logie. During the next three years he continued his researches, spending long periods of time observing psychiatric practice in mental hospitals.

He gave classes in psycho-pathology at the École Normale and, in 1954, published a short book on the subject, *Maladie mentale et person-nalité*. It falls into two parts. The first is an able, succinct account of psychiatric theory. Definitions of such terms as hysteria, paranoia, neurosis, psychosis are paraded and the usual names—Hughlings Jackson, Janet, Kraepelin, Freud—appear. The second part is an attempt to situate the theme of mental illness in a social and historical perspective. By the time of writing, Foucault had broken with the Communists—this occurred in 1951. Paradoxically, however, the analysis of this second part is a straightforwardly Marxist one that culminates in a long exposition of Pavlovian and Soviet psychological theory. Mental illness is to be traced back to the individual's real conditions of development and, ultimately, to the 'contradictions' existing in his environment, but it is not to be confused with these pre-conditions. Mental illness itself is the immediate result of a dis-turbance to the balance in brain function of excitatory and inhibiting elements. The transition from the conflict in the social world to the disturbance of the organism is neither simple, nor immediate.

Materialism, in psycho-pathology, must therefore avoid two errors: that which consists in identifying the psychological, morbid conflict with the historical contradictions of the environment, and thus to confuse social alienation and mental alienation; and that, on the other hand, which consists in trying to reduce all mental illness to a disturbance of nervous functioning, whose mechanisms, though still unknown, might, in theory, be analysed from a purely physiological point of view (p. 106).

In this, as in so many passages of *Maladie mentale et personnalité*, there is a distinct sense of self-mutilation, of the professional setting all personal feeling aside as he dons his white coat. There is prose that is dull because it is the product of a dull or dulled mind—and there is prose that seems dull by a superhuman effort of the will. No one who did not know the book would guess that Foucault could have written such passages. It was only a matter of time before the straightjacket would snap and its wearer take his revenge. Very soon the search for scientific understanding proved as illusory as the philosophical quest. Foucault was in an impasse: there seemed no way forward. A student of outstanding brilliance, he abandoned an academic career in France and took the nearest thing to a holiday he could afford: he accepted a post in the French department of Uppsala University. Sweden did not turn out to be the social and sexual paradise that its reputation suggested, but he stayed there for four years. During that time he found his way forward: it was, in a sense, to retrace his steps. Science and philosophy had a common source in reason, in a reason that had set itself up as undisputed ruler of the mind and banished all forms of unreason. Reason, too, had its history, its genealogy. The task Foucault set himself was to go back to a time beyond Descartes and the mid-seventeenth century when men were happy to entertain within themselves dialogues between Reason and Folly. What was lacking in both university and hospital was to be found in the pages of Erasmus or on Shakespeare's stage. He began work on what was to become *Historie de la folie*. In 1958 Foucault left Uppsala for Warsaw, where he became Director of the French Institute. The following year he took up a similar post in Hamburg. There he completed his History of Madness. Foucault took the manuscript to Jean Hyppolite, who suggested that it be presented as a doctoral thesis. It could not, of course, pass as philosophy, but, under the aegis of Georges Canguilhem, it might be accepted as 'history of science'. It was awarded the *doctorat d'état*, the highest degree conferred by a French univer-

sity. His revenge complete, he made his peace with academic philosophy. In 1960 he returned to France to become head of the philosophy department at the University of Clermont-Ferrand, where he
remained for six years.

Meanwhile, *Maladie mentale et personnalité* had gone out of print.
A new edition was planned. Asked if he wished to make any altera-
tions, Foucault changed the title—to *Maladie mentale et psychologie*
and replaced the entire second part with new material. As a result, the
whole thesis of the book was turned on its head. Mental pathology
cannot be modelled on organic pathology, psychology cannot have
the same scientific status as physiology, 'mental illness' is not analogous to physical illness, but a changing, historically conditioned
notion. It is not just Foucault's book, but the whole conceptual basis
of psychiatry that is turned on its head, sabotaged from within, in the
name of its victims. The real heroes are not the sober, white-coated
scientists patiently pushing back the clouds of ignorance and painfully revealing, little by little, the true nature of madness, but rather
those literary 'madmen' who, repudiating the language of reason,
crossed over into the territory of 'unreason' and, in a language
beyond and prior to both, testified to an experience that lay, not
beyond the boundary of true humanity, but at its heart.

Madness, which had for so long been overt and unrestricted, which
had for so long been present on the horizon, disappeared. It
entered a phase of silence from which it was not to emerge for a
long time; it was deprived of its language; and although one continued to speak of it, it became impossible for it to speak of itself . . .
All this is not the gradual discovery of the true nature of madness,
but simply the sedimentation of what the history of the West had
made of it for the last three hundred years. Madness is much more
historical than is usually believed, and much *younger* too . . .
This experience of Unreason in which, up to the eighteenth century, Western man encountered the night of his truth and his
absolute challenge was to become, and still remains for us, the
mode of access to the natural truth of man. . . The whole epistemological structure of modern psychology is rooted in this event,
which is contemporary with the French Revolution and which
concerns man's relation with himself. 'Psychology' is merely a thin
skin on the surface of the ethical world in which modern man seeks

7

his truth—and loses it. Nietzsche, who has been accused of saying the contrary, saw this very clearly. . . Psychology can never tell the truth about madness because it is madness that holds the truth of psychology. . . . If carried back to its roots the psychology of madness would appear to be not the mastery of mental illness and hence the possibility of its disappearance, but the destruction of psychology itself and the discovery of that essential, non-psychological because non-moralizable relation that is the relation between Reason and Unreason. It is this relation that, despite all the penury of psychology, is present and visible in the works of Hölderlin, Nerval, Roussel and Artaud, and that holds out the promise to man that one day, perhaps, he will be able to be free of all psychology and be ready for the great tragic confrontation with madness (MMP, 82, 88–9; MIP, 68–9, 74–5).

These passages could have come from *Histoire de la folie*, with which they are contemporary. They assort ill with the first half of the book, written some eight years before. Foucault has long regarded *La Maladie mentale et psychologie* as a juvenilium, unworthy to survive. When, in its second form, it again went out of print, Foucault refused to authorize its reprinting. (He even tried to prevent publication of an English translation of this revised version—successfully in Britain, unsuccessfully in the United States.) Yet, with its curious history, this book is indispensable to an understanding of Foucault's emergence as a thinker. It also contains passages of astonishing prescience.

None of this psychology would exist without the *moralizing sadism* in which nineteenth-century 'philanthropy' enclosed it, under the hypocritical appearances of 'liberation'. It might be said that all knowledge is linked to the essential forms of cruelty (MMP, 87; MIP, 73).

What we have here is not only an adumbration of the conjunction *pouvoir-savoir*, power-knowledge, the central axis of Foucault's later work, but an obscure reference to Foucault's critique of the notion of 'liberation', so fundamental to his latest enterprise, *The History of Sexuality*.

◇ PART I ◇
The Archaeology
of Knowledge

◇ I ◇

Madness, Death, and the Birth of Reason

Folie et déraison: Histoire de la folie à l'âge classique—to give the book its full, original title—was first published by Plon in 1961. Two years later, a considerably shorter version appeared in a cheap, pocketbook edition in the 10/18 series. The English edition, *Madness and Civilization*, first published in the United States in 1965 and two years later in Britain, was a translation of the shortened version, with the addition of one chapter and of other material from the original edition. (Nevertheless, the English version still represents only two-fifths of the French original.) In 1972, the first edition having long been out of print, Gallimard published a second unabridged version, *Histoire de la folie à l'âge classique*. When asked to provide a new preface for this 'already old book', Foucault refused to act as judge of his own work, to justify or to condemn positions adopted eleven years earlier. Instead, he turned out a brilliant little essay on the genre 'author's preface' in which no mention is made of the book it prefaces. What is more, he insisted that the original preface—a beautiful, illuminating piece—be suppressed. My own references will be to the second French edition and, where possible, to the English translation (HF and MC respectively). My quotations from the first preface will be indicated by the letters FD (*Folie et déraison*).

In an interview published in 1977, Foucault links the writing of *Histoire de la folie* to the political situation of the 1950s. In the wake of the Lysenko affair and the discrediting of so-called 'socialist science', left-wing intellectuals had become acutely aware of the problem of the relations between science and politics. Perhaps, thought the young Foucault, the problems posed by the relations between, say,

11

theoretical physics or organic chemistry and the political and economic structures of society are too complicated, their threshold of possible explanation beyond our reach. If, however, one took a less pure, more 'dubious' science such as psychiatry, the relations between knowledge and power might emerge more clearly. Such an explanation of the genesis of *Histoire de la folie* could have occurred to no one but Foucault himself. It is unlikely that psychiatry presented itself to Foucault as just one, among other, 'dubious' sciences. On the contrary, his attention was carried unerringly from philosophy to psychiatry, from the core of Reason to the frontiers of Reason, and beyond. Beyond because Foucault's interest in psychiatry was short-lived: it had led him towards what he chose, in all simplicity, to call 'madness'. But he soon came to see that psychiatry represented the tyranny of 'reason' over 'madness'. As he went beyond the frontiers of reason, he found himself in a sort of no-man's land. How could one speak of madness in the language of reason? There was no formal discourse, no recognized discipline within which one could speak of it. In this twilight world, beyond the light of reason, yet this side of total darkness, a few signposts loomed up: Hölderlin, Nerval, Van Gogh, Raymond Roussel, Artaud and, above all, the key, enigmatic figure of Nietzsche, the 'mad philosopher'. The names recur constantly, in different orders, sometimes with one or other of the names absent, like so many signs, touchstones, a litany. They are the great mediators between the separated worlds of 'reason' and 'madness'. They represent a phenomenon which, thanks to the tyranny exercised by the one over the other, thanks to science in general and psychiatry in particular, no longer enjoys the currency it once did. Foucault knew that he was not of their number, that his own position lay short of theirs. But he, too, could be a mediator, situated more easily in the academy than in the asylum, but one who could never sit comfortably in a professorial chair, who would never forget the straightjacket that was its silenced counterpart. In that first Preface of 1961, Foucault shows that he was amply aware of his mission. This was to be the first stage in a 'long inquiry', carried out 'under the sun of Nietzsche's great search'. Foucault mentions other areas of possible research, that, for example, of the sexual prohibitions of our own culture and the whole question of 'repression' and 'tolerance'. This is of course the subject of the six-volume 'History of Sexuality' begun some fifteen years later. But before embarking on his genealogy of

Western thought he had first to examine the act of exclusion that made the triumphs of reason possible.

The title 'History of Madness' is deceptively banal—one critic complained that it did little justice to what was, after all, a brilliantly original, even iconoclastic work. But neither of its terms is used without irony. 'History' suggests a certain assurance, sanctioned by an institution, a discipline and, ultimately, reason itself. Yet Foucault's enterprise undermines institution, discipline, and the rule of reason. Likewise, when Foucault speaks of 'madness' he does so not from the standpoint of reason. He offers no definition of the term. He refuses to see it as a constant, unchanging reality, man's growing understanding of which is reflected in an ever more refined vocabulary. The word is useful to Foucault precisely because it is non-medical, because it is used by everyone and spans the entire period with which he is concerned. Madness is not initially a fact, but a judgement—even if that judgement becomes itself a fact. It is a judgement passed by one part of the human mind on another. One person on another. The Preface to the first edition opens with two quotations, one from Pascal ('Men are so necessarily mad, that not to be mad would amount to another form of madness') and one from Dostoievsky ('It is not by confining one's neighbours that one is convinced of one's own sanity'). What we have, then, is not so much a 'history of madness' as a 'history' of 'madness', a counter-history of that 'other form of madness', that *autre tour*', that further turn or twist—Pascal's image is that of the turn of a key, or screw. Under cover of his title, the student of philosophy and psychiatry has gone over to the other side:

> We have yet to write the history of that other form of madness, by which men, in an act of sovereign reason, confine their neighbours, and communicate and recognize each other through the merciless language of non-madness (FD, i; MC, xi).

That particular 'madness' is as old, as recent, as modern science. It is as if Newtonian physics and Cartesian rationalism required that 'madness', that establishment of the sole sovereignty of reason, and the consequent expulsion of anything that constituted a threat to its rule, as a necessary condition of their birth. What is significant in the treatment accorded the 'insane' over the last three hundred years is not an increase in scientificity, nor the spread of more 'humane' attitudes and methods, but the continuing allegiance paid to 'reason' and the complete failure to listen either to one's own 'necessary' madness or to those labelled 'mad'.

> The language of psychiatry, which is a monologue of reason *about* madness, could be established only on the basis of such a silence. I have not tried to write the history of that language, but rather the archaeology of that silence (FD, ii; MC, xii-xiii).

This is the first appearance of the term 'archaeology' in Foucault's *oeuvre*. Here it is thrown off almost in passing, as if Foucault is looking around for a word to distinguish what he is doing from 'history'. The concept that is to play such a central role in his thinking, from this work through *Naissance de la clinique* (subtitled 'une archéologie du regard medical') and *Les mots et les choses* (subtitled 'une archéologie des sciences humaines') to *L'archéologie du savoir*, is clearly enough adumbrated here. For Foucault, history—and the 'history of ideas' in particular—is too deeply imbued with notions of continuity, causality and teleology, which stem from modern rationalism and ultimately from the Cartesian notion of the constitutive subject. Against the triumphant, onward, *horizontal* march of history, Foucault sets the *'constant verticality'* of the tragic, of the limits set by madness and death.

Foucault's enterprise, then, is to go back, beyond modern rationalism and science, to a time when madness was still an 'undifferentiated experience, a not yet divided experience of division itself', before Reason and Madness were relegated to separate, non-communicating cells. In exploring that 'uncomfortable region' we must, of course, renounce as far as possible the attitudes, techniques, vocabulary inherited from that division. We must abandon any notion that we now possess the truth about madness. Indeed, we must set aside anything we think we know about it, any temptation to analyse, order, classify madness from some retrospective standpoint. Not to do so would be to speak the language of exclusion, a language that Foucault himself had learnt, and rejected.

> In the serene world of mental illness, modern man no longer communicates with the madman: on the one hand, the man of reason delegates the physician to madness, thereby authorizing a relation only through the abstract universality of disease; on the other, the man of madness communicates with society only by the

intermediary of an equally abstract reason which is order, physical and moral constraint, the anonymous pressure of the group, the requirements of conformity. As for a common language, there is no such thing; or rather, there is no such thing any longer; the constitution of madness as mental illness, at the end of the eighteenth century, affords the evidence of a broken dialogue, posits the separation as already effected, and thrusts into oblivion all those stammered, imperfect words without fixed syntax in which the exchange between madness and reason was made. . .

What, then, is this confrontation beneath the language of reason? Where can an interrogation lead us that does not follow reason in its horizontal course, but seeks to retrace in time that constant verticality which confronts European culture with what it is not, establishes its range by its own derangement? What realm do we enter which is neither the history of knowledge, nor history itself; which is controlled neither by the teleology of truth nor the rational sequence of causes, since causes have value and meaning only beyond the division? A realm, no doubt, where what is in question is the limits rather than the identity of a culture (FD, ii-iii; MC, xii-xiii).

In a phrase, striking by turns for its apparent inappropriateness, inadequacy, and excess, Foucault defines the basic condition of madness, stripped of all the interpretations offered by science. It is characterized, he says, by *'une absence d'oeuvre'*, an unproductive idleness, outside human achievement, outside 'the great work of history'. It is the void on which the plenitude of history is built, a constant, unchanging 'experience' that stands perpendicular to the horizontal of history. The 'possibility of history' is linked to the 'necessity of madness'. To attempt a 'history of madness' is, therefore, a contradiction in terms. The 'experience of madness', in the raw, prior to its capture by knowledge, is, in itself, inaccessible. To observe madness is to place oneself on the side of reason—one would be better employed observing reason. Look hard enough at reason, Foucault seems to be saying, and you will find madness. That, in a sense, is the course he adopts. Fighting his way back through the shifting mass of 'notions, institutions, measures taken by judiciary and police, scientific concepts', he locates the heart of his enterprise, 'the decision that at once binds together and separates reason and madness'. His task is to uncover the 'perpetual exchange, the obscure common root, the original confrontation that gives sense to both the unity and the opposition of sense and senselessness' (FD, vii).

Once one goes back beyond the mid-seventeenth century, beyond the division between reason and madness, people no longer seem to be talking of quite the same thing when they use the word 'madness'. English speakers have an additional problem. Not only does Renaissance 'madness' seem to have a quite distinct dimension from that of madness after the rise of rationalism, but it is coupled with another word, 'folly'. Foucault's *folie*, of course, covers both senses. This problem is particularly acute for the translator—a problem that is not entirely solved in *Madness and Civilization*. For the translator, the difficulty is not that the French covers two quite different notions and that he has merely to decide which is intended. 'Folly' and 'madness' do not represent two different concepts, nor even a spectrum ranging from pure madness at one end to pure folly at the other, but a shifting confused relation in which no one seems quite certain when or why one should be more appropriate than the other. We speak of the Ship of Fools and the Feast of Fools, Erasmus praises folly, but King Lear goes mad. The last case is not as simple as it looks. Lear is not just a foolish man who goes mad (accompanied by his fool and a man feigning madness). For Kent, Lear is 'mad' at the outset: 'be Kent unmannerly, When Lear is *mad*'. A few lines later, Kent repeats exactly the same sentiment, using 'folly': 'To plainness honour's bound When majesty falls to folly'. Clearly, the two words are often interchangeable: not only can 'folly' stand for what we mean by 'madness', but 'mad' can stand for what we mean by 'foolish'. *King Lear* is no doubt the richest source for our understanding of that twilight world between distinction and synonym in which the Renaissance experienced folly and madness. Reversing the point I am making, it is salutory to realize that no distinction exists in *Le Roi Lear*. How, one wonders, do Shakespeare's translators render: 'Oh, Fool, I shall go mad!' Obviously, in the only way possible, by replacing a subtle, gentle distinction by a sublime pun: '*Ah, Fou, je deviendrai fou*'. In this instance, at least, the translation would have its own effectiveness. After all, one clear implication of the English and one that the Fool never ceases to harp on, is that Lear has exchanged his crown for a cap and bells. Majesty does fall to folly and, in folly, in madness, Lear finds the wisdom he never knew as king and which, in his own burlesque way, the Fool has possessed all along. What, then, is Foucault's translator to do with *folie* and *fou*? Clearly, 'madness', 'mad', 'madman' and 'folly', 'foolish', 'fool' must be used when they are felt to be most appropriate. But the English reader should make a mental note that whenever one set of terms is used the other is also present within it. After the mid-seventeenth century, of course, the problem does not arise. Folly/madness and its free communication with Reason disappears. In its place, there is a new Reason and a new Madness, new because one has come to dominate and exclude the other: in such a relationship neither can remain the same, even if the words do. In English, significantly, 'folly' disappears from the exalted language of philosophers and moralists altogether.

With the waning of the Middle Ages leprosy disappeared from the Western world. Its role as focus of exclusion in the European consciousness was, for a time, taken over by venereal disease. But the true heir of leprosy, says Foucault, was that 'highly complex phenomenon', madness. But it needed a period of latency, lasting almost two hundred years, before madness aroused similar reactions of isolation, exclusion and purification. Before madness was finally tamed, it had participated in 'all the major experiences of the Renaissance'. One of the most potent symbols of this participation was the *'stultifera navis'*, or Ship of Fools, that 'strange "drunken boat" that glides along the calm rivers of the Rhineland and the Flemish canals' and which gave rise to a mass of literary and artistic works. At this time madmen were not generally interned. They were often expelled from the city itself, but allowed to wander freely over the countryside. To prevent their return, they were often entrusted to groups of merchants and pilgrims, who then deposited them at a safe distance from their place of origin. Certainly considerations of public order played their part, but there were other purposes at work in this movement of madmen from one place to another. The practices associated with their departure and embarkation suggest rituals of exclusion:

> Certain madmen were publicly whipped, and in the course of a kind of game they were chased in a mock race and driven out of the city with quarterstaff blows. . . But water adds to this the dark mass of its own values; it carries off, but it does more: it purifies. Navigation delivers man to the uncertainty of fate; on water, each

of us is in the hands of his own destiny; every embarkation is, potentially, the last. It is for the other world that the madman sets sail in his fools' boat; it is from the other world that he comes when he disembarks. The madman's voyage is at once a rigorous division and an absolute Passage. In one sense, it simply develops, across a half-real, half-imaginary geography, the madman's *liminal* position on the horizon of medieval concern. . . Confined on the ship, from which there is no escape, the madman delivered to the river with its thousand arms, the sea with its thousand roads, to that great uncertainty external to everything. He is a prisoner in the midst of what is the freest, the openest of routes: bound fast at the infinite crossroads. He is the passenger *par excellence:* that is, the prisoner of the passage. And the land he will come to is unknown—as is, once he disembarks, the land from which he comes. He has his truth and his homeland only in that fruitless expanse between two countries that cannot belong to him. Is it this ritual and these values which are at the origin of the long imaginary relationship that can be traced through the whole of Western culture? Or is it, conversely, this relationship that, from time immemorial, has called into being and established the rite of embarkation? One thing at least is certain: water and madness have long been linked in the dreams of European man (HF, 21–2; MC, 10–12).

The Ship of Fools emerged, out of all proportion to its actual presence in the life of the community, as the focus of a deep-seated unease that suddenly dawned on the horizon of European culture at the end of the Middle Ages. Folly and the fool became a major preoccupation in literature and art from the mid-fifteenth to the mid-seventeenth century. First, in a mass of comic tales and moral fables, 'folly' seems to usurp the democracy of the vices and establish its own singular rule as the root of all human failings. Then, in the satirical farces, the character of the 'fool' himself assumes more and more importance.

He is no longer a ridiculous and familiar silhouette in the wings:

he stands centre stage as the guardian of truth. . . In a comedy where each man deceives the other and dupes himself, he is comedy to the second degree: the deception of deception. . . Folly also has its academic pastimes; it is the object of argument, it contends against itself; it is denounced, and defends itself by claiming that it is closer to happiness and truth than reason, that it is closer to reason than reason itself. . . Finally, at the centre of all these serious games, the great humanist texts: the *Moria rediviva* of Flayder and Erasmus's *In Praise of Folly*. And confronting all these discussions, with their tireless dialectic, confronting these discourses, constantly reworded and reworked, a long dynasty of images, from Hieronymus Bosch with *The Cure of Folly* and *The Ship of Fools*, down to Brueghel and his *Dulle Griet*; woodcuts and engravings transcribe what the theatre, what literature and art have already taken up: the intermingled themes of the Feast and of the Dance of Fools. Indeed, from the fifteenth century on, the face of madness has haunted the imagination of Western Man. . .

Up to the second half of the fifteenth century, or even a little beyond, the theme of death reigns alone. The end of man, the end of time, bear the face of pestilence and war. What overhangs human existence is this conclusion and this order from which nothing escapes. The presence that threatens even within this world is a fleshless one. Then in the last years of the century this enormous uneasiness turns on itself; the mockery of folly replaces death and its solemnity. From the discovery of that necessity which inevitably reduces man to nothing, we have shifted to the scornful contemplation of that nothing which is existence itself. Fear in the face of the absolute limit of death turns inwards in a continuous irony; man disarms it in advance, making it an object of derision by giving it an everyday, tamed form, by constantly renewing it in the spectacle of life, by scattering it throughout the vices, the difficulties and the absurdities of all men. Death's annihilation is no longer anything because it was already everything, because life itself was only futility, vain words, a squabble of cap and bells. The head that will become a skull is already empty. . . When the fool laughs, he already laughs with the laugh of death; the madman, anticipating the macabre has disarmed it. The cries of *Dulle Griet* triumph in the high Renaissance, over that *Triumph of Death* sung at the end of the Middle Ages on the walls of the Campo Santo. The substitution of the theme of folly for that of death does not mark a break, but rather a torsion within the same anxiety. What is in question is still the nothingness of existence, but this nothingness is no longer considered an external, final term, both threat and conclusion; it is experienced from within as the continuous and constant form of existence. And where once man's folly had been not to see that death's term was approaching, so that it was necessary to recall him to wisdom with the spectacle of death, now wisdom consisted of denouncing folly everywhere, teaching men that they were no more than dead already, and that if the end was near, it was to the degree that folly, become universal, would be one and the same with death itself. . . The elements are now reversed, it is no longer the end of time and of the world which will show retrospectively that men were mad not to have been prepared for them; it is the tide of folly, its secret invasion, that shows that the world is near its final catastrophe; it is man's madness that invokes and makes necessary the world's end (HF, 24–7; MC, 14–17).

However, this experience of folly/madness is not as coherent as it may seem. Image and word may refer back to one another, they may each illustrate the same fable of folly in the same moral world, Bosch's painting and Brant's poem may each be entitled *Narrenschiff*, but already they are taking two different directions. From this point of barely perceptible divergence is to grow one of the great divisions in the Western experience of madness. It is, says Foucault, in its paintings—above all in the works of Bosch, Dürer, Thierry Bouts, Grünewald, Brueghel—that the Renaissance expressed its true fear of madness and its fascination with the secret knowledge that madness was believed to conceal.

On all sides, madness fascinates man. The fantastic images it generates are not fleeting appearances that quickly disappear from the surface of things. By a strange paradox, what is born from the strangest delusion was already hidden, like a secret, like an inaccessible truth, in the bowels of the earth. When man deploys the arbitrary nature of his madness, he confronts the dark necessity of the world; the animal that haunts his nightmares and his nights of privation is his own nature, which will lay bare hell's pitiless truth; the vain images of blind idiocy—such are the world's *Magna Scientia*; and already, in this disorder, in this mad universe, is prefigured what will be the cruelty of the finale. In such images—and this is doubtless what gives them their weight, what imposes such great coherence on their fantasy—the Renaissance has expressed what it apprehended of the threats and secrets of the world (HF, 33; MC, 23–4).

What has entered the literary expression of madness, on the other hand, is an element of irony, of play that serves both to confront madness and to protect man from it. For the humanist poets and philosophers madness is linked not to the world and its subterranean forms, but rather to man, to his weakness, his dreams, his illusions—more folly, perhaps, than madness.

> Whatever obscure cosmic manifestation there was in madness as seen by Bosch is wiped out in Erasmus; madness no longer lies in wait for mankind at the four corners of the earth; it insinuates itself within man, or rather it is a subtle relation that man maintains with himself (HF, 35; MC, 26).

On the one hand, we have the silent images in which the full force of madness is unleashed. This vision depicts the incontrovertible reality of the dream-world; it also shows that one day all the reality of the world will become as insubstantial as the nightmare.

> This interweaving of appearance as secret, immediate image and concealed riddle is deployed, in the painting of the fifteenth century, as the *tragic folly of the world* (HF, 38).

On the other hand with Brant, Erasmus and the whole humanist tradition, madness is caught up in discourse.

> It becomes more refined, more subtle, but it is also disarmed. . . It is born in men's hearts, regulates and deranges their conduct; it governs cities, but it is unknown to the calm truth of things, to great nature. It disappears soon enough when the essential—life and death, justice and truth—appears. Every man may be subjected to it, but its reign will always be petty, and relative; for it will be revealed in its shabby truth when the wise man turns his eye upon it. For him, it will become an object, and in the worst possible way, for it will become the object of his laughter. . . Though it be wiser than all science, it must bow before wisdom, for whom it is folly (HF, 39).

This confrontation of critical consciousness and tragic experience animates the whole of the early Renaissance thinking on madness. Yet, by the early seventeenth century, with the privilege accorded the one over the other, this dualism has disappeared. Madness became more and more an experience in the field of language, an experience in which man was confronted by the rules of his own nature. Under the onslaught of reason, madness was forced to lay down its arms. But the price that reason paid was to incorporate madness within itself.

> Such, then, was the ambiguous role of this sceptical thought, this reason, so acutely aware of the forms that limit and the forces that contradict it: it discovered madness as one of its own figures— which is a way of conjuring away any form of external power, irreducible hostility, sign of transcendence; but at the same time it places madness at the heart of its own task, designating it as an essential moment of its own nature (HF, 46).

This enables us to understand more clearly Pascal's reflection that 'men are so necessarily mad that not to be mad would be another form of madness'. On the one hand, there is a 'mad madness' that rejects the madness proper to reason and which, by doing so, doubles itself and falls into the simplest, most enclosed, most immediate form of madness; and, on the other, a 'wise madness' that welcomes the madness of reason, allowing it to permeate its whole being, and, in doing so protects itself from the real madness that obstinate rejection would bring. This, says Foucault, is the key to the massive presence of madness and madmen in late sixteenth- and early seventeenth-century literature, 'an art which, in its effort to master this reason in search of itself, recognizes the presence of madness, of *its* madness, circumscribes it, lays siege to it and, finally, triumphs over it' (HF, 47). Foucault's first chapter is taken up with an analysis of this literature: Scudéry, Rotrou, Tristan l'Hermite and, above all, of course, Cervantes and Shakespeare.

By the middle of the seventeenth century, the triumph of the critical consciousness is complete: the Age of Reason is born.

> The great threat that dawned on the horizon of the fifteenth century subsides, the disturbing powers that inhabit Bosch's painting have lost their violence. Forms remain, now transparent and docile, forming a cortège, the inevitable procession of reason. Madness has ceased to be—at the limits of the world, of man and death—an eschatalogical figure; the darkness has dispersed on which the eyes of madness were fixed and out of which the forms of the impossible were born. Oblivion falls upon the world navigated by the free

slaves of the Ship of Fools. Madness will no longer proceed from a point within the world to a point beyond, on its strange voyage; it will never again be that fugitive and absolute limit. Behold it moored now, made fast among things and men. Retained and maintained. No longer a ship but a hospital. Scarcely a century after the career of the mad ships we note the appearance of the theme of the 'Hospital of Madmen', the 'Madhouse'. . . Here each form of madness finds its proper place. . . Everyone in this world of disorder pronounces, in perfect order, each in his turn, the Praise of Reason. Already, in this 'Hospital', *confinement* has succeeded *embarkation* (HF, 53; MC, 35–6).

During this 'Classical age' as Foucault calls it, the tragic, cosmic experience of madness was banished from the light of day. It managed to survive here and there in the works of a Goya or a Sade. It continued to haunt men's nights.

That is why the Classical experience, and through it the modern experience, of madness cannot be regarded as a total figure, one that has finally arrived at its positive truth. . . It is a figure made unbalanced by all that is lacking in it, by all that it conceals (HF, 40).

For Descartes, madness belongs with dreams and all forms of error. Yet their relation to truth and to the seeker after truth is quite different. Dreams and illusions are overcome in the structure of truth itself, while madness is excluded by the doubting subject. To the doubting philosopher, sanity is as unquestionable as the fact that he thinks and exists. Once achieved, this certainty will not easily be abandoned: madness can no longer be of concern to him. It will remain outside the concern of European philosophy until its partial re-entry in Hegel's *Phenomenology of Mind*. *Man* may become mad, but *thought*, as the exercise of a sovereign subject duty-bound to observe the true, cannot be insane. The experience, so familiar to the Renaissance, of an unreasonable Reason and a reasonable Unreason, is now precluded. Between Montaigne and Descartes, something has occurred, something concerned with the advent of a *ratio*.

This exclusion of madness from the centre of intellectual life, its demotion to the purely negative, dependent status of Unreason, is paralleled by changes in the institutional treatment of madness in the life of society. A single symbolic event marks the beginning of the

Classical experience of madness: the founding, in 1656, of the Hôpital général. But this event, and the legal and institutional reforms of which it forms part, did not concern the insane, as such, at all. What these measures amounted to was a policy for dealing with the unproductive poor. Within a matter of months, one per cent of the Paris population was interned. Among their number were many previously regarded as insane, but they did not constitute a category of inmate. They were interned not because they were 'mad', but because they were useless. The Hôpital was to take in, house and feed all those who presented themselves, all those sent by royal or judicial authority 'of both sexes, of all ages and for all localities, of whatever breeding and birth, able-bodied or invalid, sick or convalescent, curable or incurable'. It was not, clearly, a medical establishment. It was a semi-juridical, semi-autonomous institution, operating outside the normal legal machinery and possessing powers of judgement, discipline, and punishment. The model was soon imitated throughout France and spread to the rest of Europe: England soon had its workshops and Germany its *Zuchthäusen*.

> The practice of confinement represents a new reaction to poverty—in a wider sense, a new relation between man and the inhuman aspect of his existence. In the sixteenth century, a poor man, the man who could not support his own existence, assumed a figure that the Middle Ages would not have recognized. By a double movement of thought that robbed Poverty of its absolute meaning and Charity of the value derived from assisting it, the Renaissance divested poverty of its mystical positivity (HF, 67).

There can be little doubt that this policy of confining the poor was a response to the economic crisis—fall in wages, unemployment, scarcity of coinage—that spread from Spain to the whole of Europe. But, ultimately, the policy failed: it did not solve the problems of low wages and unemployment and, with the growth of industrialization at the beginning of the nineteenth century, it was largely abandoned. Its implementation and stubborn survival owed more to an ideology than to economic necessity. Labour was seen not as an integral element of the production of wealth, but rather as a general remedy for all forms of poverty. Labour and poverty stood in a simple opposition to one another. Labour derived its ability to banish poverty, not from its productive power, but by virtue of a certain moral force. In

24

the Classical age, the confinement of the idle had much the same symbolic force as the isolation of the leper once had.

> The asylum was substituted for the lazar house, in the geography of haunted places as in the landscape of the moral universe. The old rites of excommunication were revived, but in the world of production and commerce. . . It is not immaterial that madmen were included in the proscription of idleness. From its origin, they would have their place beside the poor, deserving or not, and the idle, voluntary or not. Like them, they would be subject to the rules of forced labour. . . In the workshops in which they were interned, they distinguished themselves by their inability to work and to follow the rhythms of collective life. The necessity, discovered in the eighteenth century, to provide a special régime for the insane, and the great crisis of confinement that shortly preceded the Revolution, are linked to the experience of madness available in the universal necessity of labour. Men did not wait until the seventeenth century to 'shut up' the mad, but it was in this period that they began to 'confine' or 'intern' them, along with an entire population with whom their kinship was recognized. Until the Renaissance, the sensibility to madness was linked to the presence of imaginary transcendences. In the Classical age, for the first time, madness was perceived through a condemnation of idleness and in a social immanence guaranteed by the community of labour. This community acquired an ethical power of segregation, which permitted it to eject, as into another world, all forms of social uselessness. It was in this *other world*, encircled by the sacred powers of labour, that madness would assume the status we now attribute to it. If there is, in Classical madness, something which refers elsewhere, and to *other things*, it is no longer because the madman comes from the world of the irrational and bears its stigmata; rather, it is because he crosses the frontiers of bourgeois order of his own accord and alienates himself outside the sacred limits of its ethic (HF, 84–5; MC, 57–8).

At first, confinement certainly functioned as a mechanism of social regulation. But Foucault's analysis goes much further than an explanation based on social utility. Indeed, he takes issue with a whole group of leading twentieth-century French historians on this point (HF, 92–3). According to this view, confinement was simply a spontaneous elimination of those asocial elements that we now distribute between prisons, borstals, psychiatric hospitals, and psychoanalysts' couches. Such a view presupposes an eternal, unchanging madness, already fully armed with its perennial psychological equipment, but which had to await the early years of our century for its true scientific articulation to be revealed. It also presupposes a sort of orthogenesis of scientific knowledge out of social consciousness: a belief that social experience was some kind of approximate knowledge on the road to scientific perfection. The object of a science must, therefore, exist prior to the science itself, for the object is first dimly apprehended before it is finally understood by a positive science. This evolutionist, teleological view of knowledge, which sees us standing at the threshold of a new scientific future, with the past stretching behind us as a kind of twilight zone of pre-history, is one that Foucault combats throughout his work. Madness did not wait, in immobile identity, for the advent of psychiatry to carry it from the darkness of superstition to the light of truth. The categories of modern psychiatry were not lying in a state of nature ready to be picked up by the perceptive observer: they were *produced* by that 'science' in its very act of forma-tion. Similarly, the sudden, massive resort to confinement in the mid-seventeenth century was not a necessary response to a sudden, massive upsurge of 'asocial elements'. This act was as sudden as that by which lepers were expelled from the city: but its significance cannot be reduced to its actual result. One per cent of the Paris population was not interned in 1657 in order to free the city of 'asocial' elements, any more than the lepers were expelled in order to halt the spread of the disease. Rather the 'asocial' elements were produced by the act of segregation. If in the light of our own system of thought, it seems to us that many different social categories came under the same act of segregation, it is not to our own system of thought that we must turn for an understanding of that act. For this particular phenomenon of confinement, during the hundred and fifty years of its existence, was the product, not of ignorance or confused thinking, but of a system of thought peculiar to the 'Classical age'.

Its practices and its rules constituted a domain of experience that possessed its own unity, coherence and function. It brought together, in a single field, individuals and values between which the preceding cultures had seen no resemblance; imperceptibly it moved them in the direction of madness, thus paving the way for an experience—our own experience—in which they will already appear as belonging to mental alienation. This regrouping required a whole reorganization of the ethical world, new lines of separation between good and evil, the accepted and the rejected, the establishment of new norms in social integration. . . There were certain experiences that the sixteenth century had accepted or rejected, which had been the object of its concern, or left to one side and which, now, the seventeenth century was to take up, group together and banish in a single act, send into an exile that they would share with the insane—thus forming a uniform world of Unreason (HF, 96).

These experiences concern either sexuality, in its relations with the bourgeois family, profanation, in its relations with the new view of the sacred, or 'libertinage', that is, the new relations being formed between free thinking and the passions. These three areas of experience form, with madness, in the space of confinement, a homogeneous world of mental alienation that is still, to a large extent, our own. By the end of the eighteenth century, it was regarded as self-evident that certain forms of 'libertine' thinking, such as Sade's, were closely bound up with delusion and madness. Equally, the practice of alchemy or homosexuality, for example, was seen as a manifestation of mental illness. Yet, fifty years or so earlier, both practices had been not only tolerated, but celebrated, in thought, word, and deed. Even where certain practices had been condemned—sodomy, for example, as opposed to homosexual love—the grounds for that condemnation were quite different. Perhaps in every culture, sexuality has been subjected to a system of constraint; only in our own, and from a relatively recent date, has it been divided on the basis of Reason and Unreason and, more recently still, between health and sickness, the normal and the abnormal.

Prostitution and debauchery also constituted sufficient grounds for confinement. But action was taken only when the scandal became public or the interests of the family were in question—one of the most common reasons for confining a 'debauchee' was the danger his conduct presented to the family fortune.

The family and its demands became one of the essential criteria of reason; it was above all the family that requested and obtained a confinement. What one is witnessing at this time is the great confiscation of sexual ethics by family morality. . . It is no longer love that is sacred, but marriage. . . In the nineteenth century the conflict between the individual and his family was to become a private matter and was to assume the character of a psychological problem. During the whole period of confinement the family was, on the contrary, a matter of public order. Whoever attacked it entered the world of unreason. By becoming the major occasion of unreason, the family was, one day, to become the battleground of the conflicts from which the various forms of madness would arise (HF, 104–6).

But perhaps the most curious aspect of confinement in this 'Age of Reason' was the way in which certain forms of freethinking, that is, certain modes of the exercise of reason, were to be linked with unreason. In the early seventeenth century libertinage was exclusively a form of nascent rationalism: it was also a disturbing awareness of the unreason within reason itself. From the middle of the century, this libertinage splits into two, mutually contradictory forms: on the one hand, an attempt on the part of reason to develop a rationalism in which all unreason takes on the appearance of the rational and, on the other hand, an unreason of the heart that twists the discourses of reason to its own unreasonable ends. What is now meant by the term is neither exactly freedom of thought nor freedom of morals, but, on the contrary, a state of servitude in which reason becomes enslaved to the desires of the heart. The eighteenth century produced no coherent philosophy of libertinage until Sade. And then, significantly, it emerged out of a situation of confinement; more significantly still, it saw the liberty of the libertine as a total enslavement to his own passions.

From the creation of the Hôpital général and similar institutions in England and Germany to the end of the eighteenth century, those whom our own authorities would classify as insane were found side by side with prostitutes, spendthrift fathers, prodigal sons, homosexuals, blasphemers, libertines, etc. It is easy for us to assume that the Classical age therefore misunderstood the *nature* of madness, that its state of pre-scientific ignorance prevented it from reading the symptoms aright. But such a view is itself a misunderstanding: a failure to see that what underlay the common treatment accorded those whom we would variously seek to cure, condemn to prison or leave at liberty, was a coherent view of human behaviour based on a belief in the power of reason. Indeed, compared with our own confused, contradictory and, constantly evolving, penologies, the classical concept of unreason is clarity itself.

However, because the insane were generally interned with other 'unreasonable' persons, it would be wrong to suppose that the Classical age made no distinction between the various inmates. Madness and crime were not mutually exclusive; yet each retained its identity. Together they formed a common concept, unreason, and their manifestation called for a common response, confinement. Nevertheless, the mad were often subjected to a different régime from that imposed on other prisoners; there were even institutions (the Hôtel Dieu in Paris, 'Bedlam' in London) that dealt exclusively with them. The medical profession had long regarded the study and treatment of madness as part of its province and, to a limited extent, operated within the institutions of confinement. 'Lunacy' being regarded as a cyclical illness, treatment, too, tended to follow the calendar: bleeding in late May, followed by several weekly administrations of vomit-inducing medicines, followed in turn by purges. The actual degree of medical intervention was either non-existent or minimal. Moreover, only those considered to be 'curable' were subjected to any form of medical treatment and, proportionately, not a great many of these. But it would be an error to suppose that the existence of some form of medical intervention, however crude and misinformed, represents the beginnings of a more modern attitude towards insanity, the birth of mental illness. On the contrary, the medical treatment of the insane within the Classical world of confinement represents an anachronism, the survival in hostile conditions of an older tradition stretching back, through the Renaissance, to the Middle Ages. The doctrine of confinement, on the other hand, based on the concept of unreason, was perfectly at one with the Classical *episteme*. The one system was newer, more vigorous, but the other was never totally eclipsed. Indeed, it was the physician who, effectively, made the decision as to whether or not to confine. He alone was competent to read the signs: he had at his disposal a complicated symptomatology based on the 'faculties' and their various deficiencies. It was his judgement that largely formed the basis of the legal judgement, itself based on an elaborate system of moral judgements derived from canon and Roman law. The two systems, the older elaborate system of medical/legal judgement and the newer, uniform system of confinement as implementation of that judgement existed side by side in eighteenth-century society, neither appearing to affect the other. The first saw the person as a legal subject made up of rights and obligations; the second saw the individual as a social being. In the first, there was a recognition that various forms of insanity affect the subject's freedom of moral choice; in the second, a simple awareness that 'unreasonable' behaviour itself constituted an exclusion from the society of reasonable men. For the first, the madman was to a greater or lesser degree innocent in his actions, since his reasoning faculties were impaired; for the second, the 'unreasonable' citizen, whether insane or not, could not but be guilty, since the slightest inflexion towards unreason was an exercise of the will—insanity was a consequence, rather than a cause of unreasonable behaviour. Either way, madness was perceived by the eighteenth century as a relapse into animality. In the first case, man had lost the use of reason and had sunk into the innocent, amoral condition of the animal; in the second, man had deliberately chosen to rid himself of the guidance of reason, of his very humanity. The 'furious' lunatic was seen and treated as a wild beast. Many accounts of madmen in confinement attest to their extraordinary resistance to extremes of hunger, heat, cold, and pain. This was regarded as further proof of the animality of the mad.

Yet in the mechanistic universe of the Classical age, animality had nothing of the dark, secret, almost *supernatural* powers attributed to it in so much literature, mythology, and religion. This it had lost; it was not to regain it until the Classical age itself came to an end. Throughout this period, animality was conceived essentially as *negativity*, as non-human. Yet, for Classical medicine, madness was not a single, uniform condition. In a dazzling display of erudition Foucault resurrects the forgotten names of Classical medicine (Willis, Dufour, Cullen, Sydenham, Whytt, von Haller, Boissier de Sauvages, etc.), pores over their *Treatises*, their *Observations*, their *Nosologies*, their *Dictionaries*, written in Latin, French, English, and German and brings back to something resembling a life that 'garden of the species of madness'. The metaphor is peculiarly apt, for the eighteenth century found no difficulty in regarding madness as a branch of natural history. Did not the great Linnaeus himself, in his *Genera morborum*, turn his taxonomic gifts to the unweeded garden of dementia and morosis, mania and melancholia, hysteria and hypochondria?

Madness, Death, and the Birth of Reason

Madness is one of those fundamental experiences in which a culture puts its own values at risk and, at the same time, arms those values against attack.

A culture like that of the Classical age, so many of whose values were invested in reason, had both the most and the least to lose in madness. The most because madness constituted the most immediate contradiction of all that justified it; the least, because it disarmed madness entirely, leaving it quite powerless. This maximum and minimum of risk accepted by Classical culture in madness is perfectly expressed in the word 'unreason': the simple, immediate reverse side of reason; and this empty, purely negative form, possessing neither content nor value, which bears the imprint of a reason that has just fled, but which remains for unreason the *raison d'être* of what it is (HF, 192).

For Foucault, the Classical age opened with a single symbolic event, the founding, in 1656, of the Hôpital général; it closes with another, Pinel's freeing of the inmates of Bicêtre in 1794. In the liberal hagiography of the nineteenth-century Pinel holds an honoured place: as he struck the chains off the prisoners, he appeared to work miracles on their minds. As he himself remarked on one such case, a drunken ex-soldier, suffering under the delusion of being a general, 'Never in a human intelligence was revolution more sudden, or more complete. . .' (HF, 498). Five years after the great Revolution, Pinel toppled the *ancien régime* of confinement and initiated the new, benign rule of the asylum. Pinel's action is seen as the founding act of the modern, humane treatment of mental patients and, ultimately, of modern psychology. The application of Reason to human society brought, as its inevitable consequence, both moral and scientific progress. Needless to say, Foucault does not share this view, though a revised version is implicit in most modern psychiatric theory and practice. He is concerned neither to trace the line of historical progress, nor to amass evidence against any general theory of historical change. His enterprise is, as always, to study all the available documentation of the period (Foucault's books may seem unusually well documented, but the height of his references is merely the tip of an iceberg of submerged research), with as little assistance (interference) from non-contemporary sources and notions as possible. An account of change does emerge, but it is usually a detailed and original account.

Something, undoubtedly, *did* change in society's view and treatment of madness at the close of the eighteenth century. It was not, however, as sudden as might at first appear. The roots of change lay further back both inside and outside the world of confinement. The Classical age had seen madness in terms of animality: what distinguished man from the animals was the gift of reason. When men wilfully acted contrary to the dictates of reason they sank to the level of the animals, banished themselves from the society of their fellows and exposed themselves to the danger of madness. By a curious inversion of values the late eighteenth century was to identify the possibility of madness, not with animality, but with a human society, an environment, that repressed man's natural animality. Madness came to be seen as the reverse side of progress: as civilized man became further and further removed from nature, the more he exposed himself to madness. Moreover, urban civilization threatened not only the individual citizen but the very species itself. It was confidently believed that the civilized races were suffering from a gradual degeneration from a primitive type: it was noted that 'savages' were rarely afflicted by madness. Insanity was seen more and more as something outside the individual's volition, something that struck from the outside, without warning. It is hardly surprising, therefore, that the latter half of the century was marked by a 'great fear' of madness. It was as if the evil that had been shut away out of sight for some hundred years had re-appeared in phantasy form. In 1780, an epidemic spread through Paris. It was supposed to have originated in the Hôpital général; there was even talk among the population of burning down the buildings. Madness, it was firmly believed, was on the increase. Certainly the figures for confinement show a massive increase over the previous half century (HF, 401–4). These figures are paralleled by a growth in the number of institutions dealing exclusively with the insane and by an increasing tendency within the institutions of general confinement to isolate the insane from the other inmates.

This isolation was at first more in the nature of a side-effect, deriving from a change in attitude not so much towards madness as to poverty, sickness, and public assistance. With the population explosion, the crisis in the food supply, enclosures, etc., it became more and more difficult to view poverty as a matter of purely *moral* concern. Political economy showed that poverty was a result of objective, social forces, not of individual human or divine will. The population was one of the elements of the nation's wealth. The confinement of the poor and workless was, therefore, economically unsound. Far from being extracted from the play of market forces, they should be made once more available to them. A plentiful supply of labour would keep wages low and thus encourage the growth of new industries. Where assistance was needed, it should be given in the *natural* environment of the family. (Until a new act of parliament in 1796, it was actually forbidden in England to provide assistance in the home.) As far as possible, the sick, too, should be cared for in the home. Thus madness which, throughout this period, had been associated with poverty in a general, indifferentiated world of unreason, was now divided from it: the institutions of internment were left to the insane—and the doctors. This was the work not of philanthropic intervention or scientific advance, but of a general change within the institutions themselves, in response to economic and social pressures or, rather, to men's experience of change in their social and economic relations.

As Pinel was at work reforming Bicêtre, the Quakers of York, led by Samuel Tuke, were taking steps to set up their own asylum. 'The Retreat' was based on a double principle of segregation: it housed only members of the Society of Friends and only those regarded as insane. 'It was thought,' said Tuke, 'that the indiscriminate mixture, which must occur in large public establishments, of persons of opposite religious sentiments and practices; of the profligate and the virtuous; the profane and the serious; was calculated to check the progress of returning reason, and to fix, still deeper, the melancholy and misanthropic train of ideas.' But the principal reason lay in the power of religion to operate as both spontaneity and constraint and so, in the absence of reason, counterbalance the violence that madness can harbour. Its precepts, 'where these have been strongly imbued in early life . . . become little less than principles of our nature; and their restraining power is frequently felt, even under the delirious excitement of insanity' (HF, 502; MC, 243–4). The true role of religion in the Retreat was to keep the inmate in a perpetual state of anxiety, under constant threat of transgressing the Law.

In fact Tuke created an asylum where he substituted for the free terror of madness the stifling anguish of responsibility; fear no longer reigned on the other side of the prison gates, it now raged under the seals of conscience. . . . The asylum no longer punished the madman's guilt, it is true; but it did more, it organized that guilt; it organized it for the madman as a consciousness of himself, and as a non-reciprocal relation to the keeper . . . a therapeutic intervention in the madman's existence. . . From the acknowledgment of his status as object, from the awareness of his guilt, the madman was to return to his awareness of himself as a free and responsible subject, and consequently to reason (HF, 504–5; MC, 247).

The law had long regarded the insane as minors, but this was an abstract juridical status, rather than a concrete relation between man and man. What Tuke did was to transpose this minority status into an institution modelled on the family. Thus, under the guise of parental protection, in a 'natural' and 'normal' milieu, the madman was still further enslaved. What we have here, says Foucault, is the beginning of a 'parental complex' that was to envelop the entire existence of madness up to our own time. In the 'Oedipus Complex', a modern, mythical interpretation of an ancient myth, psychoanalysis claimed to have discovered a universal structure in the constitution of the human subject. In fact, it inherited and perpetuated a structure that was already well established in the medical treatment of the insane and which, in turn, formed part of a general 'familialization' of Western societies that had been developing since the beginning of the nineteenth century.

At first sight an institution based on a belief in the efficacy of Christian principles in the treatment of insanity would seem to have little in common with Pinel's view that preoccupation with religion was itself a form of insanity. For Pinel, religion led the mind towards error, illusion and, ultimately, to delusion and hallucination. It was the imaginary forms of religion that were dangerous; its moral content, on the other hand, was as necessary to his work as to Tuke's. His asylum was 'a religious domain without religion, a domain of pure morality, of ethical uniformity'. The asylum was no longer alien country, as far removed in spirit as possible from normal social life; on the contrary, the morality on which the new social order was supposedly based extended without interruption into the heart of the asylum, where the values of family and work reigned supreme.

> The asylum of the age of positivism, which Pinel is credited with having founded, was not a free domain of observation, diagnosis and therapy; it was a juridical space where one was accused, judged and sentenced, and from which one was released only by the version of this trial that took place at a deeper, psychological level—that is, by repentance. Madness was to be punished inside the asylum, even if declared innocent outside it. For a long time to come, and until our own day at least, it was to be imprisoned in a moral world (HF, 522–3; MC, 269).

Neither Pinel nor Tuke was either a doctor or a psychiatrist. Their efficacy was based not on an objective definition of the illness or some classificatory diagnosis, but on the obscure, internal workings of the Family, Authority, Punishment, and Love. It was by assuming the mask of Father and Judge that they became the almost magical agents of cure. It is something of a paradox that medical practice entered this semi-miraculous domain just as it was laying the foundations of its own positivity.

> If we wanted to analyse the profound structures of objectivity in the knowledge and practice of nineteenth-century psychiatry from Pinel to Freud, we would have to show in fact that such objectivity was from the start a reification of a magical kind, which could only be accomplished with the complicity of the patient himself, and on the basis of an initially transparent moral practice, gradually forgotten as positivism imposed its myths of scientific objectivity; a practice forgotten in its origins and its meanings, but always used and always present. What we call psychiatric practice is a certain moral tactic contemporary with the end of the eighteenth century, preserved in the rites of asylum life, and overlaid by the myths of positivism (HF, 528; MC, 276).

Freud occupies an ambivalent position in all this. He is sufficiently the child of positivistic science to see his work as an extension of the objective structures of the physical sciences. But he was also the first to see that behind the empty forms of positive psychiatry there stood a single concrete reality: the doctor-patient relationship. He was the first to take that relationship seriously; to see it as a dynamic whole, rather than to place the patient in the position of an *object* beneath the *objective* gaze of the doctor/scientist; and to face the full implications of that realization. On the other hand, he exploited all the semi-magical powers invested in the figure of the doctor.

> He focused upon this single presence—concealed behind the patient and above him, in an absence that is also a total presence—all the powers that had been distributed in the collective existence of the asylum; he transformed this into an absolute Observation, a pure, impassive Silence, a Judge who punishes and rewards in a judgement that does not even condescend to language. . . The doctor, as an alienating figure, remains the key to psychoanalysis. It is perhaps because it did not suppress this ultimate structure, and because it referred all the others to it, that psychoanalysis has not been able, will not be able, to hear the voices of unreason, nor to decipher in their own terms the signs of the madman. Psychoanalysis can unravel some of the forms of madness; it remains a stranger to the sovereign labour of unreason. It can neither liberate nor transcribe, let alone explain, what is essential in this labour. Since the end of the eighteenth century, the life of unreason has been manifested only in the lightning-flash of works such as those of Hölderlin, of Nerval, of Nietzsche, or of Artaud—forever irreducible to those alienations that can be cured, resisting by their own strength that gigantic moral imprisonment that we are in the habit of calling, doubtless by antiphrasis, the liberation of the insane by Pinel and Tuke (HF, 529–30; MC, 277–8).

To most readers, perhaps, *Naissance de la clinique* is the least immediately attractive of Foucault's books. There is an air of specialization, of marginality about the history of medicine. As if to overcome this initial reticence on the reader's part Foucault endows this work with one of his most arresting beginnings—like all great stylists, he has an acute sense of beginnings and endings.

> This book is about space, about language, and about death; it is about the act of seeing, the gaze.
> Towards the middle of the eighteenth century, Pomme treated and cured a hysteric by making her take 'baths, ten or twelve hours a day, for ten whole months. . .' (NC, V; BC, ix).

It is a technique Foucault uses often: an abstract statement of startling breadth, followed by some equally startling anecdote. With masterly economy we are shown that a study of the 'anatomo-clinical method' need not be of concern to medical historians alone—and that the pillaging of archives need not be short on entertainment value. In the end, what emerges from this apparently inauspicious material is a new perspective on nineteenth-century science and culture, expressed in some of Foucault's most sumptuously beautiful prose.

Naissance de la clinique was first published in 1966—two years after *Histoire de la folie*. It takes as its turning-point, the mid-point of its narrative, what is the culminating point of *Histoire de la folie*. The first half of the second book overlaps, therefore, with the last section of the first. It is, in a sense, an extended postscript to the earlier work. Georges Canguilhem had 'supervised' the presentation of *Histoire de la folie* for the degree of *doctorat d'état*; it was Canguilhem who commissioned *Naissance de la clinique* for his 'Galien', a series devoted to the 'history and philosophy of biology and medicine' published by the Presses Universitaires de France. By about 1970, the book had gone out of print and for a second edition, published in 1972, Foucault made a number of changes to the text. My English translation, *The Birth of the Clinic*, appeared in 1973 and incorporates these changes. They do not represent so much as a shift of emphasis, let alone a change of direction. They amount, in effect, to little more than rewordings: 'language' becomes 'discourse'; 'a structural analysis of the signified' becomes 'the analysis of a type of discourse', the signifier/signified distinction is largely dropped. In short, terms drawn from structural linguistics have been replaced by more 'neutral' terms. The explanation is to be found not in Foucault's work as such, but rather in his attitude to certain developments in the cultural milieu. During the early 1960s, in company with many French intellectuals, Foucault absorbed, almost without realizing it, a certain vocabulary deriving from Saussure and Jakobson. For some, the study of structural linguistics had an effect, to a greater or lesser degree, on their own work. For others, and Foucault is one, modern linguistics lay completely outside their area of interest. By the end of the decade, however, 'Structuralism' had not only arrived on the intellectual scene; it seemed to dominate it. Battle-lines were drawn up: a heterogeneous band of conservative academics, non-Althusserian Marxists, phenomenologists and Sartreans, on the one hand, and, on the other, a new wave of younger academics, largely from the École Normale Supérieure, claiming various allegiance to Lévi-Strauss, Lacan, Althusser, Barthes and, despite vigorous denials of the 'Structuralist' nature of his work, Foucault. The mere use of words like 'structure' and 'signifier' were enough to brand one a 'Structuralist'. From then on, Foucault was careful to avoid them and, when opportunity offered, to excise them from earlier work. I shall return at greater length to the question of Foucault's non-relation to 'Structuralism'. For the moment, it is enough perhaps to observe that the changes in vocabulary brought to *Naissance de la clinique* expressed a desire to contain a misunderstanding that had already spread beyond recall.

Histoire de la folie spans a vast time-scale: from the end of the Middle Ages, through the Renaissance and the 'classical' period, to the 'birth' of the asylum in the early nineteenth century. Its unifying concept, 'madness', is a particularly amorphous one. *Naissance de la clinique* covers barely half a century and is centred on a single, highly delimited object. The book turns around the point—the last years of the eighteenth century—when the old classificatory medicine gave way to the anatomo-clinical method, to medicine as the 'science' we know today. It is considerably shorter than its predecessor, but its concentration of focus means that the argument is correspondingly close and, on occasion, technical. Much of the book rehearses the intricacies and interrelations of medical discourse and institution (the 'nosologies', 'tables', 'systems' of classificatory medicine; the changing relations between seeing and naming; the reforms carried out in the wake of the French Revolution in public assistance, general and teaching hospitals, medical faculties and the medical profession generally; the theoretical problems attaching to anatomical practice or the treatment of fevers). With Foucault, it is always difficult to produce a summary of the argument that has much validity and pitch independent of the supporting detail: the detail is of the essence. Here the difficulty is compounded by the fact that this detail belongs to an area that is outside the competence of the general reader. I shall not attempt, therefore, to summarize the argument of this book, but merely to indicate a number of points that arise from it, depending more than usually on Foucault's own words. What may be of especial interest to the non-medical reader is the central role that Foucault attributes to medicine in the foundation of the social and human 'sciences', on the one hand, and, on the other, the importance for both the new medicine and the contemporary Romantic movement in the arts of the interlinked notions of individuality and death. In this respect, *Naissance de la clinique* is much more than a postscript to *Histoire de la folie*: it touches on problems that are fundamental to Foucault's next major work, *Les mots et les choses*.

'Never treat a disease without first being sure of its species': Gilibert's words might be taken as a motto of eighteenth-century classificatory medicine. Diseases were organized and hierarchized into so many families, genera and species; their semi-autonomous existences seemed to have more to do with one another than with the body that gave them temporary shelter. Presence in an organ was never absolutely necessary to define a disease: this disease could travel from one point on the body's surface to another and remain identical in nature. Indeed, for the eighteenth-century physician, the patient, with his peculiarities of age, sex, and personal history, represented an interference that had first to be abstracted before the pure nosological essence of the disease could be revealed. Even the intervention of the doctor himself was regarded as an impurity, an act of violence perpetrated on nature from the outside. The ultimate disturbance was death: death was at once the limit of the doctor's ability to cure and the end of the disease.

By common consent, modern medicine dates from the last years of the eighteenth century. The founding myth of modern medicine speaks of doctors who, letting the scales of phantasy fall from their eyes, were suddenly able to see what lay before them: experience had triumphed over theory. The myth has, for Foucault, a certain truth. The new clinical medicine that emerged at the turn of the century was dominated by the gaze, the act of seeing; it was particularly attuned to the individual, abnormal event. But, says Foucault, what made that mutation possible was not 'an act of psychological and epistomological purification', but rather 'a syntactical reorganization of disease in which the limits of the visible and invisible follow a new pattern' (NC, 197; BC, 195). Suddenly doctors were able to see and to describe what for centuries had lain beneath the level of the visible and the expressible. It was not so much that doctors suddenly opened their eyes; rather that the old *codes of knowledge* had determined *what* was seen. For doctors to see what nineteenth-century doctors were trained to see those codes had to be transgressed and transformed. What

Michel Foucault: The Will to Truth

occurred was not a return, beneath the level of language to a pure, untrammelled gaze, but a simultaneous change in *seeing* and *saying*. What made that change possible was a complex of events that included the reorganization of the hospital, a new definition of the social status of the patient, a new relationship between public assistance and medical experience, between health and knowledge; the patient had to be enveloped in a collective homogeneous space. This was achieved by a convergence of the requirements of a *political ideology* and those of a *medical technology*.

> In a concerted effort, doctors and statesmen demand, in a different vocabulary but for essentially identical reasons, the suppression of every obstacle to the constitution of this new space: the hospitals, which alter the specific laws governing disease and which disturb those no less rigorous laws that define the relations between property and wealth, poverty and work; the association of doctors, which prevents the formation of a centralized medical consciousness and the free play of an experience that is allowed to reach the universal without imposed limitations; and, lastly, the Faculties, which recognize that which is true only in theoretical structures and turn knowledge into a social privilege. Liberty is the vital, unfettered force of truth (NC, 37–8; BC, 38–9).

The essential locus of the new medicine was no longer the study or lecture-hall, where the doctor transmitted the fruits of his learning to his students, at several removes in time and space from the actual experience; it was now the hospital itself, where, as the experience occurred, it was simultaneously described by doctor to student. From this situation of examining and intervening in living, diseased bodies, it was a short step to 'opening up a few corpses': anatomo-clinical medicine was born.

> For twenty years, from morning to night, you have taken notes at patients' bedsides on affections of the heart, the lungs and the gastric viscera, and all is confusion for you in the symptoms which, refusing to yield up their meaning, offer you a succession of incoherent phenomena. Open up a few corpses: you will dissipate at once the darkness that observation alone could not dissipate (Bichat, *Anatomie générale*, quoted in NC, 148; BC, 146).

40

'The living night,' Foucault adds, 'is dissipated in the brightness of death.' Later, expanding the paradox, Foucault writes:

> That which hides and envelops, the curtain of night over truth, is, paradoxically, life; and death, on the contrary, opens up to the light of day the black coffer of the body: obscure life, limpid death, the oldest imaginary values of the Western world are crossed here in a strange misconstruction that is the very meaning of pathological anatomy if one agrees to treat it as a fact of civilization of the same order as—and why not?—the transformation from an incinerating to an inhuming culture. Nineteenth-century medicine was haunted by that absolute eye that cadaverizes life and rediscovers in the corpse the frail, broken nervure of life (NC, 168; BC, 166).

For classificatory medicine, death constituted the outer limit of its conceptual structure. With the advent of pathological anatomy, death became the summit in a new triangular structure of which life and disease were the other two terms.

> It is from the height of death that one can see and analyse organic dependences and pathological sequences. . . Death is the great analyst that shows the connections by unfolding them, and bursts upon the wonders of genesis in the rigour of decomposition: and the word *decomposition* must be allowed to stagger under the weight of its meaning (NC, 146; BC, 144).

In introducing death into knowledge the new medicine rediscovered a theme that had lain dormant throughout the Classical period.

> To see death in life, immobility in its change, skeletal, fixed space beneath its smile, and, at the end of its time, the beginning of a reversed time swarming with innumerable lives, is the structure of a Baroque experience whose re-appearance was attested by the previous century four hundred years after the frescoes of Campo Santo. Is not Bichat, in fact, the contemporary of the man who suddenly, in the most discursive of languages, introduced eroticism at its most inevitable point, death? Once more, knowledge and eroticism denounce, in this coincidence, their profound kinship. Throughout the latter years of the eighteenth century, this kinship opened up death to the task, to the infinitely repeated

attempts of language. The nineteenth century will speak obstinately of death: the savage, castrated death of Goya, the visible, muscular, sculptural death offered by Géricault, the voluptuous death by fire in Delacroix, the Lamartinian death of acquatic effusions, Baudelaire's death. To know life is given only to that derisory, reductive and already infernal knowledge that only wishes it dead. The Gaze that envelops, caresses, details, atomizes the most individual flesh and enumerates its secret bites is that fixed, attentive, rather dilated gaze which, from the height of death, has already condemned life.

But the perception of death in life does not have the same function in the nineteenth century as at the Renaissance. Then it carried with it reductive significations: differences of fate, fortune and condition were effaced by its universal gesture; it drew each irrevocably to all; the dances of skeletons depicted, on the underside of life, a sort of egalitarian saturnalia; death unfailingly compensated for fortune. Now, on the contrary, it is constitutive of singularity; it is in that perception of death that the individual finds himself, escaping from a monotonous, average life; in the slow, half-subterranean, but already visible, approach of death, the dull, common life becomes an individuality at last; a black border isolates it and gives it the style of its own truth. Hence the importance of the Morbid. The *macabre* implied a homogeneous perception of death, once its threshold had been crossed. The *morbid* authorizes a subtle perception of the way in which life finds in death its most differentiated figure. The morbid is the *rarefied* form of life, in the sense that an exhausted existence works itself into the void of death, but also in the sense that in death it takes on its peculiar volume, irreducible to conformities and customs, to received necessities, a *singular* volume defined by its absolute rarity. The privilege of the consumptive: in earlier times, one contracted leprosy against a background of great waves of collective punishment; in the nineteenth century, a man, in becoming tubercular, in the fever that hastens things and betrays them, fulfills his incommunicable secret. That is why chest diseases are of exactly the same nature as diseases of love: they are the Passion, a life to which death gives a face that cannot be exchanged. Death left its old tragic heaven and became the lyrical core of man: his invisible truth, his visible secret (NC, 173–4; BC, 170–2).

Only when death became the concrete *a priori* of medical experience could the old Aristotelian law, which prohibited the application of scientific discourse to the individual, be lifted.

Bergson is strictly in error when he seeks in time and against space, in a silent grasp of the internal, in a mad ride towards immortality, the conditions with which it is possible to conceive of the living individuality. Bichat, a century earlier, gave a more severe lesson. . .

It will no doubt remain a decisive fact about our culture that its first scientific discourse concerning the individual had to pass through this stage of death. Western man could constitute himself in his own eyes as an object of science, he grasped himself within his language and gave himself, in himself and by himself, a discursive existence, only in the opening created by his own elimination: from the experience of Unreason was born psychology, the very possibility of psychology; from the integration of death into medical thought is born a medicine that is given as a science of the individual. And, generally speaking, the experience of individuality in modern culture is bound up with that of death: from Hölderlin's Empedocles to Nietzsche's Zarathustra, and on to Freudian man, an obstinate relation to death prescribes to the universal its singular face, and lends to each individual the power of being heard forever; the individual owes to death a meaning that does not cease with him. The division that it traces and the finitude whose mark it imposes link, paradoxically, the universality of language and the precarious, irreplaceable form of the individual (NC, 173, 198–9; BC, 170, 197).

Thus medicine appears as the founding science of all the sciences of man, of that proliferation of disciplines that set out to study man as an individual interacting with other individuals; it is also seen to be linked, in its epistemic configuration, with all that we mean by Romanticism, with that sense of the doomed, isolated individual, with his dark, secret interiority. The changes brought about in medicine herald the major developments in nineteenth-century science and art.

It is understandable, then, that medicine should have had such importance in the constitution of the sciences of man—an importance that is not only methodological, but ontological, in that it concerns man's being as object of positive knowledge.

The possibility for the individual of being both subject and object of his own knowledge implies an inversion in the structure of finitude. For classical thought, finitude had no other content than the negation of the infinite, while the thought that was formed at the end of the eighteenth century gave it the powers of the positive: the anthropological structure that then appeared played both the critical role of limit and the founding role of origin. It was this reversal that served as the philosophical condition for the organiza- tion of a positive medicine; conversely, this positive medicine marked, at the empirical level, the beginning of that fundamental relation that binds modern man to his original finitude. Hence the fundamental place of medicine in the over-all architecture of the human sciences: it is closer than any of them to the anthropological structure that sustains them all. Hence, too, its prestige in the concrete forms of existence: health replaces salvation, said Guar- dia. This is because medicine offers modern man the obstinate, yet reassuring face of his finitude; in it, death is endlessly repeated, but it is also exorcized; and although it ceaselessly reminds man of the limit that he bears within him, it also speaks to him of that technical world that is the armed, positive, full form of his finitude. At that point in time, medical gestures, words, gazes took on a philosophi- cal density that had formerly belonged only to mathematical thought. The importance of Bichat, Jackson and Freud in European culture does not prove that they were philosophers as well as doctors, but that, in this culture, medical thought is fully engaged in the philosophical status of man.

This medical experience is therefore akin even to a lyrical experi- ence that his language sought, from Hölderlin to Rilke. This experi- ence, which began in the eighteenth century, and from which we have not yet escaped, is bound up with a return to the forms of finitude, of which death is no doubt the most menacing, but also the fullest. Hölderlin's Empedocles, reaching, by voluntary steps, the very edge of Etna, is the death of the last mediator between mortals and Olympus, the end of the infinite on earth, the flame returning to its native fire, leaving as its sole remaining trace that which had precisely to be abolished by his death: the beautiful, enclosed form of individuality; after Empedocles, the world is placed under the sign of finitude, in that irreconcilable, intermediate state in which reigns the Law, the harsh law of limit; the destiny of individuality will be to appear always in the objectivity that manifests and conceals it, that denies it and yet forms its basis. . . In what at first sight might seem a very strange way, the movement that sustained lyricism in the nineteenth century was one and the same as that by which man obtained positive knowledge of himself; but is it surprising that the figure of knowledge and those of language should obey the same profound law and that the irruption of finitude should dominate, in the same way, this relation of man to death, which, in the first case, authorizes a scientific discourse in a rational form and, in the second, opens up the source of a language that unfolds endlessly in the void left by the absence of the gods? (NC, 199–200; BC, 197–8).

◊ 2 ◊

The World, Representation, Man

This book first arose out of a passage in Borges, out of the laughter that shattered, as I read the passage, all the familiar landmarks of thought—*our* thought, the thought that bears the stamp of our age and our geography—breaking up all the ordered surfaces and all the planes with which we are accustomed to tame the wild profusion of existing things and continuing long afterwards to disturb and threaten with collapse our age-old distinction between the Same and the Other. This passage quotes 'a certain Chinese encyclopaedia' in which it is written that 'animals are divided into: (a) belonging to the Emperor, (b) embalmed, (c) tame, (d) sucking pigs, (e) sirens, (f) fabulous, (g) stray dogs, (h) included in the present classification, (i) frenzied, (j) innumerable, (k) drawn with a very fine camelhair brush, (l) *et cetera*, (m) having just broken the water pitcher, (n) that from a long way off look like flies'. In the wonderment of this taxonomy, the thing we apprehend in one great leap, the thing that, by means of the fable, is demonstrated as the exotic charm of another system of thought, is the limitation of our own, the stark impossibility of thinking *that*. But what is it impossible to think, and what kind of impossibility are we faced with here? (MC, 7; OT, xv).

Les mots et les choses was first published in 1966, four years after *Naissance de la clinique* and the short book on Raymond Roussel. In the intervening years Foucault published a number of articles and reviews, notably four long pieces on writers that had particularly claimed his attention: 'Le non du père' (on Hölderlin), 'Préface à la

46

transgression' (on Georges Bataille), 'Le langage à l'infini' (on Maurice Blanchot), 'La prose d'Actéon' (on Pierre Klossowski). (The first three have been translated into English and appear in Bouchard's *Language, Counter-Memory, Practice*.) In the most obvious, superficial sense *Les mots et les choses* marked a turning-point in Foucault's career. *Histoire de la folie* had been turned down by two leading Paris publishers and, somewhat grudgingly, accepted by its eventual publisher. The original edition had not sold well: the cheaper, abridged version had sold better, though not as well as such a book in that format might be expected to. Reviews were few, tardy, and largely uncomprehending. There were exceptions, notably Roland Barthes' in *Critique* and Maurice Blanchot's in the *NRF* (appearing several weeks after an earlier, uncomplimentary review in the same journal). *Naissance de la clinique* fared still worse: lower sales, virtually no reviews. *Raymond Roussel* almost totally escaped attention save for a curious review by Alain Robbe-Grillet in which, for reasons best known to himself, the reviewer contrived to say nothing about Foucault's book. In the circumstances, Gallimard can hardly be blamed for publishing *Les mots et les choses* in a modest first edition of 3,000 copies. The book was sold out within a week. A further 5,000 copies were printed, which were sold within six weeks. In the end, 50,000 copies of the French edition alone were sold. What is more, Foucault's other books rapidly went out of print and have since been reissued several times. I mention such matters not out of scholarly scruple, still less in a spirit of idle gossip, but because a book is not a closed system of significations, existing in a pure, ideal state inhabited by a single, disembodied consciousness, but an event in a real, complex cultural situation. *How* it is read (misread or not read) is an integral part of that event. Moreover, the phenomenon I have described was not confined to Foucault. The year 1966 also saw the publication of Lacan's long-awaited *Écrits*, which managed to be at once a runaway commercial success and one of the most inaccessible collections of texts ever written. A similar fate awaited books by Barthes, Lévi-Strauss, Deleuze and Guattari, and others.

The English translation of *Les mots et les choses* appeared in 1970. Since two books were already in print bearing the title *Words and Things*, Foucault was asked to supply an alternative. He suggested *The Order of Things*, adding that it was a title he preferred to the original one. In a foreword to the English edition Foucault provides a succinct account of his aims. The history of science has given a certain primacy to the sciences of the abstract and inorganic, to mathematics, cosmology, physics, for example—sciences, in fact, that embody most completely the ideal model of scientific endeavour. The other disciplines, those in which the human being figures, to a greater or lesser extent, as object as well as subject, are thought to be too impure, too resistant to objective criteria, too deeply imbued with the human colouring of error, superstition, and prejudice to provide anything but an irregular, confused history. Foucault's initial hypothesis was that perhaps on the contrary, all the intellectual activity of a given period obeyed the laws of a certain code of knowledge. He took a period stretching from the end of the Renaissance to the end of the nineteenth century and three distinct discourses, those concerning living beings, language, and wealth. The second hypothesis concerned chronology: to what extent would the periodization employed in the studies of madness and medicine—a 'Classical' age beginning in the mid-seventeenth century and ending with the eighteenth, preceded by the Renaissance and followed by the modern period—be applicable to the three kinds of discourse under examination? If the mutation around 1800 that occurred in the history of medicine were found to be valid also for our three disciplines, then there would be a sense in which one could hardly speak of eighteenth-century discourse on economic exchange (the 'analysis of wealth') as belonging to the same discipline as nineteenth-century discourse on the same subject (political economy). The same can be said for the other two pairs, natural history/biology and general grammar/philology. Indeed, the reverse would probably be true; that is, the three nineteenth-century disciplines would reveal common underlying structures that were quite alien to their three eighteenth-century predecessors. This common basis is what Foucault calls the 'archaeological' level or system. It consists of a set of rules of formation that determine the conditions of possibility of all that can be said within the particular discourse at any given time. It is this 'archaeological' method that distinguishes Foucault's analyses from those of the historians of science.

On the one hand, the history of science traces the progress of discovery, the formulation of problems and the clash of controversy; it also analyses theories in their internal economy; in short, it describes the processes and products of the scientific consciousness. But, on the other hand, it tries to restore what eluded that consciousness: the influences that affected it, the implicit philosophies that were subjacent to it, the unformulated thematics, the unseen obstacles; it describes the unconscious of science. This unconscious is always the negative side of science— that which resists it, deflects it or disturbs it. What I would like to do, however, is to reveal a *positive unconscious* of knowledge: a level that eludes the consciousness of the scientist and yet is part of scientific discourse, instead of disputing its validity and seeking to diminish its scientific nature. What was common to the natural history, the economics and the grammar of the Classical period was certainly not present to the consciousness of the scientist; or that part of it that was conscious was superficial, limited and almost fanciful, but, unknown to themselves, the naturalists, economists and grammarians employed the same rules to define the objects proper to their own study, to form their concepts, to build their theories (OT, xi).

What, more than anything else, provides the coherence of Classical theories of language, living beings and wealth is a philosophical theory of representation, in which language is seen as the *tabula*, the space, on which things, in the form of their verbal representations, are ordered. With the turn of the century, the theory of representation is replaced by a theory of historicity, which imposes on things a form of order implied by the continuity of time, by development. The analysis of wealth and its circulation gives way to a study of how wealth is produced; the search for the taxonomic 'characters' of natural entities to an examination of organism as function; language ceases to be the universal medium of representation and becomes itself a historical phenomenon, subject to change, as dense and obscure as the interior of any living being. It is easy to see the significance for Foucault of Borges' 'Chinese Encyclopaedia'. That ordered list of nineteen sub-categories of the category 'animal' acts as total violation of any rational classification known to us: its apparently measured progress through the alphabet, from '(a) belonging to the Emperor' to '(n) that from a long way off look like flies' has all the trappings of rational analysis while subverting reason itself. It seems to conflate 'our age-old distinction between the Same and the Other'. One could comment at length on the various ways Borges' 'classification' does this, but basically its impossibility rests on the absence of any space in which such categories could coexist. What is missing is the 'operating table' on which, however improbably, Lautréamont's 'umbrella' and 'sewing-machine' could rest. Or, rather, that space is provided by language alone. That coexistence of the minutely specific ('drawn with a very fine camelhair brush', for example, which is, itself, not a category of real animal), the almost universal ('innumerable', *'et cetera'*) and a category that includes all the others can only be an autonomously linguistic one.

If Borges' 'classification' stands as an extreme instance of the breakdown of representation, Velázquez's *Las Meninas*, which is reproduced in the book, and which occupies the whole of Foucault's first chapter, may be taken as a perfect image of Classical representation. The scene is Velázquez's studio—paintings line the two visible walls. On the left, the painter stands, brush in hand, facing a huge canvas, of which only the reverse side is visible to us. Other figures stand or kneel in the foreground: the young Infanta Margarita, a dwarf, a jester, a dog, courtiers, and the eponymous maids-of-honour. At the rear of the studio, a man is standing in a lighted doorway. The painter's gaze is directed at an invisible point beyond the foreground of the picture, to that point that we, the spectators, occupy. (Most of the other figures in the picture are also looking at the same point.) In short, we are looking at a picture in which the painter is in turn looking out at us. Moreover, we occupy the same position as that of his subject. But what is the subject of the painting within the painting whose position we have, as it were, usurped? On the rear wall of the studio is a 'picture' that appears more clearly defined, more brightly lit than the others. In fact, it is a mirror: reflected in it is an image of a man and a woman. They, Philip IV of Spain and his wife, Mariana, are the true subjects of the painting. The picture is only ironically, misleadingly named after the quite incidental maids-of-honour in the foreground. The mirror is the reverse side, or, rather, the right side of the canvas: from behind the painter, it shows us what he sees and what he is in the process of depicting on his canvas. All the elements of representation are represented here—the gaze, the palette and brush, the canvas, the finished paintings, the reflections, light—all except the subject of that representation. In the most obvious sense, it is a self-portrait of Velázquez's work. Painted in 1658, it stands at the threshold of the Classical age as a representation of Classical representation itself.

But before embarking on his analysis of Classical culture, Foucault lays before us a description of the Renaissance notion of 'the prose of the world', the world held together by the power of resemblance.

It was resemblance that largely guided exegesis and the interpreta-tion of texts; it was resemblance that organized the play of symbols, made possible knowledge of things visible and invisible, and con-trolled the art of representing them. The universe was folded in upon itself: the earth echoing the sky, faces seeing themselves reflected in the stars and plants holding within their stems secrets that were of use to man. Painting imitated space. And repres-entation—whether in the service of pleasure or knowledge—was positioned as a form of repetition: the theatre of life or the mirror of nature, that was the claim made by all languages, its manner of declaring its existence and of formulating its right of speech (MC, 32; OT, 17).

In its various forms of *convenientia* (adjacency), *aemulatio*, analogy, and sympathy, resemblance maintained the world in its identity. But the power of the last of these, sympathy, was so strong, so all-pervasive, that it required an equally powerful counter-force, antipathy, to hold things apart, to prevent a total assimilation of everything in the Same. This system of resemblances, which held everything together, yet distinct, was inscribed in the universe itself in the form of signs. Human knowledge was a matter of unearthing and deciphering these signatures. But this knowledge was not self-evident, not accessible to the untutored eye. In the sixteenth century, no distinction was drawn between the observation of natural phenomena, on the one hand, and, on the other, magic, Scripture, and the writings of the Ancients. In both cases there were signs that had to be discovered and interpreted. In its original form, language was perfectly transparent: word and thing were one, because created simultaneously by God. After Babel, language became fragmented into human languages and the original resemblance to things was lost. Even Hebrew, the language closest to that original language, was but a dim memory of that original naming of things. At the Renaissance signs were organized in a three-fold system: the marks themselves, the things designated by those marks and the similitudes that joined them together. However, since resemblance constituted both the form and the content of the sign, the three elements operated as a single figure. During the seventeenth century the arrangement of signs became binary: the connection of a *significans* (signifier) with a *significandum* (signified). The world was no longer seen as itself a depository of language; language was wrested free of things, entered an arbitrary relation to them as *representation*, as one form of representation. There is one literary masterpiece that, perhaps more than any other, embodies the old interplay of signs of resemblance, while containing the beginnings of new relations.

> Don Quixote is not a man given to extravagance, but rather a diligent pilgrim breaking his journey before all the marks of similitude. He is the hero of the Same. He never manages to escape from the familiar plain stretching out on all sides of the Analogue, any more than he does from his own small province. He travels endlessly over that plain, without ever crossing the clearly defined frontiers of difference or reaching the heart of identity. . . His whole being is nothing but language, text, printed pages, stories that already have been written down. He is made up of interwoven words; he is writing itself, wandering through the world among the resemblances of things. . . Don Quixote reads the world in order to prove his books. . . His whole journey is a quest for similitudes: the slightest analogies are pressed into service as dormant signs that must be reawakened and made to speak once more. Flocks, serving girls and inns become more the language of books to the imperceptible degree to which they resemble castles, ladies and armies—a perpetually untenable resemblance that transforms the sought-for proof into derision and leaves the words of the books forever hollow (MC, 60–1; OT, 46–7).

But *Don Quixote* is also a negative as well as an ironic farewell to it.

> Writing has ceased to be the prose of the world; resemblances and signs have dissolved their former alliance; similitudes have become deceptive and verge upon the visionary or madness; things still remain stubbornly within their ironic identity: they are no longer anything but what they are; words wander off on their own, without content, without resemblance to fill their emptiness; they are no longer the marks of things; they lie sleeping between the pages of

books and covered in dust. Magic, which permitted the decipher-
ment of the world by revealing the secret resemblances beneath its
signs, is no longer of any use except as an explanation, in terms of
madness, of why analogies are always proved false. The erudition
that once read nature and books alike as parts of a single text has
been relegated to the same category as its own chimeras: lodged in
the yellowed pages of books, the signs of language no longer have
any value apart from the slender fiction that they represent. The
written word and things no longer resemble one another. And
between them, Don Quixote wanders off on his own (MC, 61–2; OT,
47–8).

From being the source of knowledge, similitude becomes, in the
seventeenth century, an occasion of error, the charming phantasy of
a knowledge that had not yet reached the age of reason. Bacon, with
his examination of 'idols' launched one of the first attacks on resemblance. A more thoroughgoing and far-reaching critique came from
Descartes. For him, resemblance was little more than a confused
mixture of different categories that had to be analysed in terms of
identity and difference. More particularly, the notion of resemblance
is replaced by that of comparison, of which there are two kinds: that of
measurement and that of order. The one analyses into units with a
view to forming relations of equality and inequality; the other establishes the simplest possible elements and arranges differences according to the smallest possible degrees. As a result, the entire *episteme* of
Western culture was transformed in its most fundamental arrangement. At the most superficial level this new *episteme* might find
expression in a number of different, even conflicting schools of
thought. In the late seventeenth century 'mechanism' provided a
theoretical knowledge in certain fields, such as physiology and
medicine. There was also a more widespread attempt to reduce all
empirical knowledge to the laws of mathematics. But, at the
archaeological level, says Foucault, what is constant throughout the
Classical age, what governs all scientific endeavour is the belief that
the relations betweeen things are to be conceived in the form of order,
it being understood that problems of measurement are also reducible
to problems of order. In this sense, analysis soon acquired the value of
a universal method. However, this relation to the mathesis, or general science of order, does not mean that all knowledge was absorbed

into mathematics. On the contrary, side by side with this search for a mathesis, a number of empirical fields were being established in which no trace of mathematics was to be found. Nevertheless, they are all based on the notion of order. General grammar, natural history, and the analysis of wealth were sciences of order in the domain of words, beings, and needs. All three are coextensive with the Classical period, their limits being marked, around 1660, by Lancelot, Ray, and Petty, and, around 1800–10 by Bopp, Cuvier, and Ricardo respectively. Although all dependent on the analysis of order, their particular method was not the algebraic method, but the system of signs. The ordering of things by means of signs characterized all empirical knowledge as knowledge based upon identity and difference. In the case of simple natures ordering takes the form of mathesis, in particular the algebraic method. When ordering complex natures (representations in general, as given in experience) one has recourse to a *taxonomy*, which requires a system of signs. Having analysed the mutation in the Western *episteme* that took place in the mid-seventeenth century, from a general theory of signs and resemblance to one based on signs and representation, Foucault is in a position to embark on his detailed analysis of the Classical theories of language, classification, and money. No culture is able to grasp in its coherence the general system of knowledge that generates and constricts its more visible forms of knowledge. In this respect, however, the Classical age was particularly percipient at seeing the connections between the various branches of empirical knowledge. Writers in one field frequently wrote, with equal authority, on others. Condillac and Dustutt de Tracy included in their theory of knowledge and language the theory of wealth and exchange; Turgot wrote the article on 'Etymology' for the *Encyclopédie* and the first systematic parallel between money and words as systems of exchange; Rousseau wrote on botany as well as on the origin of languages.

'The existence of language in the Classical age is both pre-eminent and unobtrusive' (MC, 92; OT, 78). It occupies the foremost position because its task is to represent thought. Such representation is not, however, an act of translation or an exact physical replica of mental phenomena. Thought does not exist in a pure, disembodied condition prior to its expression in language. It is in the nature of thought to represent itself, that is, to analyse itself into parts, to place one part beside another, to make one part stand in place of another. Representations do not derive their meaning from the world; language and meaning are inherent within them. Language *is* thought. As a result, its very existence ceases to be a problem.

> The Renaissance came to a halt before the brute fact that language existed: in the density of the world, a graphism mingling with things or flowing beneath them; marks made upon manuscripts or the pages of books. And all these insistent marks summoned up a secondary language—that of commentary, exegesis, erudition—in order to stir the language that lay dormant within them and to make it speak at last; the existence of language preceded, as if by a mute stubbornness, what one could read in it and the words that gave it sound. From the seventeenth century, it is this massive and intriguing existence of language that is eliminated. It no longer appears hidden in the enigma of the mark. . . From an extreme point of view, one might say that language in the Classical era does not exist: it functions. Its whole existence is located in its representative role, is limited precisely to that role and finally exhausts it. Language has no other locus, no other value, than in representation (MC, 93; OT, 79).

Language is not a being, but a function: a system of verbal signs that represents representation. What distinguishes language from other sign-systems is not so much that it is individual or collective, natural or arbitrary, but that it analyses representation in a necessarily successive order. It cannot represent thought instantly, in its totality: it must arrange it, part by part, in a linear order. The study of this verbal order in its relation to the simultaneity of thought is what the Classical age called 'general grammar'. However, it does not attempt to define the *laws* underlying all languages, but to examine each particular language in turn, as a mode of representation. It defines the system of identities and differences that its peculiar set of 'characters' presuppose and employ. It establishes the *taxonomy* of each language, the mechanism by which discourse is made possible. This activity may be broken down into what Foucault calls the 'quadrilateral of language', a four-sided figure made up the proposition, designation, articulation and derivation. The proposition is the essential object of general grammar: it is to language what representation is to thought. The theory of the proposition is more particularly the theory of the verb, for without the verb there can be no discourse. Furthermore, all verbs

55

are reducible to the single verb *to be*, which is the representation of being in language. It is also the representative being *of* language—that which makes it susceptible to truth or error. Language is *discourse* by virtue of the power of the word to leap across the system of signs towards the being of the signified. The word also designates: it is by nature a name, a noun. In its simplest form it is a proper noun, a particular representation, the name of one thing only. There ought to be as many of them as there are things to name. But if that were the case discourse would remain at a very primitive, inefficient, unordered and, ultimately, confused level. The acquiring and transmission of knowledge is dependent on a form of language in which nouns represent not only individuals, but also qualities common to several individuals. Thus a distinguishing activity comes into play, grouping together individuals that have certain identities in common and separating those that are different. From these substantival distinctions all the other forms of distinction, including syntax itself, derive. These taxonomic, ordering functions are called articulation. This leads to the question of the arbitrariness of the sign (since that which designates may be as different from that which it indicates as a gesture from the object towards which it is directed) and the profound link with that which it names (since a particular word has always been chosen to designate a particular thing). The first concerns the analysis of the language of action, the second the study of roots. Language originates in the spontaneous cries emitted by primitive man, but it is also a separation from their natural origin. Roots are those rudimentary words that are to be found in a similar form in a number of languages. Their universality is attributable to their appropriateness to that which they represent, the most obvious form of which is onomatopoeia. The theory of derivation concerns the capacity of words not only to move away from their original signification and to acquire wider (or narrower) meanings, but also to alter their sounds and, even, to disappear altogether. At the centre of the quadrilateral is the *name*. To name is to give the verbal representation of a mental representation; it is also to place it in a general table. The entire Classical theory of language is organized around this central, privileged entity.

At the beginning of his section on 'natural history', Foucault takes issue with various interpretations of the Classical period offered by historians of science or ideas. What these amount to is a 'horizontal' view of scientific development, in contrast with Foucault's 'vertical', archaeological analysis. Thus eighteenth-century 'natural history' is seen, not as a system coherent in itself and coherent with other widely removed, yet contemporary disciplines, but as the pre-history of nineteenth-century biology, as a heterogeneous amalgam of notions that were to prove useful or otherwise in the advance towards a truly scientific biology. Foucault points out some of the methodological problems inherent in writing this kind of history:

> The difficulty of apprehending the network that is able to link such diverse investigations as attempts to establish a taxonomy and microscopic observations; the necessity of recording as observed facts the conflicts between those who were fixists and those who were not, or between the experimentalists and the partisans of the system; the obligation to divide knowledge into two interwoven fabrics where in fact they were alien to one another—the first being defined by what was known already and from elsewhere (the Aristotelian or scholastic inheritance, the weight of Cartesianism, the prestige of Newton), the second by what still remained to be known (evolution, the specificity of life, the notion of organism); and above all the application of categories that are strictly ana-chronistic in relation to this knowledge. Obviously, the most important of all these refers to life. Historians want to write his-tories of biology in the eighteenth century; but they do not realize that biology did not exist then, and that the pattern of knowledge that has been familiar to us for a hundred and fifty years is not valid for a previous period. And that, if biology was unknown, there was a very simple reason for it: that life itself did not exist. All that existed were living beings, which were viewed through a grid of knowledge constituted by *natural history* (MC, 139; OT, 127–8).

Contrary to a view commonly expressed, natural history did not appear to fill the gap left by Cartesian mechanism, at the point when it became clear that the complexity of the vegetable and animal king-doms could not be made to fit the laws of rectilinear movement. In fact, the very possibility of natural history as found in the work of Ray and Jonston is contemporaneous with Cartesianism itself, not with its decline. Mechanism from Descartes to d'Alembert and natural his-tory from Tournefort to Daubenton were authorized by the same *episteme*. What characterizes Jonston's *Natural History of the Quadruped* in relation to, say, Aldrovandi half a century earlier is not an increase in knowledge, but rather a profound change in the assumptions upon which such knowledge is based. Indeed the most striking difference between the two writers is that Jonston has scaled down rather than expanded the range of concerns considered appropriate. The six-teenth century made no distinction between, on the one hand, description of the parts or organs of a plant or animal and, on the other, its supposed virtues, the legends associated with it, its place in heraldry, medicine, or cooking and what the Ancients or travellers happen to have written about it. Jonston was able to ignore so much of what appeared in Aldrovandi not because science had at last discovered its rational vocation and was able to slough off the dead weight of superstition, but rather because signs were no longer regarded as part of things themselves; they had become rep-resentations of things. Because one could now *say* things in a new way, one could see things in a new way. At the height of the Classical period Linnaeus laid down the method for natural description. Every living being should be analysed in the following order: name, theory, kind, species, attributes, use, and *Litteraria*. Old habits die hard. Even Linnaeus considered it a part of his task to mention the cultural accretions that had formed around the objects of his observation. But they were kept quite separate, banished, as it were, to a harmless appendage at the end. The thing itself is allowed to appear, analysed in its various parts, related to other more or less similar things, but only according to a process initiated by the name. Why natural *his-tory*? Until the mid-seventeenth century writing about living beings was a sub-division of history. The historian's task was essentially that of a compiler of documents and signs: he did not say what he saw, but retold what others had written. Classical natural history inherited the title, but gave it a new, or rather revived its original, meaning. (In Greek, the term 'history' has the broader sense of any form of inquiry.) It set itself the very different task of examining things with meticulous care and transcribing what was seen in smooth, neutral, accurate language. The 'documents' of this natural history were not written words, but free spaces in which things were juxtaposed: herbariums, collections, gardens.

> The locus of this history is a non-temporal rectangle in which, stripped of all commentary, of all enveloping language, creatures

present themselves one beside another, their surfaces visible, grouped according to their common features and thus already virtually analysed, and bearers of nothing but their own individual names. It is often said that the establishment of botanical gardens and zoological collections expressed a new curiosity about exotic plants and animals. In fact, these had already claimed men's interest for a long while. What had changed was the space in which it was possible to see them and from which it was possible to describe them. To the Renaissance, the strangeness of animals was a spectacle: it was featured in fairs, in tournaments, in fictitious or real combats, in reconstitutions of legends in which the bestiary displayed its ageless fables. The natural history room and the garden, as created in the Classical period, replaced the circular procession of the 'show' with the arrangement of things in a 'table'. What came surreptitiously into being between the age of the theatre and that of the catalogue was not the desire for knowledge, but a new way of connecting things both to the eye and to discourse (MC, 143; OT, 131).

Natural history became possible not because men looked more carefully, more closely at things, but rather because the requirement of naming things necessarily involved the concentration on certain parts of what one saw to the exclusion of others. Literary accretions had already been excluded, but so also had the evidence of most of the senses. Taste and smell were considered too variable, too imprecise to furnish a universally accepted description. The sense of touch was limited to a few fairly evident distinctions, such as that between rough and smooth. Even colour was excluded from the area of relevant visual information. What remained was a series of carefully screened black and white objects that could be analysed according to four variables: the form of the component parts, their quantity, their relative distribution, and their relative size. The simplicity of such an analysis makes it readily communicable and comprehensible to all. Words and things have come together in a simultaneous act of seeing and naming that excludes all uncertainty. This articulation of the object was what botanists called its structure. So inseparable was its structure from the words that comprised it that Linnaeus even proposed a form of description in which the actual arrangement of words on the page would mirror the arrangement of their visual counterparts on the object. Thus structure also linked natural history to the mathesis. By reducing the visible to a system of variables susceptible, if not to quantity, at least to a clear, finite description, it became possible to establish an order of identities and differences between natural entities. Natural history concerned itself with surfaces and lines, but not with functions or invisible tissues. The plant or animal was seen not so much as an organic unity as a visible articulation of organs. Throughout the Classical period, anatomy had lost the prestige it had enjoyed during the Renaissance and which it was to acquire again at the end of the eighteenth century. This was not because curiosity had diminished or knowledge declined; rather that the fundamental arrangement of the visible and expressible no longer passed through the thickness of the body. This explains why so much more attention was paid to botanical than to zoological study in the eighteenth century. The organs of plants are generally more visible than those of animals and thus yield a richer, more coherent set of perceptible variables.

The complete set of elements selected from a particular plant or animal for description was called its *structure*. Its *character* was composed of those elements that distinguished it from and linked it to other natural entities. Using the linguistic analogy, structure constituted a proper noun, character a common noun. Classical natural history knew two ways of determining character, each having its own adherents. One could take a number of entities possessing fairly obvious similarities, select one of them, describe all its various parts (its structure), then proceed to the second, omitting all parts previously enumerated in the first entity, then the third, and so on. Finally, by a process of comparison, the character that distinguishes each species or genus is the one differential feature that stands out from the background of identities. This procedure, known as the Method, was practised by, among others, Buffon and Adanson. The alternative was to select a limited group of elements whose variations and constants could be studied in any individual entity. Differences not related to one of these elements would be regarded as irrelevant. When such elements were found in two individuals they were given a common name. This procedure, known as the System, was chiefly associated with Linnaeus. However, the opposition of the two schools was a relatively superficial phenomenon. System and Method rested on the same epistemological base, which distinguished them from the pre- and post-Classical study of living beings. They both required a knowledge of individual natural entities deriving from the continuous, ordered tabulation of differences. With the beginnings of modern biology differences were to be deduced not so much from sets of external variables as from a consideration of internal systems (skeleton, respiration, circulation). Classification occupied a gap of some hundred and fifty years between the Renaissance theory of the *mark* and the modern theory of the *organism*.

Just as there is no biology or philology in the Classical period, so there is no political economy in the sense understood, since Ricardo, of a discipline based on the concept of production. The economic discourse contemporary with general grammar and natural history was based, not on production or labour, but on the notions of money and exchange; it was known as the 'analysis of wealth'. In the sixteenth century economic thought was mainly concerned with the problem of prices and that of the best monetary substance. These problems were made more acute by the effect of successive devaluations and the influx of Spanish gold into the European economy. The metals used in coins were not commodities, but signs, signs of wealth. But just as words belonged to the same order of reality as the things they signified, so the signs that indicated wealth were in themselves valuable. The two functions of money, as a common measure of commodities and as a substitute in exchange, were based on its material reality. With the advent of the Classical age this analysis is turned upside down: it is its function in exchange that provides the basis for its other two characteristics. This reversal, by which money became the instrument of the representation and analysis of wealth, is usually referred to as mercantilism. Just as the word is a representation of the thing and the verbal description of structure a representation of the living being, so the metal coin is the sign of a certain quantity of wealth. And just as the individual word or natural character is capable of being articulated in a language— whether a natural language or the artificial language of taxonomy—and used in communication, so money has its own form of language, exchange. This exchangeability was conceived by the Classical period as a 'pledge', that is, money was simply a token accepted by common consent. But this token was also reversible: coinage could also buy back that for which it was exchanged. That, at least, was the theory. However, old suspicions lingered in men's minds and these

61

were further aggravated by the advent of paper money. How could one be sure that money in relation to commodities was not an empty sign devoid of real value? It was on this issue that one of the great controversies in the Classical analysis of wealth was centred. There were those who believed that money was guaranteed by the marketable material from which it was made. Others, led by Law, thought that the value of money could be linked to the quantity of some other commodity, guaranteed by collective consent or the will of the prince. Yet, in relation to the single arrangement that made all such controversies possible, this opposition was a mere surface effect. The other major controversy of the period was between the Physiocrats and their opponents; it concerned the theory of value. Yet, here again, the theoretical elements are the same in each case.

> All wealth springs from the land; the value of things is linked with exchange; money has value as the representation of the wealth in circulation; circulation should be as simple and as complete as possible. But these theoretical segments are arranged by the Physiocrats and by the 'ultilitarians' in reverse order. . . What plays a positive role in one theory becomes negative in the other. Condillac, Galiani and Graslin start from the exchange of utilities as the subjective and positive foundation of all values; all that satisfies a need has, therefore, a value and any transformation or transference that makes it possible to satisfy a greater number of needs constitutes an increase of value: it is this increase that makes it possible to remunerate workers, by giving them an amount deducted from this increase, which is equivalent to their subsistence. But all these positive elements that constitute value are based upon a certain state of need present in men and therefore upon the finite character of nature's fecundity. For the Physiocrats, the same sequence must be gone through in the opposite direction: all transformation of the products of the land and all work on them is remunerated by the worker's subsistence; it must therefore be debited to the totality of goods as a diminution; value arises only where there is consumption. For value to be created, then, nature must be endowed with endless fecundity (MC, 212–13: OT, 199).

At this point Foucault remarks, not without a touch of irony, that perhaps it would have been simpler to say that the Physiocrats represented the landowners and the 'ultilitarians' the merchants and entrepreneurs. He goes on to sketch a possible analysis of the two opposing ideologies in terms of class conflict. Foucault in no way disputes the validity of such an approach. Membership of a social group may explain why a particular individual espouses one system of thought rather than another, but the conditions that make it possible for that system to be thought do not reside in the existence of the group. Physiocrat and Anti-Physiocrat share the same set of concepts and the ways in which those concepts are articulated are subject to the same restrictions. This set of concepts and rules is what is known as 'analysis of wealth'.

At a still deeper level, as it were, the analysis of wealth shares a common ground with general and natural history. All three empirical disciplines are made possible by a general philosophical concept, that of representation. The end of Classical thought will coincide with the decline of representation, or rather with the emancipation of language, of the living being and of need from the limitation of representation.

> The obscure but stubborn spirit of a people who talk, the violence and the endless effort of life, the hidden energy of needs, were all to escape from the mode of being of representation. And representation itself was to be paralleled, limited, circumscribed, mocked perhaps, but in any case regulated from the outside, by the enormous thrust of a freedom, a desire or a will, posited as the metaphysical converse of consciousness. Something like a will or force was to arise in the modern experience—constituting it perhaps but in any case indicating that the Classical age was now over, and with it the reign of representative discourse, the dynasty of a representation signifying itself and giving voice in the sequence of its words to the order that lay dormant within things. This reversal is contemporaneous with Sade. . . (MC, 222; OT, 209).

No bathos is intended. The English-speaking reader, unaware perhaps of the importance attributed to Sade's work in France, may well wonder what the albeit 'divine' Marquis is doing in such august company. Foucault chooses to end his analysis of the Classical age with a discussion of Sade, not *pour épater le bourgeois*, but because he sees Sade as occupying a position at the end of this period isomorphic with that attributed to Cervantes at its outset. To be more precise, just as the first part of *Don Quixote* exemplifies a sixteenth-century view of

63

the world and the second, in some measure, a world of representation, so *Justine* embodies a classical world of representation and *Juliette* the collapse of that world.

In Justine, desire and representation communicate only through the presence of Another who represents the heroine to himself as an object of desire, while she herself knows nothing of desire other than its diaphanous, distant, exterior and icy form as representation. Such is her misfortune: her innocence acts as a perpetual chaperone between desire and its representation. Juliette, on the other hand, is no more than the subject of all possible desires; but those desires are carried over, without any residue, into the representation that provides them with a reasonable foundation in *discourse* and transforms them spontaneously into *scenes*. So that the great narrative of Juliette's life reveals, throughout its catalogue of desire, violence, savagery and death, the glittering table of representation. But this table is so thin, so transparent to all the figures of desire that untiringly accumulate within it and multiply there simply by the force of their combination, that it is just as lacking in reason as that of Don Quixote, when he believed himself to be progressing, from similitude to similitude, along the commingled paths of the world and books, but was in fact getting more and more entangled in the labyrinth of his own representations. *Juliette* thins out this inspissation of the represented so that, without the slightest blemish, the slightest reticence, the slightest veil, all the possibilities of desire may rise to the surface. . . And though it is true that this is the last discourse that undertakes to 'represent', to *name*, we are well enough aware that it simultaneously reduces this ceremony to the utmost precision (it calls things by their strict name, thus eliminating the space occupied by rhetoric) and extends it to infinity (by naming everything, including the slightest of possibilities, for they are all traversed in accordance with the Universal Characteristic of Desire). Sade attains the end of Classical discourse and thought. He holds sway precisely upon their frontier. After him, violence, life and death, desire and sexuality will extend, below the level of representation, an immense expanse of shade that we are now attempting to regain, as far as we can, in our discourse, in our freedom, in our thought. But our thought is so brief, our freedom so enslaved, our discourse so repetitive, that we must face the fact that that expanse of shade below is really a bottomless sea. The prosperities of *Juliette* are still more solitary—and endless (MC,223–4; OT, 210–11).

Classical order distributed across a permanent space a network of identities and differences that separated and united things; it was this order that governed the theories of discourse, natural beings, and the exchange of wealth. What occurred at the end of the eighteenth century was a change in the foundations of knowledge as far-reaching as that which accompanied the advent of the Classical period. The world is now seen to be made up, not of isolated elements related by identity and difference, but of organic structures, of internal relations between elements whose totality performs a function. The link between one organic structure and another is no longer the identity of one or more elements but the analogy of the relation between the elements (a relation no longer based on visibility) and the functions they perform. This notion of function makes time of central concern, whereas for Classical thought time was conceived only as intervening from the outside in otherwise timeless structures. History performs a fundamental role in modern thought similar to that of Order in Classical thought. History, in this sense, is not the mere description of events: there was, of course, nothing new in this. By History is meant that fundamental arrangement of knowledge, involving notions of time, development, 'becoming', that is common to all the empirical sciences that arose in the closing years of the eighteenth century. One of these disciplines, however, was constituted by the systematic study of events.

History becomes divided, in accordance with an ambiguity that it is probably impossible to control, into an empirical science of events and that radical mode of being that prescribes their destiny to all empirical beings, to those particular beings that we are. History, as we know, is certainly the most erudite, the most aware, the most conscious and possibly the most cluttered area of our memory; but it is equally the depths on which all beings emerge into their precarious, glittering existence. Since it is the mode of being of all that is given us in experience, History has become the unavoidable element in our thought. . . In the nineteenth century, philosophy was to reside in the gap between history and History, between events and the Origin, between evolution and the first rending open of the source, between oblivion and the Return. It will be Metaphysics, therefore, but only in so far as it is Memory, and it will necessarily lead thought back to the question of knowing what it means for thought to have a history. This question was to bear down upon philosophy, heavily and tirelessly, from Hegel to Nietzsche and beyond (MC, 231–2; OT, 219–20).

Foucault's analysis of this second great turning point in the Western *episteme* reveals not, as in the case of the first, a single, but a double operation. Or, rather, the transformation of the archaeological foundations takes place in two stages. In the first, an attempt is made to incorporate new concepts while remaining within the basic system of representation. It is only in the second stage that representation itself is abandoned.

In the economic area, this first phase is largely associated with Adam Smith. Indeed, Smith is often credited with introducing the concept of labour into the analysis of wealth and so founding modern political economy. In fact, Smith did not invent labour as an economic concept—it is already present in the work of Cantillon, Quesnay, and Condillac. What is new in Smith is the relative position attributed to labour in economic theory. Wealth is still analysed in terms of objects of need (objects of representation), but he establishes at the heart of his analysis a principle of order (labour) that is irreducible to representation. Objects of desire can no longer be represented solely by other objects of desire. The principle of their value is to be found, outside the representative framework of exchange, in labour, conceived as toil and time, the working-day that divides up, and uses up, men's lives. Moreover, labour is no longer seen atomistically, solely in terms of individuals' abilities and self-interest; it is now subject to conditions that go beyond the bounds of representation, to industrial progress, the growing division of labour, the accumulation of capital. Smith lays the foundations for a political economy that will no longer be based on the exchange of wealth, but on its real production: on the interior time of an organic structure formed by labour and capital.

Similar changes occurred at this time in natural history. The principle of classification was not called in question. However, the method used to establish the character, the relation between visible structure and criteria of identity, was modified in the same way as Adam Smith modified the relations of need or price. With Jussieu,

Lamarck, and Viq d'Azyr, character was to be based on a principle alien to the visible—an internal principle irreducible to the interaction of representations. This principle, which corresponds to labour in the economic sphere, is organic structure. The notions of life and function now become fundamental to the ordering of natural beings: superficial organs had to be related to those internal organs that performed the essential functions. Now that character could classify only by prior reference to the organic structure of individuals, to the totality of relations between internal and external, classification could no longer be based on the naming of observable structural elements. A wedge had been driven between the unities of names and genera, designation and classification, language and nature.

In the study of language, similar changes occurred if with a slight time-lag as in the other two fields. This delay is no doubt due to the special position enjoyed by language in representation. Technical modifications, such as new ways of measuring exchange values or of establishing 'characters', were enough to bring considerable changes to the analysis of wealth or natural history. Something more profound was required if the science of language was to undergo comparable changes. The theory of the name had provided representation with a model and thus governed not only general grammar but the other two disciplines as well. It was natural, therefore, that it should survive longest, breaking up only when representation itself was modified at its deepest archaeological level. The notion on which the transition from the analysis of grammar to the new philology was focused was that of *inflection*. But, as in the other disciplines, it was not the notion itself that was new, but the use to which it was put. Until the end of the eighteenth century inflectional modifications were seen as a representational mechanism (for example, the letters *m*, *s*, *t*, in the verbal ending of Latin languages represented the first, second, and third persons). With the collapse of representation, language ceased to be unchanging discourse and became languages, living, changing 'organisms' possessed of a history, a dark, internal structure. It was inflection that provided the evidence for this new view of language.

But this is to anticipate a rearrangement of the field of knowledge that had not yet been fully accomplished. The notions of labour, organic structure, and inflectional analysis were not used by Smith, Jussieu, and William Jones in order to break out of the tabular space provided by Classical thought or to escape the limitations of representation. The quest, beyond representation, for the being of that which is represented had not yet begun; only the place from which that quest would become possible had so far been established. This uncertainty, this ambiguity, is also to be found in the philosophy of the late eighteenth century. Destutt de Tracy and the *Idéologues* extended their reflection over the entire field of human knowledge and tried to resume in the form of representation what had been formed and reformed outside representation. In this sense, Ideology is the last of the Classical philosophies. Contemporary with the *Idéologues*, however, Kant was making the first truly modern attempt to break through the limits of representation.

The Kantian critique. . .questions representation, not in accordance with the endless movement that proceeds from the simple element to all its possible combinations, but on the basis of its rightful limits. Thus it sanctions for the first time that event in European culture which coincides with the end of the eighteenth century: the withdrawal of knowledge and thought outside the space of representation. That space is brought into question in its foundation, its origin and its limits: and by this very fact, the unlimited field of representation, which Classical thought had established, which Ideology had attempted to scan in accordance with a step-by-step, discursive, scientific method, now appears as a metaphysics. But as a metaphysics that had never stepped outside itself, that had posited itself in an uninformed dogmatism and that had never brought into the light the question of its right. In this sense, Criticism brings out the metaphysical dimension that eighteenth-century philosophy had attempted to reduce solely by means of the analysis of representation. But it opens up at the same time the possibility of another metaphysics; one whose purpose will be to question, apart from representation, all that is the source and origin of representation; it makes possible those philosophies of Life, the Will and the Word that the nineteenth-century is to deploy in the wake of criticism (MC, 255–6; OT, 242–3).

Adam Smith's analysis marks the first stage in the great epistemic transformation of economic discourse. By making labour the constant measure of exchange value he laid the foundations for a political economy that could be based not on exchange (representation), but on production. But, in Smith, labour is still regarded as itself a commodity that can be bought and sold. As long as representation retained its precedence all commodities represented a certain labour and all labour a certain quantity of commodities. The second stage of the founding of modern political economy was the work of David Ricardo. Ricardo pointed out that labour could not be used as a constant measure since it is 'subject to as many fluctuations as the commodities compared with it'. This insight led him to make the productive activity of labour itself, not the *measure* of value but the *source* of value. Value is no longer a sign in the system of equivalences, but a product of labour, which is prior to any system of exchange. The theory of production must now precede that of circulation. Circular causality has been replaced by linear causality. Ricardo has made possible the articulation of economics on histroy. Another consequence of his analysis is that he inverts the Classical view of scarcity. In Classical thought scarcity comes about because men represent to themselves objects that they do not have, but this scarcity is underwritten, as it were, by the infinite wealth of the land. For Ricardo, this generosity of the land is due to its growing avarice. Labour, economic activity, came into being as an attempt to overcome the inability of the land to feed the population 'naturally'. As the population increases so more and more of the earth's resources are eaten up. Without work, men die. The more work is performed, the closer the ultimate threat of total extinction for mankind.

Thus economics refers us to that order of somewhat ambiguous considerations that may be termed anthropological: it is related, in fact, to the biological properties of a human species, which, as Malthus showed in the same period as Ricardo, tends always to increase unless prevented by some remedy or constraint; it is related also to the situation of those living beings that run the risk of not finding in their natural environment enough to ensure their existence; lastly, it designates in labour and in the very hardship of that labour, the only means of overcoming the fundamental inefficiency of nature and triumphing for an instant over death. . . *Homo oeconomicus* is not the human being who represents to himself his own needs and the objects capable of satisfying them; he is the human being who spends, wears out and wastes his life in evading the imminence of death. He is a finite being: and just as, since Kant,

<u>the question of finitude has become more fundamental than the analysis of representations</u> (the latter now being necessarily a derivation of the former), since Ricardo, economics has rested, in a more or less explicit fashion, upon an anthropology that attempts to assign concrete forms to finitude (MC, 269; OT, 257).

Paradoxically, it is the historicity introduced into economics by Ricardo that makes it possible to conceive of an end of history, of the inability of mankind as a whole to sustain itself. Ricardo's 'pessimistic' analysis is the starting-point, of course, of Marx's economic theory. The relation between History and what Foucault calls 'anthropological finitude' is construed by Marx in the opposite direction. In the Marxist analysis History plays a negative role, increasing need, and therefore the labour required to satisfy that need, while giving the labourer more or less than a subsistence wage. The difference between the full value of the worker's labour and his wage becomes profit, which enables the capitalist to buy more labour to produce yet more profit. An ever growing class of men experiences need, hunger, and labour. What men have hitherto attributed to the natural order, they are able to recognize as a result of historical development and are thus equipped for reversing that development. Then alone will the truth of the unalienated human essence be restored. In Foucault's view, Marx's analysis does not represent—as Marxists believe—a fundamental rupture with previous views of society and history. <u>The true epistemic break occurs with Ricardo: Marx's alternative to Ricardo's pessimism belongs, fundamentally, to the same mode of thought.</u>

At the deepest level of Western knowledge, Marxism introduced no real discontinuity; it found its place without difficulty, as a full, quiet, comfortable and, goodness knows, satisfying form for a time (its own), within an epistemological arrangement that welcomed it gladly (since it was this arrangement that was in fact making room for it) and that it, in return, had no intention of disturbing and, above all, no power to modify, even one jot, since it rested entirely upon it. <u>Marxism exists in nineteenth-century thought like a fish in water: that is, it is unable to breathe anywhere else.</u> Though it is in opposition to the 'bourgeois' theories of economics and though this opposition leads it to use the project of a radical reversal of History as a weapon against them, that conflict and that project nevertheless have as their condition of possibility, not the reworking of all History, but an event that archaeology can situate with precision and that prescribes simultaneously, and according to the same mode, both nineteenth-century bourgeois economics and nineteenth-century revolutionary economics. The controversies may have stirred up a few waves and caused a few surface ripples; but they are no more than storms in a children's paddling pool (MC, 274; CT, 261–2).

As can readily be imagined, this is one of the most frequently quoted passages in the book. As so often when Foucault is saying something that runs counter to received opinion, his language verges on the hyperbolic. The imagery is certainly provocative, but the degree of intended provocation was in proportion to the degree of resistance that then existed throughout the French Left to any questioning of Marx's position. Such remarks certainly led to misunderstanding of Foucault's views on Marx: they alienated many potential admirers and attracted certain unwanted attentions. Certainly they stirred up a few storms whether or not they were bounded by the dimensions of a paddling pool or, for that matter, a teacup. The quarrel between Marxist and 'bourgeois' economic analyses is seen as one of those surface effects in relation to more fundamental, archaeological events.

What is essential is that at the beginning of the nineteenth century a new arrangement of knowledge was constituted, which accomodated simultaneously the historicity of economics (in relation to the forms of production), the finitude of human existence (in relation to scarcity and labour) and the fulfilment of an end to History— whether in the form of an indefinite deceleration or in that of a radical reversal. History, anthropology and the suspension of development are all linked together in accordance with a figure that defines one of the major networks of nineteenth-century thought. We know, for example, the role that this arrangement played in reviving the weary good intentions of the humanisms; we know how it brought the utopias of ultimate development back to life. In Classical thought, the utopia functioned rather as a fantasy of origins: this was because the freshness of the world had to provide the ideal unfolding of a table in which everything would be present in its proper place, with its adjacencies, its peculiar differences and its immediate equivalences; in this primal light, representations could not yet have been separated from the living, sharp, perceptible presence of what they represent. In the nineteenth century, the utopia is concerned with the final decline of time rather than with its morning: this is because knowledge is no longer constituted in the form of a table but in that of series, sequential connection, development: when, with the promised evening, the shadow of the *dénouement* comes, the slow erosion or violent eruption of History will cause man's anthropological truth to spring forth in its stony immobility; calendar time will be able to continue; but it will be, as it were, void, for historicity will have been superimposed exactly upon the human essence. The flow of development, with all its resources of drama, oblivion, alienation, will be held within an anthropological finitude that finds in them, in turn, its own illuminated expression. Finitude, with its truth, is posited in *time;* and *time* is therefore *finite*. The great dream of an end to History is the utopia of causal systems of thought, just as the dream of the world's beginnings was the utopia of the classifying systems of thought.

This arrangement maintained its firm grip on thought for a long while; and Nietzsche, at the end of the nineteenth century, made it glow into brightness again for the last time by setting fire to it. He took the end of time and transformed it into the death of God and the odyssey of the last man; he took up anthropological finitude once again, but in order to use it as a basis for the prodigious leap of the superman; he took up once again the great continuous chain of History, but in order to bend it round into the infinity of the eternal return. It is in vain that the death of God, the imminence of the superman and the promise and terror of the great year take up once more, as it were term by term, the elements that are arranged in nineteenth-century thought and form its archaeological framework. The fact remains that they sent all those stable forms up in flames, that they used their charred remains to draw strange and perhaps impossible faces; and by a light that may be either—we do not yet know which—the reviving flame of the last great fire or an indication of the dawn, we see the emergence of what may perhaps be the space of contemporary thought. It was Nietzsche, in any case, who burned for us, even before we were born, the intermingled promises of the dialectic and anthropology (MC, 274–5; OT, 262–3.

72

The implications are clear enough. <u>Marxist thought is irremediably</u> <u>confined by an *episteme* that is coming to an end</u>. <u>This does not mean</u> <u>that Marx's contribution to economic and political theory are not</u> of <u>enduring interest, but that it is anachronistic at this point in time</u> to <u>call oneself a Marxist</u>. Nietzsche, so central a figure in *Histoire de la folie*, the great mediator between Reason and Unreason, appears here as the great liberator from the Hegelian (Marxist) dialectic and from what Foucault calls 'anthropology'. This was an astonishing analysis for an intellectual who regarded himself as a committed man of the Left—and no reformist—to make in 1965. Three years later the events of 1968 erupted to reveal alongside the various heretical Marxisms, a Leftism that held Marx at an unaccustomed distance. The phenomenon has proliferated since, but it was Foucault who first gave it voice.

Just as Ricardo freed labour from its role as constant measure of value by placing it prior to all exchange, in the process of production, so Cuvier freed character from its taxonomic function in order to introduce it, prior to any classification, into the organic structures of living beings. Life, in its non-perceptible, purely functional aspect, now provides the basis for classification. The classification of living beings is no longer to be found in the great expanse of order; it now arises from the depths of life, from those elements hidden from view. Inextricably linked with this new biology is, of course, the medical use of comparative anatomy. It was the use of dissection that made possible the distinction, crucial to the new discipline, between the secondary organs, situated on the surface of the body, and the primary, vital organs hidden within the outer surface. The creation of the Classical taxonomies was a problem of *linguistic patterning:* parts had to be simultaneously isolated and named. The new biology is a matter of *anatomic disarticulation*: the major functional system has to be isolated and the ordering of living beings is now based on the real divisions of anatomy. Thus the historical *a priori* of the science of living beings is overthrown and replaced by another—and it is Cuvier who performs the final act in that transformation. However, as Foucault points out, this view is not shared by many historians of science. This is because, unlike Foucault, they remain on the surface of an individual's ideas, opinions, and theories, comparing them with those of other individuals of other times. Thus Cuvier's overall view of living beings is regarded as 'fixist' in contrast, for example, with Lamarck's 'transformism'. Now, it is true that the latter is related to evolutionism and that the former is not. Superficially, therefore, Cuvier is labelled a 'reactionary' and Lamarck a 'revolutionary' in relation to the evolutionism that was to triumph in the subsequent history of biology. Yet, at the level with which Foucault is dealing, it is Cuvier, not Lamarck, who provides the indispensable element that makes the future of biology possible. By introducing a radical discontinuity into the Classical order of beings, Cuvier gave rise to such notions as biological incompatibility, relations with external elements, conditions of existence and, above all, the notion of a life force that brings with it the threat of death. It became possible to replace natural history with a 'history' of nature.

> The animal maintains its existence on the frontiers of life and death. Death besieges it on all sides; furthermore, it threatens it also from within, for only the organisms can die and it is from the depths of their lives that death overtakes living beings. Hence, no doubt, the ambiguous values assumed by animality towards the end of the eighteenth century: the animal appears as the bearer of that death to which it is, at the same time, subjected; it contains a perpetual devouring of life by life. It belongs to nature only at the price of containing within itself a nucleus of anti-nature. Transferring its most secret essence from the vegetable to the animal kingdom, life has left the tabulated space of order and become wild once more. The same movement that dooms it to death reveals it as murderous. It kills because it lives. Nature can no longer be good. That life can no longer be separated from murder, nature from evil or desires from anti-nature, Sade proclaimed in the eighteenth century, whose language he drained dry, and to the modern age, which has for so long attempted to stifle his voice. I hope the insolence (for whom?) is excusable, but *Les 120 Journées de Sodome* is the velvety, marvellous obverse of the *Leçons d'anatomie comparée*. At all events, in our archaeological calendar they are the same age (MT, 290; OT, 277–8).

As Schlegel, one of the founders of the new philology himself pointed out, historicity was introduced into the study of languages in the same way as into the science of living beings. This is hardly surprising, since in the Classical view, the words that were thought to make up language had the same status as the characters that made up the taxonomies of natural history: they played the same role as representations. Just as with Cuvier the character finally lost its representative function, so in the study of language the word underwent a similar transformation. The word continued, of course, to represent the thing it referred to, but this act of representation no longer constituted its essential function. The 'meaning' of a word no longer derives from the same fixed, abstract decision that constitutes it thus, but from the particular history that dictates the way in which it was formed and altered in the course of time and the way it acts as one element of a complicated grammatical structure. Foucault points out how little attention has been paid to this momentous event in Western culture, compared with the ultimately no more important transformations of political economy and biology. For Bopp, words represent not so much what one sees as what one does and feels. Language is rooted not in the thing perceived, but in the active subject. It is the product of will and energy, rather than of perception and memory. It has an irreducible expressive value that no arbitrariness, no grammatical convention can obliterate. Languages, accordingly, are expressive of the people who fashion them and recognize themselves in them—and peoples rather than learned élites. Language is no longer linked to the knowing of things, but to men's freedom (Grimm). Throughout the nineteenth century the language question was to have a whole political dimension.

Language has now lost the primal function it enjoyed in the Classical period as the medium in which signs first originate and things can be known. In the nineteenth century, language folded in upon itself, as it were, acquired its own density, history, laws, objectivity. It became one object of knowledge among others. However, as if by way of compensation for this demotion, language acquired added status in other ways. It was the necessary medium for scientific discourse—necessary, but no longer adequate to its task. This led to the attempt to neutralize, purify language of all its alien, subjective elements and, ultimately, to the 'positivist' dream of a language keeping strictly to what was known, purged of all error, uncertainty, and supposition. It also led to the search for a 'language' independent of the natural languages, with all their treacherous densities, a language of pure, symbolic logic. Because language had lost its primacy and transparency, it returned in a sense to the mysterious, inexhaustible condition it enjoyed in the Renaissance. Language had become, once again, a problem, a barrier as well as a medium of expression; hence the revival in techniques of interpretation and exegesis.

> The first book of *Das Kapital* is an exegesis of 'value'; all Nietzsche is an exegesis of a few Greek words; Freud, the exegesis of all those unspoken phrases that support and at the same time undermine our apparent discourse, our phantasies, our dreams, our bodies. Philology, as the analysis of what is said in the depths of discourse, has become the modern form of criticism. Where, at the end of the eighteenth century, it was a matter of fixing the frontiers of knowledge, it will now be one of seeking to destroy syntax, to shatter tyrannical modes of speech, to turn words around in order to perceive all that is being said through them and despite them. God is perhaps not so much a region beyond knowledge as something prior to the sentences we speak; and if Western man is inseparable from him it is not because of some invincible propensity to go beyond the frontiers of experience, but because his language ceaselessly foments him in the shadow of his laws: 'I fear indeed that we will never rid ourselves of God, since we still believe in grammar' (Nietzsche) (MC, 311; OT, 298).

The unity of language has thus been shattered; its reacquired density gives rise to attempts, on the one hand, to overcome that density (the scientific enterprise) and, on the other, to explore that density (philology, interpretation, criticism). Concomitant with the latter is the appearance of the notion of 'literature'.

> Literature is the contestation of philology (of which it is nevertheless the twin figure): it leads language back from grammar to the naked power of speech, and there it encounters the untamed, imperious being of words. From the Romantic revolt against a discourse frozen in its own ritual pomp, to the Mallarméan discovery of the word in its impotent power, it becomes clear what the function of literature was, in the nineteenth century, in relation to the modern mode of being of language. Against the background of this essential interaction, the rest is merely effect: literature becomes progressively more differentiated from the discourse of ideas and encloses itself within a radical intransitivity; it becomes detached from all the values that were able to keep it in general circulation during the Classical age (taste, pleasure, naturalness,

truth) and creates within its own space everything that will ensure a ludic denial of them (the scandalous, the ugly, the impossible); it breaks with the whole definition of *genres* as forms adapted to an order of representations and becomes merely a manifestation of a language that has no other law than that of affirming—in opposition to all other forms of discourse—its own precipitous existence; and so there is nothing for it to do but to curve back in a perpetual return upon itself, as if its discourse could have no other content than the expression of its own form; it addresses itself to itself as a writing subjectivity, or seeks to re-apprehend the essence of all literature in the movement that brought it into being; and thus all its threads converge upon the finest of points—singular, instantaneous and yet absolutely universal—upon the simple act of writing. At the moment when language, as spoken and scattered words, becomes an object of knowledge, we see it reappearing in a strictly opposite modality: a silent, cautious deposition of the word upon the whiteness of a piece of paper, where it can possess neither sound nor interlocutor, where it has nothing to say but itself, nothing to do but shine in the brightness of its being (MC, 313; OT, 300).

By 'literature' Foucault does not mean, of course, all the poetry, fiction, drama etc., written in the nineteenth century and after. He means a certain radically new notion that begins with the Romantic poets and reaches its purest, most extreme form in Mallarmé. Indeed, the whole Realist or Naturalist project, which forms one of the most important elements in the nineteenth-century novel, runs quite counter to this notion. But this confirms, rather than contradicts, Foucault's analysis. For part, at least, of what Balzac, Dickens, George Eliot, and Tolstoy are doing is related to the positivist aim of providing a 'scientific' account of society and its workings. It is related not to 'literature' in Foucault's sense, but to the various sociological aspirations that were one other part of the now fragmented body of language. Indeed, throughout most of the nineteenth century, language itself was paid relatively little attention, except, perhaps, in the negative sense of various attempts to overcome its inadequacy as a vehicle of truth. It was Nietzsche, the classical philologist, who first linked the task of philosophy to a radical reflection on language. For him, it was not a question of knowing what, in themselves, good and evil were, but rather who was speaking and about whom when, for example, one uses the word *agathos* (well-born, noble—but also good, brave) of oneself and *deilos* (low-born, wretched—but also bad, cowardly) of others. The conditions of possibility for such questions were established at the beginning of the nineteenth century when language, detached from representation, was fragmented. They became inevitable when Nietzsche and Mallarmé brought thought back to language itself. Is our present awareness of language, our almost excessive preoccupation with it, Foucault asks, the closing chapter of a work that began a century and a half ago or the beginnings of a new re-arrangement of our knowledge? It is because Foucault believes that we can never know the precise archaeological structure of our present knowledge that he is condemned to ask questions.

The question of language is intimately bound up with the question of man himself. Just as in Classical thought language as a problem did not exist, because it was at once ubiquitous and transparent, so man, as an object of knowledge, did not exist. Man, for whom and by whom representations existed, was himself absent from the table of knowledge. Man, as the object of scientific knowledge, makes his appearance when language ceases to be the unquestioned universal model of knowledge. When language becomes opaque, problematic, an object to be known, man follows in its wake. Various aspects of man—the problem of the different races, for example—had been touched on in the eighteenth century, but there was no epistemological consciousness of man as such, no specific domain of knowledge proper to man. The very concept of human nature precluded any possibility of a Classical science of man. The modern notion of a creature who lives, speaks, and works in accordance with the laws of biology, philology, and economics, but who has also acquired the right, through the interplay of these very laws, to know them and to know himself—all that we understand today by the 'human sciences'—was excluded by Classical thought. But the three new sciences that emerged from the final overthrow of representation all required man as their object as well as their subject. It is man who now speaks, who now resides among the animals and who is now the principle of all production. But his position in all this is an ambiguous one. His concrete existence is determined by life, labour, and language: knowledge of him is acquired through his organism, his products, and his words, as if he were merely a temporary vehicle for forms that existed before him and which would outlive him. Modern man—the man that stands at the centre of the three sciences to emerge from the collapse of representation, man in his corporeal, labouring, and speaking existence—is possible only as 'a figuration of finitude'.

Modern culture can conceive of man because it conceives of the finite on the basis of itself. Given these conditions, it is understandable that Classical thought and all the forms of thought that preceded it, were able to speak of the mind and the body, of the human being, of how restricted a place he occupies in the universe, of all the limitations by which his knowledge or his freedom must be measured, but that not one of them was able to know man as he is posited in modern knowledge. Renaissance 'humanism' and Classical 'rationalism' were indeed able to allot human beings a privileged position in the order of the world, but they were not able to conceive of man (MC, 329; OT, 318).

Man, by which is meant here man as an operational concept in the sciences and philosophy that emerged in the early nineteenth century, is what Foucault calls 'a strange empirico-transcendental doublet'. This concept operates, that is to say, in two areas: that of the body, where knowledge is seen to have conditions imposed upon it by man's physiological mechanisms, and that of man's history, where knowledge is seen to be dependent on particular historical, social, and economic conditions. But together with this figure of man and his knowledge of himself there emerged the element of the 'unthought'.

Man has not been able to describe himself as a configuration in the *episteme* without thought at the same time discovering, both in itself and outside itself, at its borders yet also in its very warp and woof, an element of darkness, an apparently inert density in which it is embedded, an unthought which it contains entirely, yet in which it is also caught . . . Since it was really never more than an insistent double, it has never been the object of reflection in an autonomous way; it has received the complementary form and the inverted name of that for which it was the Other and shadow: in Hegelian phenomenology, it was the *An sich* as opposed to the *Für sich*; for Schopenhauer it was the *Unbewusste*; for Marx it was alienated man; in Husserl's analysis it was the implicit, the inactual, the sedimented, the non-effected—in every case, the inexhaustible double that presents itself to reflection as the blurred projection of what man is in his truth, but that also plays the role of a preliminary ground upon which man must collect himself and recall himself in order to attain his truth (MC, 337–8; OT, 326–7).

Throughout the modern period it has been the task of thought to think the unthought, to bring the unknown within the sphere of knowledge, to end man's alienation by reconciling him with his own innocence, whether it be in the sphere of alienated labour or in the unconscious region of repressed desires. Thought can no longer stand back, separated and protected from that which it thinks. In transforming the unthought, thought also transforms itself, for the modern epistemic figure of man encloses both. Modern thought cannot but be a form of action. This is why, says Foucault, modern thought cannot produce a morality: its sole ethical commitment lies in the mutual transformation of the thought and the unthought.

> Even before prescribing, suggesting a future, saying what must be done, even before exhorting or merely sounding an alarm, thought, at the level of its existence, in its very dawning, is in itself an action—a perilous act. Sade, Nietzsche, Artaud and Bataille have understood this on behalf of all those who tried to ignore it; but it is also certain that Hegel, Marx and Freud knew it. Can we say that it is not known by those who, in their profound stupidity, assert that there is no philosophy without political choice, that all thought is either 'progressive' or 'reactionary'? Their foolishness is to believe that all thought 'expresses' the ideology of a class; their involuntary profundity is that they point directly at the modern mode of being of thought. Superficially, one might say that knowledge of man, unlike the sciences of nature, is always linked, even in its vaguest form, to ethics or politics; more fundamentally, modern thought is advancing towards that region where man's Other must become the Same as himself (MC, 339; OT, 328).

Thus we are brought back, as if by a further turn of the spiral, to the principal thesis of *Histoire de la folie*, that the ascendency of reason and science brought with it a certain impoverishment of human experience, that a Reason that banished Unreason in order to set up its own undivided rule becomes defensive and constantly exposed to attacks from the outside. It is because the successive reigns of reason and science are drawing to a close, because, since Nietzsche, cracks in the humanist edifice have been getting more and more apparent, that what Foucault is saying can be said at all.

Perhaps we should see the first attempt at this uprooting of Anthropology—to which, no doubt, contemporary thought is dedicated—in the Nietzschean experience: by means of a philological critique, by means of a certain form of biologism, Nietzsche rediscovered the point at which man and God belong to one another, at which the death of the second is synonymous with the disappearance of the first, and at which the promise of the superman signifies first and foremost the imminence of the death of man. In this, Nietzsche, offering this future to us as both promise and task, marks the threshold beyond which contemporary philosophy can begin thinking again; and he will no doubt continue for a long while to dominate its advance. If the discovery of the Return is indeed the end of philosophy, then the end of man is the return of the beginning of philosophy. It is no longer possible to think in our day other than in the void left by man's disappearance. For this void does not create a deficiency; it does not constitute a lacuna that must be filled. It is nothing more, and nothing less, than the unfolding of a space in which it is once more possible to think.

Anthropology constitutes perhaps the fundamental arrangement that has governed and controlled the path of philosophical thought from Kant until our own day. This arrangement is essential, since it forms part of our history; but it is disintegrating before our eyes, since we are beginning to recognize and denounce in it, in a critical mode, both a forgetfulness of the opening that made it possible and a stubborn obstacle standing obstinately in the way of an imminent new form of thought. To all those who still wish to talk about man, about his reign or his liberation, to all those who still ask themselves questions about what man is in his essence, to all those who wish to take him as their starting-point in their attempts to reach the truth, to all those who, on the other hand, refer all knowledge back to the truths of man himself, to all those who refuse to formalize without anthropologizing, who refuse to mythologize without demystifying, who refuse to think without immediately thinking that it is man who is thinking, to all these warped and twisted forms of reflection we can answer only with a philosophical laugh—which means, to a certain extent, a silent one (MC, 353–4; OT, 342–3).

Characteristically, this master of the Gay Science ends what is possibly one of the most daring and potentially productive sections of *Les mots et les choses* as he began the entire book, with a laugh. The sense of release at finding himself, after three hundred and fifty years (and as many pages) once more in the present where he began, springs out from the printed word. For as he said years later in an interview, he has no interest in history for its own sake. He is not one of those who, repelled by an unsympathetic present, turn their faces to the past. Nor is he one of those who seek solace in better worlds to come—which, because such utopias derive from already superannuated modes of thought, is simply a more mystificatory form of reaction. His essential concern has always been to understand the present, the present as a product of the past and as the seed-bed of the new.

Les mots et les choses is subtitled 'une archéologie des sciences humaines', as if the immense labour that went into the writing of this book were directed towards the end of providing the recently conceived, vaguely demarcated, and insecurely based 'human sciences' with an archaeology, an account of their formation and conditions of possibility. For by 'human sciences', Foucault does not mean the three empiricities that emerged out of the collapse of representation and the establishment of 'man' as an operational concept (biology, political economy, and philology), but those later derivatives, psychology, sociology, and literary/cultural studies, together with the mass of proliferating disciplines formed from their sub-divisions and cross-fertilization. What occurs at the point at which the 'empirical' sciences give rise to the 'human' sciences is, in a sense, a return to representation. This does not mean, however, that the latter are in any way the heirs of Classical knowledge: their very existence is dependent on the change in the *episteme* that brought Classical representation to an end. Classical representation was a universal, neutral, conscious, 'objective' mode of thought in which, though it was operated by and for men, 'man' as a concept was absent. This new form of representation, on the other hand, derives not from man's consciousness of the world or of himself operating in the world, but rather from a sense of something taking place in himself, often at an unconscious level, in his subjectivity, in his values, that traverses the whole of his action in the world. It is this domain, in which men *represent* to themselves their *experience* as living, labouring and speaking beings, that is opened up in the human sciences. It is a domain that maintains its tripartite origin in the form of three regions: a 'psychological region', in which man represents to himself his experience as a living being in the world; a 'sociological region', in which the labouring, producing, and consuming individual offers himself a representation of the society in which this activity occurs, of the practices and beliefs by which it is maintained and regulated; a 'linguistic region', in which, in the form of literature, myth, and history, man leaves representations in the form of verbal traces.

This three-fold origin of the human sciences also accounts for their use of three analytic models. From biology, they received the notion of *function*: receiving and reacting to stimuli, adapting to the environment, compensating for imbalances, in short, establishing and obeying *norms*. Economics, which depicts man seeking satisfaction for his needs and desires, provides the notion of *conflict* and, by way of containment of conflict, that of *rules*. Language provides the notions of *signification* and *system*, which is an ordering of signs. However, these three pairs of concepts do not remain exclusively within their fields of origin: conflict and rule do not apply only to the sociological domain, or signification and system only to phenomena of a more or less linguistic nature. Though fundamental to the region in which it occurs, each pair of concepts is valid for either of the other two regions. This accounts for frequent difficulty in fixing the limits of a particular discipline or the methods appropriate to it. Thus all the human sciences interlock and can be used to interpret one another: intermediary and composite disciplines multiply endlessly. Furthermore, one or other of the models has tended, since the early nineteenth century, to dominate the whole range of human sciences. First, the biological model was dominant (man, his psyche, his group, his society, his language, all tended in the Romantic period to be conceived as organic beings and analysed in terms of function); then came the reign of the economic model (the whole of human activity was conceived in terms of conflict); lastly, human activity came to be seen in terms of the interpretation of hidden meanings (philology) or signifying structures (linguistics). In any case, all the human sciences employ a form of representation that breaks with the

Classical association of representation and consciousness. As a result, they seem to be constantly employed in a process of demystification, of unveiling a reality that is less apparent, but more profound. The problem of the unconscious—its possibility, its status, mode of existence, the means of bringing it to knowledge—is ultimately of the very essence of the human sciences. A 'human science' exists, not where man is in question, but wherever there is analysis of unconscious processes in terms of norms, rules, and signifying systems. It is because they are parasitic, in the models that they use, on the three sciences of biology, economics, and linguistics, that Foucault believes them to be misnamed: they are not really sciences at all. This is not because their object, man, is too complex or too obscure, nor because they are still at a pre-scientific stage, but because by their very constitution they cannot emerge as autonomous sciences.

Foucault ends with a discussion of two disciplines that have enjoyed particular attention in recent years: psychoanalysis and ethnology (or social anthropology as it is more usually called in the English-speaking world). This is not because they have established their scientificity any more firmly than the other 'human sciences', but because they provide an 'inexhaustible treasure-hoard of experience and concepts' and because they exercise a strongly critical role in relation to apparently established notions. In psychoanalysis the task of unveiling unconscious processes, which is implicit in all human sciences, is explicitly at the very centre of its concerns. In this sense it has a unique relation to representation and to the 'analytics of finitude.'

Psychoanalysis advances and leaps over representation, overflows it on the side of finitude, and thus reveals, where one had expected functions bearing their norms, conflicts burdened with rules and significations forming a system, the simple fact that it is possible for there to be system (therefore signification), rule (therefore conflict), norm (therefore function). And in this region where representation remains in suspense, on the edge of itself, open, in a sense, to the closed boundary of finitude, we find outlined the three figures by means of which life, with its function and norms, attains its foundation in the mute repetition of Death, conflicts and rules their foundation in the naked opening of Desire, significations and systems their foundation in a language that is at the same time Law. We know that psychologists and philosophers have dismissed all this as Freudian mythology. It was indeed inevitable that this approach of Freud's should have appeared to them in this way; to a know-ledge situated within the representable, all that frames and defines, on the outside, the very possibility of representation can be nothing other than mythology. But when one follows the movement of psychoanalysis as it progresses, or when one traverses the epis-temological space as a whole, one sees that these figures are in fact . . . the very forms of finitude, as it is analysed in modern thought. Is death not that upon the basis of which knowledge in general is possible—so much so that we can think of it as being, in the area of psychoanalysis, the figure of that empirico-transcendental *duplica-tion* that characterizes man's mode of being within finitude? Is desire not that which remains always *unthought* at the heart of thought? And the law-language (at once word and word-system) that psychoanalysis takes such pains to make speak, is it not that in which all signification assumes an *origin* more distant that itself, but also that whose return is promised in the very act of analysis? It is indeed true that this Death, and this Desire, and this Law can never meet within the knowledge that traverses in its positivity the empirical domain of man; but the reason for this is that they desig-nate the conditions of possibility of all knowledge about man (MC, 386; OT, 374–5).

Like psychoanalysis, ethnology questions not so much man himself as the region that makes possible knowledge about man in general. Just as psychoanalysis situates itself in the dimension of the uncon-scious (disturbing the whole domain of the human sciences from within), ethnology situates itself in the dimension of historicity (chal-lenging the human sciences by reference to their relativity). Super-ficially, ethnology appears to be ahistorical: its objects are relatively unchanging societies prior to the advent of history. In fact, it has its roots in a possibility that belongs to our culture: only *our* history could have given rise to it and it accompanies the intervention of history into the societies that are its object. (Its connection with colonialism is merely a contingent expression of a deeper relation.) It is situated within the particular relation that the Western *ratio* establishes with other cultures and is able, therefore, to avoid the representations that men make of themselves in their own civilization. What ethnology and psychoanalysis share is not some concern to penetrate the depths of human nature, but rather a common position in relation to the modern notion of 'man'. They stand at the frontier, as it were, between man and that 'Otherness' that undermines the entire concept of man as a unitary, knowable being. They are not so much human sciences that take up their positions among others, as two 'counter-sciences' that traverse and penetrate the entire domain of the human sciences, bringing them back to their epistemological foundation, unmaking that very man who constitutes their ground. In *Totem and Taboo* Freud laid the foundation in which psychoanalysis could form a common field, the possibility of a discourse that could move without discontinuity from one to the other, 'the double articulation of the history of individuals upon the unconscious of culture and of the historicity of those cultures upon the unconscious of those individuals'. This cross-fertilization between ethnology and psychoanalysis found more recent examples in the work of Lévi-Strauss and Lacan. But, contemporary with this phenomenon, was the penetration into both disciplines of a third, linguistics. Here we have a science perfectly founded in the order of positivities—although its object is human language, man himself does not come into play as an operational concept, language being treated as a self-contained system. It can thus offer what seems like an unimpeachably scientific base for those human sciences that choose to incorporate it.

But the present supremacy of language is not confined to the role of linguistics in the human sciences. Literature, too, is fascinated by language itself, by its self-conscious awareness of its own medium. The extreme points of this phenomenon are represented, perhaps, by Artaud and Roussel: the former rejected language as discourse and returned to the primal condition of language as cry, as physical act; the latter produced a parody of discourse, based not on expression but on a carefully constituted system of random relations. In each case, this relentless experience of finitude led to 'madness' (Artaud was locked up, Roussel killed himself). However, Foucault sees this phenomenon neither as a sign of the approaching doom of a literature that no longer has anything to say, nor as the radicalization of a literature that has discovered (or rediscovered) its true vocation.

It is, in fact, the strict unfolding of Western culture in accordance with the necessity it imposed upon itself at the beginning of the nineteenth century. It would be false to see in this general indication of our experience, which may be termed 'formalism', the sign of a drying up, of a rarefaction of thought losing its capacity for re-apprehending the plenitude of contents; it would be no less false to place it from the outset upon the horizon of some new thought or new knowledge. It is within the very tight-knit, very coherent outlines of the modern *episteme* that this contemporary experience found its possibility (MC, 395; OT, 384).

Yet Foucault does sense that the archaeological ground is once more moving under our feet.

> Rather than the death of God—or, rather, in the wake of that death and in a profound correlation with it—what Nietzsche's thought heralds is the end of his murderer; it is the explosion of man's face in laughter and the return of masks. . . Throughout the nineteenth century, the end of philosophy and the promise of an approaching culture were no doubt one and the same thing as the thought of finitude and the appearance of man in the field of knowledge; in our day, the fact that philosophy is still—and again—in the process of coming to an end and the fact that in it, perhaps though even more outside and against it, in literature as well as in formal reflection, the question of language is being posed, prove no doubt that man is in the process of disappearing.
>
> For the entire modern *episteme*—that which was formed towards the end of the eighteenth century and still serves as the positive ground of our knowledge, that which constituted man's particular mode of being and the possibility of knowing empirically—that entire *episteme* was bound up with the disappearance of Discourse and its featureless reign, with the shift of language towards objectivity and with its reappearance in multiple form. If this same language is now emerging with greater and greater insistence in a unity that we ought to think but cannot as yet do so, is this not the sign that the whole of this configuration is now about to topple and that man is in the process of perishing as the being of language continues to shine ever brighter upon our horizon? Since man was constituted at a time when language was doomed to dispersion, will he not be dispersed when language regains its unity? And if that were true, would it not be an error—a profound error, since it could hide from us what should now be thought—to interpret our

contemporary experience as an application of the forms of language to the human order? Ought we not rather to give up thinking of man, or, to be more strict, to think of this disappearance of man—and the ground of possibility of all the sciences of man—as closely as possible in correlation with our concern with language? Ought we not to admit that since language is here once more, man will return to that serene non-existence in which he was formerly maintained by the imperious unity of Discourse? Man had been a figure occurring between two modes of language; or, rather, he was constituted only when language, having been situated within representation and, as it were, dissolved in it, freed itself from that situation at the cost of its own fragmentation: man composed his own figure in the interstices of that fragmented language. . . As the archaeology of our thought easily shows, man is an invention of recent date. And perhaps one nearing its end. If those arrangements were to disappear as they appeared, if some event of which we can at the moment do no more than sense the possibility—without knowing either what its form will be or what it promises—were to cause them to crumble as the ground of Classical thought did, at the end of the eighteenth century, then one can certainly wager that man would be erased, like a face drawn in sand at the edge of the sea (MC, 396–8; OT, 385–7).

What was surely the most unexpected and most cherished of the responses Foucault received to the publication of *Les mots et les choses* was a letter from René Magritte, in which the painter comments on the use of the terms 'resemblance' and 'similitude'. Foucault replied and a few days later received a second letter from Magritte. In 1973, Foucault published a short fascinating study of Magritte entitled, after the artist's own works, *Ceci n'est pas une pipe*. The two letters from Magritte to Foucault are included in an appendix to that book.

◇ 3 ◇

The Archaeological Theory of Knowledge

L'archéologie du savoir appeared in 1969, three years after *Les mots et les choses*. It is not, strictly speaking, a book in its own right, rather an extended theoretical postscript to the earlier work. Its very existence is dependent upon its predecessor in another sense: it is the work of a man who knows that whatever he writes will be published and, by any normal standards, will be a best seller. No one but a publisher, his enthusiasm chilled by sales figures of the author's previous work, would have failed to see that *Les mots et les choses* would be an intellectual event of the first order. As it turned out, it enjoyed an extraordinary commercial as well as critical success. Under the relentless promotion of the 'higher' mass media the idea had got about that Structuralism was the biggest thing since Existentialism and that *Les mots et les choses* was the best place to find it. The French, as we know, are very good at concocting movements. Usually, these movements are a response to some real shift in the artistic or intellectual climate, but they are accompanied by much fudging of issues, blurring of distinctions, and yoking by violence together of heterogeneous ideas. The Structuralist fad was no exception. Foucault was revered and reviled as a leading light of the new movement: the fact that he was not, nor could be, anything of the kind did not, for the moment, become clear. Some, at least, of the success of *Les mots et les choses* must be attributed to a misunderstanding. Certainly, the book would have received less attention if the truth had been recognized. It is a measure of Foucault's devotion to that truth that his next book should be a painfully rigorous elucidation of his methods. It would have been foolish to expect the success of *Les mots et les choses* to be repeated, but few could have anticipated so unsparing an attempt to undermine it. The austerities—the aridities, some said—of *L'archéologie du savoir* could not fail to dissapoint. *Les mots et les choses* had a potential audience the extent of the French educated public itself; its sequel could appeal only to a small body of specialists for whom the theoretical implications of Foucault's work were *in themselves* of passionate concern. One such reader, the philosopher Gilles Deleuze, in what is probably the most original and most illuminating review of a book by Foucault, described *L'archéologie du savoir* as 'not so much a discourse on his method as the poem of his previous work'. In it, Foucault had 'reached the point at which philosophy was necessarily poetry, the severe poetry of its own steps, the inscription of its own surface'—a deliciously typical example of Deleuzian perversity.

The kind of elucidation embarked on in *L'archéologie du savoir* is of broadly two kinds. First, Foucault had to set the record straight on the fundamental misunderstandings (whether favourable or unfavourable) to which his work had given rise. These all revolve around a single problem: the status and role of the human subject, the concept of 'man', in history and in the 'human sciences'. Now it was precisely a desire to displace the human subject, consciousness, from the centre of theoretical concern—a position it had enjoyed in French philosophy during the three hundred years separating Descartes and Sartre—rather than a concern to extend the application of the concepts and methods of structural linguistics, that Foucault shared with the so-called 'Structuralists'. The confusion arose because, in addition to a basic 'anti-humanist' position, each of these thinkers had a certain relation to notions of language and structure. However, it was a *different* relation in each case. (I shall take up the question of Structuralism and its role in recent French thought in my conclusion.) Foucault's own position is more complicated. There is a sense in which his work is profoundly anti-Structuralist. Far from wishing to 'freeze' the movement of history in structures, his whole work has been an examination of the nature of historical change. Far from being a consideration of language as structure, it sees language as *act*, as *event*. But it is easy to see how the confusion arose. In his earlier books—which were written prior to the Structuralist phenomenon and have never been called Structuralist—Foucault did use the term 'structural' to denote the kind of analysis he was carrying out. However, the term was applied loosely, almost tautologically: 'analysis' would have done just as well as 'structural analysis'. When he came to use the terms sign, signifier, signified, it was because they were part of the material with which he was dealing. They were not the invention of Saussure; on the contrary, they are as old as Western civilization. In particular, they are of central concern to the seventeenth-century *Grammaire de Port-Royal*. Indeed, what emerged from Foucault's study of general grammar, natural history, and the analysis of wealth was that, in a sense, the whole Classical period was 'structuralist' in that its knowledge was based on representation and the sign, on an analysis of relations between fixed elements that exclude the concepts of 'man' and 'history' as understood in the nineteenth century. Foucault's analysis of Classical thought reveals a 'structuralist' framework; his analysis of modern thought since 1800 does not. The structural elements belong to the object of Foucault's research, not to his method.

The first kind of elucidation attempted in *L'archéologie du savoir*, then, concerned certain misunderstandings as to the very nature of Foucault's enterprise. The second was a matter of certain difficulties left unresolved in *Les mots et les choses* and which had occurred to Foucault himself or been brought to his attention by others. A number of these relate to the question of periodization, which Foucault refers to in his opening discussion of the status of certain concepts in the historical disciplines generally. This problem may be approached in one of two ways. On the one hand, history may be seen as a succession of isolated events with no self-evident connection. The historian is then obliged to set about discovering patterns of connection, perhaps of causality; on the basis of his revealed (or imposed) patterns, he divides up the mass of events into manageable periods. Alternatively, history may be seen initially as an endless, seamless web in which one event leads relentlessly to the next in causal succession. In this case, the historian sets about undermining this apparently smooth continuity by establishing thresholds, ruptures, mutations, and transformations. Foucault points out that in recent years those studies that may be broadly termed the 'history of ideas' have changed sides, as it were, with history proper. The history of ideas, which tended to stress continuities, has now been seeking and discovering more and more discontinuities (he cites the work of Gaston Bachelard, Georges Canguilhem, Michel Serres, and Louis Althusser). History proper, on the other hand, is tending more and more to abandon 'the eruption of events in favour of stable structures' (the historians of the *Annales* school). Foucault goes on to show that this apparent reversal is a mere surface effect, that both the history of thought and history in the strict sense are concerned with the same problems: it was because the existing situation in each was so different that recent work in both had to take opposite courses of correction. Traditionally, the discontinuous was a quality inherent in the material of history itself, an obstacle that it was the historian's task to overcome as he revealed the continuous relations of causality, circular determination, antagonism, or expression that underlay the surface dispersal of isolated events. More recently, the discontinuous has been shifted from the obstacle to the work itself; it is no longer an external condition, but an analytical tool of the historian, a positive rather than a negative concept. Thus the notion of a 'total history' has ceded to what Foucault calls 'general history'. 'Total history' drew all phenomena around a single centre—the principle, meaning, spirit, world-view, overall form of a society or civilization. The same form of historicity operated on economic, social, political, and religious beliefs and practices, subjecting them to the same type of transformation and dividing up the temporal succession of events into great periods, each possessing its own principle of cohesion. 'General history', on the other hand, speaks of 'series, segmentations, limits, difference of level, time-lags, anachronistic survivals, possible types of relation'. It is not simply a juxtaposition of different histories or series—economic, political, cultural, etc.—nor the search for analogies or coincidences between them. The task proposed by general history is to determine what forms of relation may legitimately be made between them.

The epistemological change that is being operated within history is not yet complete; but it is not of recent origin either. The first attack to be made on a history of uninterrupted continuities, a history based ultimately on the founding function of the subject, of human consciousness, was made by Marx. His analysis of economic, social, and political relations sought to show that all man's activities, even his cherished beliefs, are, in the final analysis, determined outside the consciousness of the individual subject. A further blow at the centrality of man's ideas was dealt by Nietzsche's genealogy, which traced the 'purest' human morality back to the most naked of power struggles. Lastly, psychoanalysis, linguistics, and ethnology have decentred the human subject in relation to the laws of his desire, the forms of his language, and the rules of his beliefs and practices. Yet, consistently, Foucault believes, these radical attempts to undermine the primacy of the subject have been countered, not only by outright opposition, but also by a recuperational process at work within. Thus Marx is turned into a historian of totalities and an apostle of humanism, Nietzsche into a transcendental philosopher of orgins, and Freud into a means of individual 'fulfilment' in a context of moral and social conformity.

> The cry goes up that one is murdering history whenever, in a historical analysis—and especially if it is concerned with thought, ideas or knowledge—one is seen to be using in too obvious a way the categories of discontinuity and difference, the notions of threshold, rupture, and transformation, the description of series and limits. One will be denounced for attacking the inalienable rights of history and the very foundations of any possible historicity. But one must not be deceived: what is being bewailed with such vehemence is not the disappearance of history, but the eclipse of that form of history that was secretly, but entirely related to the synthetic activity of the subject. . . that ideological use of history by which one tries to restore to man everything that has unceasingly eluded him for over a hundred years. All the treasure of bygone days was crammed into the old citadel of this history; it was thought to be secure; it was sacralized; it was made the last resting-place of anthropological thought; it was even thought that its most inveterate enemies could be captured and turned into vigilant guardians (AS, 24; AK, 14).

L'archéologie du savoir, then, is a study of the theoretical problems posed by the use of such concepts as discontinuity, rupture, threshold, limit, series and transformation in the history of ideas. But before embarking on this work Foucault examines a number of concepts that express the theme of continuity. The notion of *tradition* allows us to reduce 'the difference proper to every beginning. . . to isolate the new against a background of permanence and to transfer its merit to originality, to genius, to the decisions proper to individuals' (AS, 31; AK, 21). The notion of *influence*, 'of too magical a kind to be very amenable to analysis', provides a support for the facts of transmission and communication. It attributes an apparently causal, but unexamined, process to the phenomena of resemblance and repetition. It links, though time and by propagation, such unities as individuals, *oeuvres*, notions, theories. Using the model of biology, the notions of *development* and even *evolution* make it possible to group together a series of dispersed events under a single organizing principle. The notion of *spirit* makes it possible to establish between the phenomena of a given period a common, coherent body of beliefs, thus allowing the emergence of the collective consciousness as principle of unity and explanations. None of these notions, says Foucault, must be accepted at face value: they must, on the contrary, be regarded as objects of the historian's concern rather than as methodological tools.

Then there are those large discursive groupings such as 'science', 'literature', 'philosophy', 'religion', 'history', 'fiction', etc. These are not as distinctive or as timeless as they sometimes appear. Each has its own complicated, even confused history. Some, such as 'literature' or 'politics', are of recent origin and can be applied to earlier periods 'only by a retrospective hypothesis. . . an interplay of formal analogies or semantic resemblances'. But the most treacherous categories, in Foucault's view, because the most apparently self-evident, are those of the *book* and the *oeuvre*. The material support of a book—the individual volume—is not, of course, the book itself. Even the volume is not a simple unity: it forms part of an edition. It may be an anthology—the work of many authors, but the creation of another, the editor—or part of a greater work in several volumes. But the 'discursive unity' of which the volume is the material support is even more problematic.

> A novel by Stendhal and a novel by Dostoievsky do not have the same relations of individuality as that between two novels belonging to Balzac's cycle *La Comédie humaine*; and the relation between Balzac's novels is not the same as that existing between Joyce's *Ulysses* and the *Odyssey*. The frontiers of a book are never clear-cut: beyond the title, the first line and the last full stop, beyond its internal configuration, its autonomous form, it is caught up in a system of references to other books, other texts, other sentences: it is a node within a network. And this network of references is not the same in the case of a mathematical treatise, a textual commentary, a historical account and an episode in a novel cycle; the unity

of the book, even in the sense of a group of relations, cannot be regarded as identical in each case. The book is simply not the object that one holds in one's hands; and it cannot remain within the little parallelepiped that contains it: its unity is variable and relative. As soon as one questions that unity it loses its self-evidence; it indicates itself, constructs itself, only on the basis of a complex field of discourse (AS, 34; AK, 23).

The notion of *oeuvre* is still more complicated. It may be defined as a collection of texts appearing under a single proper name. But does the name of an author carry the same weight in the case of a book published under his own name, another under a pseudonym, an unfinished draft, a notebook? The establishment of a complete *oeuvre* presupposes a number of choices that are difficult to justify, but the implicit assumption of all these choices is that of a common, *expressive* function.

One is admitting that there must be a level (as deep as it is necessary to imagine it) at which the *oeuvre* emerges, in all its fragments, even the smallest, most inessential ones, as the expression of the thought, the experience, the imagination or the unconscious of the author, or, indeed, of the historical determinations that operated upon him. But it is at once apparent that such a unity, far from being given immediately, is the result of an operation; this operation is interpretative (since it deciphers, in the text, the transcription of something that it both conceals and manifests); and that the operation that determines the *opus*, in its unity, and consequently the *oeuvre* itself, will not be the same in the case of the author of *Le Théâtre et son Double* (Artaud) and the author of the *Tractatus* (Wittgenstein), and therefore when one speaks of an *oeuvre* in each case one is using the word in a different sense. The *oeuvre* can be regarded neither as an immediate unity, nor as a certain unity, nor as a homogeneous unity (AS, 35–6; AK, 24).

Foucault proposes to take as his starting-point such unities as are given (medicine or political economy, for example), but he will not remain inside them. They will be scrutinized, their familiar unity broken down. For each discipline, *oeuvre*, book may be regarded in its raw, neutral state as a collection of 'statements'—a term Foucault refrains, for the moment, from defining, other than to stress its character as *event*. One begins to see, more clearly perhaps than before, how inappropriate are the terms 'history of ideas' or 'history of thought' to Foucault's enterprise. For they suggest the existence, beyond the statements themselves, of the intention, conscious or unconscious, of an individual human subject, another, latent discourse beneath the manifest one. But the purpose of Foucault's isolation of the occurrences of the statement is not to leave a mass of facts that cannot be related to one another.

> It is in order to be sure that this occurrence is not linked with synthesizing operations of a purely psychological kind (the intention of the author, the form of his mind, the rigour of his thought, the themes that obsess him, the project that traverses his existence and gives it meaning) and to be able to grasp other forms of regularity, other types of relations. Relations between statements (even if the author is unaware of them; even if the statements do not have the same author; even if the authors were unaware of each other's existence); relations between groups of statements thus established (even if these groups do not concern the same, or even adjacent fields; even if they do not possess the same formal level; even if they are not the locus of assignable exchanges); relations between statements and groups of statements and events of a quite different kind (technical, economic, social, political) (AS, 41; AK 28–9).

Reviewing his previous work in the light of these theoretical preoccupations, Foucault concludes that the apparent unity on which such large groups of statements as medicine, economics, or general grammar were based was in fact illusory. What he found was rather 'series full of gaps, intertwined with one another, interplays of differences, distances, substitutions, transformations'. The types of statements found were much too heterogeneous to be linked together in a single figure, and to stimulate, from one period to another, beyond individual *oeuvres*, 'a sort of uninterrupted text'. So he was led to describe these discontinuities, these dispersions, themselves and to see whether, nevertheless, one cannot find certain regularities, 'an order in their successive appearance, correlations in their simultaneity, assignable positions in a common space, a reciprocal functioning, linked and hierarchized transformations'. Such an analysis would describe *systems of dispersion*. When such a system is seen at work in a group of statements, Foucault proposes to use the term *discursive formation*, preferring this neutral term to such older, misleading terms as 'science', 'discipline', 'theory', etc. The conditions to which the elements of this formation are subjected will be called the *rules of formation*. Taking the three areas of medicine, economics, and grammar, already treated in earlier work, Foucault proposes to test these new concepts and to see what others will prove necessary to a clear formulation of a theory of historical discourse. It may well be that 'unities' suspended at the outset, as a matter of methodological rigour, will be abandoned altogether. Foucault suggests—and fails to conceal his pleasure at it—the bleak prospect that his iconoclasm will present to the traditionally minded.

> Is there not a danger that everything that has so far protected the historian in his daily journey and accompanied him until nightfall (the destiny of rationality and the teleology of the sciences, the long, continuous labour of thought from period to period, the awakening and the progress of consciousness, its perpetual resumption of itself, the uncompleted, but uninterrupted movement of totalizations, the return to an ever-open source and finally the historico-transcendental thematic) may disappear, leaving for analysis a blank, indifferent space, lacking in both interiority and promise? (AS, 54; AK, 39).

Taking a particular discursive formation, psychopathology, Foucault asks how such an object of discourse comes to be formed, what precisely are its rules of formation. He names three types of rule. First, there are *surfaces of emergence*, or social and cultural areas in which a particular discursive formation makes its appearance. In the case of nineteenth-century psychopathology, these were the family, the immediate social group, the work situation, and the religious community. All these had certain thresholds of acceptability in behaviour beyond which the term 'madness' would have applied, confinement been demanded and the responsibility for explanation, if not for care and cure, placed on the medical profession. None of these areas was new in the nineteenth century, though each was organized in a stricter, more regulated fashion than previously. Moreover, they were combined with quite new surfaces of emergence, namely, sexuality, which, with its deviations from accepted norms, became for the first time an object of medical observation and analysis, and penality, in which criminal behaviour, hitherto distinguished from madness, came to be regarded as a form of deviance more or less related to madness. The second kind of rule of formation was that practised by the *authorities of delimitation*. The medical profession, as an insitutional body possessed of a certain knowledge and authority recognized by public opinion, law, and government, was obviously the major one in this case. But the law (with its attribution of responsibility, etc.) and the church (as the authority qualified to distinguish between the mystical and the pathological, for example) also played a part. The third rule of formation was what Foucault calls *grids of specification*: the systems according to which different kinds of madness could be specified and related to one another in psychiatric discourse. These included the soul (conceived as a group of faculties), the body (a three-dimensional volume of related organs) and the personal history of individuals (a linear succession of phases). However, the three rules of formation specified do not provide fully formed objects, which the discourse of psychopathology can then set about naming and classifying. The objects of a discourse and the discourse itself emerged together, in the same process. Similarly, the three kinds of rule do not exist in isolation but interact with one another in a highly complex way to form the conditions of possibility of a discourse. This means that 'one cannot speak of anything at any time; it is not easy to say something new; it is not enough to open our eyes. . . for a new object suddenly to light up and emerge out of the ground'. This difficulty is not merely a negative one: it provides the very conditions in which new objects appear. Nevertheless, these relations—between institutions, economic and social processes, beliefs and practices, etc.—are not present in the object itself: they do not constitute it. The object of a discourse is not, of course, to be confused with what linguists call the referent, the actual thing referred to by a verbal sign. Discourse is not about objects: rather, discourse constitutes them.

> We are not trying to find out who was mad at a particular period, or in what his madness consisted, or whether his disorders were identical with those known to us today. . . whether witches were unrecognized and persecuted madmen and madwomen or whether, at a different period, a mystical or aesthetic experience was not unduly medicalized (AS, 64; AK, 47).

He does not deny the possibility of such a 'history of the referent', but his aim is quite different: to dispense with 'things', in order not to make discourse the sign of something else.

Foucault has still not reached the stage of determining what it is that binds together the various forms of statement that make a discourse like nineteenth-century medicine. Before doing so, he shifts attention away from the statement (*énoncé*) to the enunciation (*énonciation*) in a section entitled 'The Formation of Enunciative Modalities ('La formation des modalités énonciatives'). It will be noted that all three key-words here have a common root—a situation that proved impossible to reproduce in English translation, thus losing the play of distinction within similarity of the French nouns and the intermediary position of the adjective between them. *Énoncé* really has to be translated as 'statement', the only word that covers its uses in English. 'Proposition' is overly philosophical and suggests a meaning beneath the actual words; 'sentence' is too grammatical, too linguistic a concept; the first sacrifices form, the second content. (Indeed, in an attempt to define what he means by *énoncé*, Foucault is at pains to show how it differs in certain crucial respects from these two notions.) By *énonciation*, Foucault means not the words spoken or written, but the act of speaking or writing them, the context in which they are uttered, the status or position of their author. ('Utterance', because it makes no distinction between *énoncé* and *énonciation*, is a suitable rendering for neither word.) By 'enunciative modality', then, Foucault means the laws operating behind the formation of things. These concern the *status of the speaker* ('medical statements cannot come from anybody; their value, efficacy, even their therapeutic powers. . . cannot be dissociated from the statutorily defined person who has the right to make them'); the *sites from which* the statements are made (hospital, laboratory, library); the *positions of* the subjects of medical discourse (in relation to the perceptual field, new systems of registration, description, and classification, new teaching methods, other institutions). Far from referring back to the synthesis performed by a unifying subject, these different statuses, sites, positions of discourse manifest his dispersion. The unity of a discursive practice is given not by conscious subjectivities, but by a system of relations prior and external to the individual, conscious activity.

What, then, is a 'statement'? It is neither a proposition nor a sentence; it is not even the unit, or atom, of a discourse. It is not so much one element among others as a function that operates vertically, cutting through the horizontal series of signs that are its embodiment. A sentence belongs to a text and is defined by the laws of a language; a proposition belongs to a larger argument and is governed by the laws of logic: a statement belongs to a discursive formation, by which it is also defined. A statement also has a relation to its subject that is quite different from that existing between a subject and a proposition or sentence.

> The subject of the statement should not be regarded as identical with the author of the formulation—either in substance or in function. It is not in fact the cause, origin or starting-point of the phenomenon of the written or spoken articulation of a sentence; nor is it that meaningful intention which, silently anticipating words, orders them like the visible body of its intuition. . . It is a particular, vacant place that may in fact be filled by different individuals; but, instead of being defined once and for all and maintaining itself as such throughout a text, a book or an *oeuvre*, this place varies—or rather it is variable enough to be able either to persevere, unchanging, through several sentences, or to alter with each one. . . To describe a formulation *qua* statement does not consist in analysing the relations between the author and what he says (or wanted to say, or said without wanting to); but in determining what position can and must be occupied by any individual if he is to be the subject of it (AS, 125–6; AK, 95–6).

A statement also differs from a sentence or a proposition in that it cannot operate in isolation. A sentence or proposition can only become a statement within an associated field, a complex whole made up of all the other formulations among which the statement appears and forms one element ('the network or spoken formulations that make up a conversation, the architecture of a demonstration, bound on the one side by its premises and on the other by its conclusion, the series of affirmations that make up a narrative'); and this network embraces not only such an immediate, apparent context, but also those other, past formulations to which it refers, if even implicitly, and those future formulations that it makes possible. Lastly, a statement must have a material existence. But this materiality is not added to it, its formation already achieved: it is part of its very constitution. A sentence composed of exactly the same words is not the same statement if spoken by someone in conversation or printed in a novel. An enunciation takes place whenever a group of signs is emitted; it is, by definition, unrepeatable. A statement, on the other hand, may, in certain conditions, be repeated; in others, the repetition of the same formulation constitutes a new statement.

> This repeatable materiality that characterizes the enunciative function reveals the statement as a specific and paradoxical object, but also as one of those objects that men produce, manipulate, use, transform, exchange, combine, decompose and recompose, and possibly destroy. Instead of being something once and for all—and lost in the past like the result of a battle, a geological catastrophe, or the death of a king—the statement, as it emerges in its materiality, appears with a status, enters various networks and various fields of use, is subjected to transferences or modifications, is integrated into operations and strategies in which its identity is maintained or effaced. Thus the statement circulates, is used, disappears, allows or prevents the realization of a desire, serves or resists various interests, participates in challenge and struggle, and becomes a theme of appropriation or rivalry (AS, 138; AK, 105).

Statements exist in conditions of rarity, exteriority, and accumulation. Usually, discourse is analysed in such a way that different texts are organized into a single figure, coherent with contemporary institutions and practices and expressive of a whole period. Thus beneath the diversity of the things said is uncovered 'a sort of great uniform text', revealing for the first time what men 'really meant'. Because this underlying meaning is arrived at by an individual act of interpretation, a single manifest formulation may also give rise to an endless number of latent meanings. Between these opposite poles of interpretative analysis, by which the many are reduced to the one or the one expanded to reveal the many, Foucault's analysis remains at the level of what is said, at the level of the *few* statements possible in relation to the unlimited number of possible sentences and propositions. This condition of the statement Foucault calls its 'rarity'.

> In this sense, discourse ceases to be what it is for the exegetic attitude: an inexhaustible treasure from which one can always draw new and always unpredictable riches. . . It appears as an asset—finite, limited, desirable, useful—that has its own rules of

appearance, but also its own conditions of appropriation and operation (AS, 158; AK, 120).

And Foucault adds, in a few phrases that indicate how clearly he has seen the future development of his work:

> an asset that consequently, from the moment of its existence (and not only in its 'practical applications'), poses the question of power; an asset that is, by nature, the object of a struggle, a political struggle.

Instead of positing an interiority from which the intention or expression of a founding, transcendental subjectivity may be intuited, Foucault's analysis of discourse places statements in the dispersion of an *exteriority*. Similarly, rather than seeing statements as forms of memory or traces of some lost origin, it sees their survival as an *accumulation*, constantly subjected to reactivation, loss, and even destruction.

In Foucault's examination of the conditions governing the production of statements three very closely related terms arise that require definition: positivity, the historical *a priori*, and the archive. The *positivity* of a discourse or discipline is that which characterizes its unity through a specific period of time, that which enables us to say that Buffon and Linnaeus, for example, were talking about 'the same thing' or were engaged upon 'the same field of battle' and, by the same token, prevents us from saying that Darwin is talking about the same thing as Diderot. It is 'a limited space of communication', not as extensive as a 'science', with its long historical development, but more so than the mere play of 'influences'. What forms such a positivity, what makes it possible, Foucault calls the 'historical *a priori*'. The juxtaposition of the two terms is admittedly 'startling'. The adjective is required because what is being described is not 'a condition of validity for judgements, but a condition of reality for statements'. It may be defined as the group of rules that characterize a discursive practice—rules not imposed from the outside, but inherent in its operation. The systems of statements produced by the different positivities, in accordance with historical *a prioris*, are what Foucault calls the *archive*. The archive is not, as its name might suggest, an inert depository of past statements preserved for future use. It is the very system that makes the emergence of statements possible. The archive of a period, let alone a society, cannot be described exhaustively and it is not possible at all to describe the archive of our own period, since it is within these rules that we speak, they that give us what we can say.

At this stage Foucault takes stock of his progress so far. In an attempt to replace the old unities of discourse—*oeuvre*, authors, books themes—he has set up a mass of 'bizarre machinery', which he himself admits is a source of embarrassment. What is this new form of analysis that he 'rather solemnly' calls 'archaeology'? Is it sufficiently different from the history of ideas to require a new name and an 'arsenal' of new weapons? Clearly Foucault thinks it is, though his subsequent works show that the battery of newfangled terms, while remaining implicit in his methods of analysis, need hardly intrude into the surface of the text at all. The history of ideas, that 'uncertain object with badly drawn frontiers', operates in two ways.

> It recounts the by-ways and margins of history. Not the history of the sciences, but that of imperfect, ill-based knowledge, which could never in the whole of its long, persistent life attain the form of scientificity (the history of alchemy rather than chemistry, of animal spirits or phrenology rather than physiology, the history of atomistic themes rather than physics). The history of those shady philosophies that haunt literature, art, the sciences, law, ethics and even man's daily life; the history of those age-old themes that are never crystallized in a rigorous and individual system, but which have formed the spontaneous philosophy of those who did not philosophize. . . The analysis of opinions rather than of knowledge, of errors rather than of truth, of types of mentality rather than of forms of thought (AS, 179; AK, 136–7).

But it also sets out to cross the boundaries of existing disciplines, to link them together, to reinterpret them from the outside. It shows how the systems and *oeuvres* of science, philosophy, and literature emerge from the immediate, unreflective experience of the period, how these systems break up, disappear or are reshaped in new ways, how ideas and themes move from one domain, one period, to another. These two roles of the history of ideas are articulated one upon the other. It describes the transition from loosely formulated notions to philosophy, science, and literature. It is dominated by three major themes: genesis, continuity, totalization. Archaeology, on the other hand, is 'an abandonment of the history of ideas, a systematic rejection of its postulates and procedures, an attempt to practise a quite different history of what men have said'.

Foucault elicits four methodological principles that distinguish the archaeological enterprise. They concern the attribution of innovation, the analysis of contradictions, comparative descriptions, and the mapping of transformations. The history of ideas treats discourse in terms of two values: old and new, traditional and original, ordinary and exceptional. There are formulations that are highly valued on account of their rarity and thus serve as models; there are others that are ordinary, everyday, derivative. In describing the first, the history of ideas speaks of inventions, changes, transformations, the slow emergence of truth from error; in the case of the second, it treats statements in terms of what they have in common, the extent to which they contribute to the 'slow accumulation of the past', the 'silent sedimentation of things said'. However, this approach poses two methodological problems. It presupposes the possibility of establishing a single, homogeneous series in which every formulation would be accorded a single, dated position, whereas the fact that one formulation appears before another is no help in distinguishing the original from the repetitive. Similarly, the resemblance between two or more formulations is no index of originality or lack of it.

> It is not legitimate, then, to demand, point-blank, of the texts that one is studying their title to originality and whether they possess those degrees of nobility that are measured here by the absence of ancestors. . . To seek in the great accumulation of the already-said the text that resembles 'in advance' a later text, to ransack history in order to rediscover the play of anticipations or echoes, to go right back to the first seeds or to go forward to the last traces, to reveal in a work its fidelity to tradition or its irreducible uniqueness, to raise or lower its stock of originality, to say that the Port-Royal grammarians invented nothing, to discover that Cuvier had more predecessors than one thought, these are harmless enough amusements for historians who refuse to grow up. . . Archaeology is not in search of inventions. . . What it seeks in the texts of Linnaeus or Buffon, Petty or Ricardo, Pinel or Bichat, is not to draw up a list of founding saints; it is to uncover the regularity of a discursive practice. A practice that is in operation, in the same way, in the

work of their predecessors; a practice that takes account in their work not only of the most original affirmations (those that no one else dreamt of before them), but also of those that they borrowed, even copied, from their predecessors. A discovery is no less regular, from the enunciative point of view, than the text that repeats and diffuses it; regularity is no less operant, no less effective and active, in a banal as in a unique formation (AS, 187–9; AK, 143–5).

The history of ideas usually attributes a certain coherence to the discourse it analyses. If this coherence is not apparent at a manifest level, it finds a hidden unity at a deeper level: in the internal organization of a text, the form of development of an *oeuvre*, the collective spirit of a period, type of society or civilization. Alternatively, a single, fundamental contradition may be found at the very origin of the system. Such a contradiction, far from being an appearance or accident of discourse, constitutes the very law of its existence, the principle of its historicity. For archaeological analysis, however, contradictions are neither appearances to be overcome, nor secret principles to be uncovered. They are objects to be described for themselves. Foucault offers an example: the 'contradiction' between Linnaeus's 'fixist' principle and the 'evolutionist' formulations to be found in Buffon, Diderot, Bordeu, Maillet, and others. The theory of structure is not a common postulate shared by both sides that reduces to a secondary level the conflict between evolutionism and fixism; it is the principle of their incompatibility, the law that governs their co-existence.

Archaeological analysis involves comparison: comparison of one discursive practice with another and a discursive practice with the non-discursive practices (institutions, political events, economic and social processes) that surround it. Thus *Les mots et les choses*, an example of the first type of comparison compares the states of several discursive formations at a particular period, but not with a view to reconstructing on this basis a complete picture of, say, Classical science or the 'Classical spirit'. The intention is not to show that eighteenth-century man was more interested in order than history, in classification than development, in signs than in causality. The aim is to reveal a number of specific relations existing between a limited set of discursive formations. They are valid only for the three positivities being studied, which form an 'interdiscursive configuration', which in turn is related to the analysis of representation, the general theory of signs and 'ideology', on the one hand, and to mathematics and the attempt to establish a *mathesis* on the other. It is not, therefore, a criticism of Foucault's work to claim that evidence from this or that other discipline would have invalidated its conclusions. His analysis is limited by choice, since any *total* analysis is deliberately excluded. What he describes is an interpositivity existing between three specific discursive formations. The replacement of one of them by another, say Biblical criticism or the theory of the fine arts, or the addition of a fourth, would have produced an interdiscursive configuration that would be different to a greater or lesser degree.

Archaeology also analyses relations between discursive practices and what Foucault calls non-discursive practices. But just as the comparison between different discursive formations was not intended to establish cultural unities for entire periods, so the second type of comparison is not intended to uncover great cultural continuities or mechanisms of causality. Foucault exemplifies this type by reference to *Naissance de la clinique*. The reference is also of particular importance in its own right, since it touches on one of Foucault's most crucial contributions to the theory of discourse: the attempt to discover a system of articulation between discursive and non-discursive practices that avoids, on the one hand, failure (the mere citing of homologies or coincidences) and the spurious success offered by certain analyses of Marxist inspiration (whereby the discursive formations are *caused* by the non-discursive practices, of which they are the expression). Nowhere, in this analysis, does Foucault refer explicitly to 'historical materialism': his criticisms are offered rather in the spirit of 'if the cap fits'. He is well aware, of course, of the attempt made by his former teacher and colleague, Louis Althusser, to salvage the theory of determination by replacing the two-tier model of base and superstructure by a number of semi-autonomous *instances*, linked together by causal reciprocity. But Althusser never operates on other than an abstract level and the work of Marxists on the ground, as they themselves are always the first to say, remains as crudely reductionist as ever. In any case, the Althusserian revival of the celebrated 'determination in the final analysis' by the mode of production (which, as Engels mischievously remarked, is often so final that it is never reached) has proved, for many, to be the thin end of the wedge of its abandonment, rather than its saving grace. Meanwhile, Foucault, attacked by Marxist readers of *Les mots et les choses* for ignoring the political, social, and economic practices of the period (as if by some oversight, when, as he explicitly stated, it was by deliberate choice), had already, in *Naissance de la clinique*, shown how a discursive practice can be related to its contemporary non-discursive practices. (And, of course, all Foucault's subsequent work is to be a further exploration of this relation.) Confronted by the changes in medicine that took place around 1800, an analysis of a causal type would try

> to discover to what extent political changes or economic processes could determine the consciousness of scientists— the horizon and direction of their interest, their system of values, their way of perceiving things, the style of their rationality; thus, at a period in which industrial capitalism was beginning to recalculate its manpower requirements, disease took on a social dimension; the maintenance of health, cure, public assistance for the poor and sick, the search for pathological causes and sites, became a collective responsibility that must be assumed by the state. Hence the value placed upon the body as a work tool, the care to rationalize medicine on the basis of the other sciences, the efforts to maintain the levels of health of a population, the attention paid to therapy, after-care and the recording of long-term phenomena (AS, 212–13; AK, 163).

old

An archaeological analysis would situate the problem rather differently.

> If archaeology brings medical discourse closer to a number of practices, it is in order to discover. . . far more direct relations than those of a causality communicated through the consciousness of the speaking subjects. It wishes to show not how political practice has determined the meaning and form of medical discourse, but how and in what form it takes part in its conditions of emergence, insertion and functioning. This relation may be assigned to several levels. First to that of the division and delimitation of the medical object: not, of course, that it was political practice that from the early nineteenth century imposed on medicine such a new object as tissular lesions or the anatomo-physiological correlations; but it opened up new fields for the mapping of medical objects (these fields are constituted by the mass of the population administratively

new

compartmented and supervised, gauged according to certain norms of life and health, and analysed according to documentary and statistical forms of registration; they are also constituted by the great conscript armies of the Revolutionary and Napoleonic period, with their specific form of medical control; they are also constituted by the institutions of hospital assistance that were defined at the end of the eighteenth and the beginning of the nineteenth centuries, in relation to the economic needs of the time and to the reciprocal position of the social classes). One can also see the appearance of this relation of political practice to medical discourse in the status accorded to the doctor, who becomes not only the privileged, but also virtually the exclusive, enunciator of this discourse, in the form of institutional relation that the doctor may have with the hospitalized patient or with his private practice, in the modalities of teaching and diffusion that are prescribed or authorized for this knowledge. Lastly, one can grasp this relation in the function that is attributed to medical discourse, or in the role that is required of it, when it is a question of judging individuals, making administrative decisions, laying down the norms of a society. . . It is not a question, then, of showing how the political practice of a given society constituted or modified the medical concepts and theoretical structure of pathology; but how medical discourse as a practice concerned with a particular field of objects, finding itself in the hands of a certain number of statutorily designated individuals and having certain functions to exercise in society, is articulated on practices that are external to it and which are not themselves of a discursive order. If in this analysis archaeology suspends. . . a causal analysis, if it wishes to avoid the necessary connection through the speaking subject, it is not in order to guarantee the sovereign, sole independence of discourse; it is in order to discover the domain of existence and functioning of a discursive practice. In other words, the archaeological description of discourses is deployed in the dimension of a general history; it seeks to discover that whole domain of institutions, economic processes and social relations on which a discursive formation can be articulated; it tries to show how the autonomy of discourse and its specificity nevertheless do not give it the status of pure ideality and total historical independence; what it wishes to uncover is the particular level in which history can give place to definite types of discourse, which have their own type of historicity and which are related to a whole set of various historicities (AS, 213–15; AK, 163–5).

Lastly, archaeological analysis is a description of change. But it is not enough simply to indicate changes and relate them to the theological, aesthetic model of creation (transcendence, originality, invention), or to the psychological model of sudden acts of awareness, or to the biological model of evolution. The undifferentiated notion of change as either a general container for all events or the abstract principle of their succession must be replaced by the analysis of different types of *transformation*. But the establishment of discontinuities is not an end in itself. For the history of ideas, the appearance of difference indicates a failure: it was the historian's task to reduce it. Archaeology takes as the object of its description what is usually regarded as an obstacle: its aim is not to overcome differences, but to analyse them. Those who say that he invents differences, says Foucault, can never have opened *La nosographie philosophique* (Pinel) and the *Traité des membranes* (Bichat). Archaeology is simply trying to take such differences seriously. Nor does archaeology try to freeze the continuous flow of history in synchronic systems that remain motionless between one transformation and the next. Again, it respects what it finds: the existence of rules of formation common to a number of positivities over a period of time. In any case, Foucault charts in scrupulous detail any minor shifts and changes occurring within the interdiscursivity uncovered. Nor does archaeology say that when one discursive formation gives place to another a whole new world of objects, concepts, or theoretical choices appears. A number of elements may remain unchanged, yet form part of a new discursive formation.

In a final chapter, Foucault examines the question of the scope and possible limitations of the archaeological enterprise. Archaeology cuts right across the science/non-science distinction. It does not occupy an area prior or external to that of the sciences, the area of the pseudo-sciences (like psycho-pathology), sciences at the pre-historical stage (like Natural History) or sciences permeated with ideology (like political economy). Its criterion is not that of scientificity or truth: it makes distinctions, not of value but of function, between 'scientific' and 'non-scientific' disciplines. Discursive practices give rise to 'knowledge', whether or not they aspire to or achieve scientific status. The territory of archaeology extends to literary or philosophical texts as well as scientific ones. Non-scientific knowledge is not to be judged by the criteria of science: it is not to be relegated to an erroneous, deceptive, interested domain such as that defined by the Althusserian concept of 'ideology'. On the contrary, the sciences are thoroughly imbued with ideology. A science does not diminish its relations with ideology by rectifying its errors.

In the 'dialogue' with which the book ends, Foucault asks his imaginary opponent:

> What is that fear that makes you reply in terms of consciousness when someone talks to you about a practice, its conditions, its rules and its historical transformations? What is that fear that makes you see, beyond all boundaries, ruptures, shifts and divisions, the great historico-transcendental destiny of the West?

He answers his own question, rather cryptically:

> It seems to me that the only reply to this question is a political one. But let us leave that to one side for today. Perhaps we will take it up again soon in another way (AS, 273; AK, 209–10).

It is significant that *L'archéologie du savior*, which in so many ways is a *summa* of one stage of his work, should end on so prophetically political a note.

PART II

The Genealogy of Power

Discourse, Power, and Knowledge

L'archéologie du savoir was completed before the events of May 1968. Foucault did not witness, let alone participate in, those events. (He was teaching in Tunisia at the time.) But like many French intellectuals he was profoundly affected by the ferment of questioning and self-questioning that followed. Not that May came to Foucault as quite the shock that it must have to many: or rather, if a shock, a shock of recognition. The author of *Histoire de la folie* must have been better prepared than most. Moreover, he was not one of those who expected its 'success', or were disillusioned by its 'failure'. For 'success', in the eyes of many of its participants and of its enemies, would have meant the seizure of state power by 'the people'. In those terms, it was doomed to failure, as the Communists saw very clearly: they did not even try to take control of it. To the extent that the participants believed that they could succeed in this sense, they were prisoners of an outmoded rhetoric of 'revolution'. What *was* truly revolutionary was the realization that the state was not sufficiently in one place to be seized, that the state was everywhere and that therefore the 'revolution' had to be everywhere, ubiquitous as well as permanent. The success of the May events was the discovery by small groups of people of an unsuspected creativity, the capacity for inventing new forms of social relations, a desire and an ability to run their own affairs. The true failure would have been the immediate, limited 'success' apostrophized in the rhetoric, a success that would certainly have been usurped by the Communists, or, which would have amounted to much the same thing, ended in bloody repression. It was Petrograd 1917 that failed, not Paris 1968. That Foucault had already learnt these lessons is apparent in the remarkable conversation with Gilles Deleuze published by *L'Arc* in 1972. 'You were the first,' Deleuze remarks, 'to teach us something absolutely fundamental: the indignity of speaking for others. We ridiculed representation and said it was finished, but we failed to draw the consequences of this "theoretical" conversion—to appreciate the theoretical fact that only those directly concerned can speak in a practical way on their own behalf' (B5, 3–10; LCP, 205–17).

When, in the aftermath of May, the French government decided to disperse the concentration of the University of Paris in the Latin Quarter and set up a number of autonomous campuses on the periphery of the city, Foucault was invited to head the philosophy department at Vincennes. There, in a ghetto of almost total internal freedom the *gauchistes* were given their head and, it was hoped, would be kept out of harm's way—or so it appeared. The truth was less simple. In fact, the government had made sure that, in addition to an impressive array of Leftist intellectuals, the staff included substantial numbers of Communists. Before long the Vincennes campus became the battleground for an unremitting confrontation between the forces of 'anarchy' (*gauchistes*) and the forces of 'order' (the CP). Thus the Communists, who had stood by uncomprehendingly in May, were allowed to assume the role they have fitted themselves to perform best, that of self-appointed vanguard of a phantom proletariat. The similarity between the 'order' of the CP and that of the Gaullist State was not lost on the *gauchistes*. What was lost on so many of them was the extent to which their practice was in advance of their theory. For a generation or more, revolutionary discourse had been so thoroughly imbued with the Stalinism of the French Party that *gauchistes* often spoke a language indistinguishable from that of the Communists. Foucault was exceptional in this regard. While showing the greatest respect for Marx himself, he refused to pay lip service to the verbal small change of Marxism and never ceased to question the usefulness of 'historical materialism' for a twentieth-century analysis of social, economic, and political forms. In a place where one was theoretically free to say anything, but where in practice everyone said much the same thing, if only because conformism was indispensable to being heard at all, it was a brave spirit who dared to speak well of Nietzsche, let alone devote an entire course to his philosophy. Only now are many of the 1968 generation beginning to learn the lessons that Foucault had tried to teach them. It is sad, nonetheless, when self-styled *nouveaux philosophes*, who discovered Marxism-Leninism *after* 1968, some of them travelling from Moscow to Peking in the process, should end up in 1978 discovering Christianity. Russians who have been forced to live their Marxism-Leninism may be allowed their extreme unction; when Parisian intellectuals follow suit it looks like charades.

The heart of Foucault's Vincennes lectures was to appear as 'Nietzsche, la généalogie, l'histoire' in a collection of essays, by various hands, published in memory of Jean Hyppolite. Hitherto in Foucault's work the name of Nietzsche was invoked rather like a sign, as a short-hand reference in an argument that required his presence, but not his voice. That presence is dominant in *Histoire de la folie* and in *Les mots et les choses* and even occurs at a crucial point in the closing pages of *Naissance de la clinique*. Yet, in *L'archéologie du savoir*, where Foucault sets out to theorize his methods of work, Nietzsche appears only in two passages, in neither case in a way that is central to the argument. It is true that the principal roles in this work are not the proper names, but a conceptual apparatus of abstract nouns. Yet an examination of the index will reveal over a hundred names of individuals, many cited far more frequently than Nietzsche. It may be argued that Nietzsche is so all-pervasive in *L'archéologie du savoir*, so subterranean, that it requires no sign-posting. Certainly what strikes the reader of 'Nietzsche, la généalogie, l'histoire' is how closely Foucault's description of Nietzschean genealogy applies to his own archaeology. Yet there is one element in the genealogy—and it is the most fundamental one—that remains at an implicit level in the archaeology. In an interview published in 1977, M. Fontana raised the question of power, suggesting that Foucault was the first to introduce it into the analysis of discourse. Foucault declined the compliment and added:

On the contrary, I am struck by the difficulty I had formulating it. When I think about it now I ask myself what I could have been talking about, in *Histoire de la folie*, for example, or *Naissance de la clinique*, if not power? Yet I am perfectly well aware that I practically never used the word and did not have that field of analysis at my disposal. This inability was certainly bound up with the political situation in which we found ourselves (B5, 19).

Earlier in the same interview Foucault admits that this tendency to ignore the power relations in discourse had led him to confuse the *'régime discursif'* with 'systematicity, theoretical form or something like the paradigm'. This, clearly, is a veiled criticism of *L'archéologie du savoir*. For, if the operation of power is so fundamental to the production of discourse, then it was there—in a work specifically devoted to the elaboration of discursive theory—that its presence should have been most clearly apparent. Conversely, in those books where discourse is described in conjunction with its contemporary institutions (the studies of madness and medicine) its explicit absence is less felt because it is so implicitly present. It is now clear why Foucault never again uses the term archaeology, or any of the 'panoply of terms' so laboriously elaborated in *L'archéologie du savoir*. This new realization of the role of power in discourse was so important to Foucault that he felt impelled to abandon altogether the terms he had fashioned for himself and to adopt, unashamedly, the Nietzschean term 'genealogy'.

Two years earlier, in another interview, Foucault was asked to comment on the way in which, during the previous decade, Nietzsche had gradually come to challenge the hegemony enjoyed by Marx in the minds of French intellectuals. Foucault replied:

It was Nietzsche who specified the power relation as the general focus, shall we say, of philosophical discourse—whereas for Marx it was the production relation. Nietzsche is the philosopher of power, but he managed to think power without confining himself within a political theory to do so. . . If I wanted to be pretentious, I would give 'the genealogy of morals' as a general title of what I am doing.

But already—it is 1975—Foucault senses the wheels of conformism grinding into action and is ready to back away:

Nowadays I prefer to remain silent about Nietzsche. When I was teaching, I often gave courses on Nietzsche, but I couldn't do that today. . . I'm tired of people studying him only in order to produce the kind of commentaries that are written on Mallarmé and Hegel. For myself, I prefer to utilize the writers I like. The only valid tribute to thought such as Nietzsche's is precisely to use it, to deform it, to make it groan and protest. And if the commentators say that I am being unfaithful to Nietzsche that is of absolutely no interest (B8, 33).

Yet, however much 'Nietzsche, la généalogie, l'histoire' could be retitled 'Foucault, la généalogie, l'histoire', this essay remains rigorously close to Nietzsche's texts. Hardly a sentence is without a quotation or a reference.

> Genealogy is gray, meticulous, and patiently documentary. It operates on a field of entangled and confused parchments, on documents that have been scratched over and recopied many times. . . Genealogy, consequently, requires patience and a knowledge of details and it depends on a vast accumulation of source material. Its 'cyclopean monuments' are constructed from 'discreet and apparently insignificant truths and according to a rigorous method'; they cannot be the product of 'large and well-meaning errors'. In short, genealogy demands relentless erudition. Genealogy does not oppose itself to history as the lofty and profound gaze of the philosopher might compare to the molelike perspective of the scholar; on the contrary, it rejects the metahistorical deployment of ideal significations and indefinite teleologies. It opposes itself to the search for 'origins' (HJH, 145–6; LCP, 139–40).

The last sentence may surprise. But if 'all Nietzsche is an exegesis of a few Greek words' (MC, 311; OT, 298), Foucault's Nietzsche is an exegesis of a few German words. His inverted commas around the word 'origin' were placed advisedly. In effect, Foucault uncovers two quite different senses of a number of German words all of which are translated into French as '*origine*' (and into English as 'origin'). But it is not simply that the translators are unable to see the difference between *Herkunft* (and *Enstehung, Abkunft, Geburt*), on the one hand, and *Ursprung*, on the other, and so declined to render them differently. It is rather that Nietzsche himself uses the term *Ursprung* in both senses, thus indicating his own ambivalent attitude to the notion of origin. Foucault locates the interrelations between these terms in the Preface to the *Genealogy of Morals*. Nietzsche first defines the genealogical enterprise as an examination of the origin (*Herkunft*) of moral prejudices. He then goes on to retrace his personal involvement with this question. He remembers how he would ask himself

such questions as, 'Is God to be held responsible for the origin of evil?'
He now finds this question amusing and characterizes it as a search
for *Ursprung*.

> Further on, he invokes the analyses that are characteristically
> Nietzschean and that began with *Human, All Too Human*. Here, he
> speaks of *Herkunfthypothesen*. This use of the word *Herkunft* cannot
> be arbitrary, since it serves to designate a number of texts beginning
> with *Human, All Too Human*, which deal with the origin of morality,
> asceticism, justice, and punishment. And yet, the word used in all
> these works had been *Ursprung*. It would seem at this point in the
> *Genealogy* Nietzsche wished to validate an opposition between
> *Herkunft* and *Ursprung* that did not exist ten years earlier (HJH, 147;
> LCP, 141).

Foucault goes on to show why Nietzsche felt the need to make this
distinction. The pursuit of the origin, *Ursprung*, is

> an attempt to capture the exact essence of things, their purest
> possibilities and their carefully protected identities, because this
> search assumes the existence of immobile forms that precede the
> external world of accident and succession. This search is directed to
> 'that which was already there', the image of a primordial truth fully
> adequate to its nature, and it necessitates the removal of every
> mask to ultimately disclose an original identity. However, if the
> genealogist refuses to extend his faith in metaphysics, if he listens
> to history, he finds that there is 'something altogether different'
> behind things: not a timeless and essential secret, but the secret that
> they have no essence or that their essence was fabricated in a
> piecemeal fashion from alien forms. Examining the history of
> reason, he learns that it was born in an altogether 'reasonable'
> fashion—from chance; devotion to truth and the precision of scien-
> tific method arose from the passion of scholars, their reciprocal
> hatred, their fanatical and unending discussions and their spirit of
> competition—the personal conflicts that slowly forged the
> weapons of reason. Further, genealogical analysis shows that the
> concept of liberty is an 'invention of the ruling classes' and not
> fundamental to man's nature or at the root of his attachment to
> being and truth. What is found at the historical beginning of things

is not the inviolable identity of their origin; it is the dissension of other things. It is disparity (HJH, 148; LCP, 142).

With immense subtlety Foucault goes on to elucidate each of the German words referred to. He diagnoses Nietzsche's ambivalent attitude not only to the concept of origin but also to the notion of history itself (a parallel to his own), contrasting the *'wirkliche Historie'* of genealogy with a history imbued with metaphysical notions of totality, identity, beginning, development, and end. (*Wirkliche* means real or true, but *Wirk* has the same etymological provenance as *Werk*, work.) He shows how Nietzsche's *'wirkliche Historie'* roots out all man's illusions concerning his immortality or immutability. Not only do the 'noblest' of his feelings have a less than honourable history, even his body 'is molded by a great many distinct regimes; it is broken down by the rhythms of work, rest and holidays; it is poisoned by food or values, through eating habits or moral laws: it constructs resistances'. It is easy to see the connection between this summary of a passage from *The Gay Science* and Foucault's next major work, *Surveiller et punir*. Similarly, not only does the title of Foucault's most recently published book, *La volonté de savoir*, form the last words of this essay on Nietzsche, but the Nietzschean concept of a 'will to knowledge' lies at the foundation of all Foucault's subsequent thought.

In appearance, or rather, according to the mask it bears, historical consciousness is neutral, devoid of passions and committed solely to truth. But if it examines itself and if, more generally, it interrogates the various forms of scientific consciousness in its history, it finds that all these forms and transformations are aspects of the will to knowledge: instinct, passion, the inquisitor's devotion, cruel subtlety and malice. . . The historical analysis of this rancorous will to knowledge reveals that all knowledge rests upon injustice (that there is no right, not even in the act of knowing, to truth or a foundation for truth) and that the instinct for knowledge is malicious (something murderous, opposed to the happiness of mankind). Even in the greatly expanded form it assumes today, the will to knowledge does not achieve a universal truth; man is not given an exact and serene mastery of nature. On the contrary, it ceaselessly multiplies the risks, creates dangers in every area; it breaks down illusory defences; it dissolves the unity of the subject; it releases those elements of itself that are devoted to its subversion and destruction. Knowledge does not slowly detach itself from its empirical roots, the initial needs from which it arose, to become pure speculation subject only to the demands of reason; its development is not tied to the constitution and affirmation of a free subject; rather, it creates a progressive enslavement to its instinctive violence. Where religion once demanded the sacrifice of bodies, knowledge now calls for experimentation on ourselves, calls us to the sacrifice of the subject of knowledge. 'The desire for knowledge has been transformed among us into a passion which fears no sacrifice, which fears nothing but its own extinction. It may be that mankind may eventually perish from this passion for knowledge. . ' (HJH, 170–1; LCP, 162–3).

I find it difficult not to accept Foucault's 'revaluation' of Nietzsche, but that is hardly the point. As Foucault says, it is of no interest whether the commentators find his interpretation faithful or not to Nietzsche. It will be equally profitless to speculate as to the part played by Nietzsche in Foucault's view of history, as against the part played by Foucault's view of history in his interpretation of Nietzsche. Perhaps it is enough to say that the 'reactivation' of Nietzsche in contemporary French thought owes much to the active role Nietzsche has played in the formation of Foucault's thinking.

In 1970 Foucault left the battle-torn plain of Vincennes for the Olympian calm of the Collège de France. At the age of forty-four he had been awarded one of France's most coveted academic positions, one usually attained only at the end of the most distinguished of careers. Twenty years before he had left Paris intending never to return, never to teach philosophy. Two years before he had been teaching at the University of Tunis. Prior to that his only academic position in France itself had been at Clermont-Ferrand, not one of France's most celebrated universities. When he did return to Paris it was in the quite exceptional circumstances of the foundation of Vincennes. At the Collège de France, there is no administration, no teaching; there are not even any students. The only obligation is to deliver ten lectures a year, which are open to the public. Foucault's inaugural lecture was published a year later as *L'ordre du discours*. (A translation, 'Orders of Discourse', by Rupert Swyer, appeared in *Social Science Information*, X 2, April 1971, pp. 7–30. Under a new title,

'The Discourse on Language', it was added, as an appendix, to the American—though not the British—edition of *The Archaeology of Knowlege*. In the quotations from *L'ordre du discours* I have preferred to use my own translations.) The work is a little masterpiece of self-conscious, ironic art: a discourse about discourse, an inaugural lecture about beginnings, a speech delivered in one of France's most hallowed institutions about the institutional constraints that operate on discourse not only from without but from within, delivered by the schoolboy who took up philosophy because it promised the ultimate knowledge and who now finds himself expected to reveal it. This master of beginnings chooses not the initial shock, but the difficulty of beginning at all:

> I wish I could have slipped unnoticed into this lecture that I am supposed to be giving today—and into those that I will have to give here, perhaps for many years to come. I wish I did not have to begin, but rather had found myself surrounded by words, taken up and carried beyond any possible beginning. I wish there had been a nameless voice speaking before me, for a long time, so that when my turn came I had only to take up what it was saying, continue the sentence, lodge myself in its gaps, without anyone noticing, as if it had made some sign to me to begin by pausing for a moment (OD, 7).

Rather than be 'him from whom discourse proceeds', he would prefer to be 'a tiny gap' in discourse, 'the point of its possible disappearance'. But the 'institution' is there, ready to lend support, to show him how his role is to be carried out, to tell him what can and cannot be said and to remind him that if what he says has any power then power proceeds from the institution. Foucault sets out an initial hypothesis:

> in any society the production of discourse is at once controlled, selected, organized and redistributed according to a number of procedures whose role is to avert its powers and its dangers, to master the unpredictable event. . . (OD, 10–11).

There are a number of 'procedures of exclusion' operating in discourse. The most obvious is prohibition:

We know very well that we are not free to say anything, that we cannot speak of anything when and where we like, and that just anyone, in short, cannot speak of just anything (OD, 11).

These three types of prohibition—the taboo of the object, the ritual of circumstance, the privileged or exclusive right of the speaking subject—intersect and reinforce one another in a complex, ever-changing network. Foucault notes that the two areas where this network operates at its strictest in our society are sexuality and politics:

as if discourse, far from being a transparent or neutral element in which sexuality is disarmed and politics pacified, were one of those privileged places where sexuality and politics exercise some of their more dangerous powers. Discourse may seem of little account, but the prohibitions to which it is subject reveal soon enough its links with desire and power (OD, 11–12).

Foucault's second principle of exclusion is that of division and rejection. Such a principle operated in the opposition between reason and madness. The discourse of the madman was not treated in the same way as that of the reasonable man. On the one hand, it was regarded as unimportant, untrue, or ineffective: the madman could neither sign a contract, nor perform the act of transubstantiation at Mass. On the other hand, it was attributed with strange powers or hidden truths. Either it was rejected out of hand as unreasonable or it was thought to contain a special reason more reasonable than that of reasonable men and women. In either case, no attempt was made before the end of the eighteenth century, to collect this discourse of madmen, even though madmen were recognized by that discourse. They were listened to seriously only in the symbolic form of the theatre, where madmen were acted by those who were not mad. Before one adds that things are different today, that a great deal of attention is now paid to the words of the mad, Foucault reminds us that

so much attention is no proof that the old division no longer applies; we have only to think of the whole framework of knowledge through which we decipher this speech . . . the whole network of institutions that allows someone—a doctor or psychoanalyst, for example—to listen to this speech and which, at the same time, allows the patient to come and speak, or desperately to withhold his meagre words (OD, 14–15).

A third, perhaps more curious, system of exclusion is the opposition between the true and the false. How, one might ask, can the constraints of truth be compared with those that are either arbitrary or historically conditioned? At the level of the proposition, within a particular discourse, the division between true and false is neither arbitrary, modifiable, institutional, nor violent. But if one steps outside the system of logic and asks, at a genealogical level, why we wish to know, on what type of division this will to knowledge is based, something like a system of exclusion emerges. In Greece, even as late as the sixth century BC, the truth—and power—of discourse resided, not in *what* was said, but in *who* said it and *how* it was said.

> True discourse, that which inspired respect and terror, that to which all had to submit because it held sway over all, was the discourse spoken by men as of right and in accordance with the required ritual; it was the discourse that meted out justice . . . that, prophesying the future, not only foretold what would come to pass, but participated in its coming, bringing to it men's acquiescence and thus weaving itself into the fabric of fate (OD, 17).

A century later, the highest truth resided not in what discourse *was* or in what it *did*, but in what it *said*. To use Foucault's distinction, truth had moved from the enunciation (*énonciation*), the ritualized act, to the statement (*énoncé*), to its meaning and to its reference to the world. This new division between true and false discourse meant that true discourse was no longer linked to the exercise of power. Our own will to knowledge, with all the transformations it has undergone, ultimately derives from that division. The truth does not impose itself on a pure, receptive human mind: it is sought after. Each of the great mutations in scientific knowledge, those in the early seventeenth or early nineteenth centuries, for example, may be seen as new forms of that will to truth: new arrangements of the objects to be studied, new functions and positions of the knowing subject, new material investments in the pursuit of knowledge. There is a whole institutional base on which the will to truth operates: the educational system, the distribution of information through libraries, learned societies, laboratories, the values set by different social systems on different forms of knowledge. Such a will to truth also tends to affect other discourses. For centuries, Western literature has sought to base itself on such notions as nature, verisimilitude, sincerity, even science itself—in short, on true discourse. Similarly, economic practices, codified into a mass of practical, even moral precepts, have sought since the seventeenth century to find a rational, scientific validation in a theory of wealth and production. Even the penal system has gradually loosened its ties with religious morality and looked to a burgeoning mass of social sciences for justification 'as if even the word of law had authority in our society only in so far as it is grounded in a discourse of truth'. Of the three systems of exclusion analysed by Foucault, it is the third—the will to truth—that has proved to be the most dominant and the most all-pervasive. Yet, perhaps for that very reason, it is the least apparent, the least discussed, as if it could operate most effectively only when masked. It is as if true discourse cannot recognize the will to truth that informs it, as if the will that has dominated Western civilization is such that the truth it seeks cannot but mask it. Those who seek to tear away that mask—Foucault cites Nietzsche, Artaud, and Bataille—are usually engaged in a struggle against prohibition and the definitions of madness, and often fall victim to them.

Foucault then turns to another set of procedures that limit and control discourse. Unlike the systems of exclusions, which act on discourse from the outside, these operate from within discourse itself, classifying, ordering, distributing, as if to master another dimension of discourse: that of discourse as irruption, as unpredictable event. The first of these is *commentary*. Most societies possess narratives or texts of some kind or another that become the object of variation, transformation, or commentary. In our own culture, these 'primary' works are religious, legal, literary and, to some extent, scientific texts. But there is no stable or absolute distinction between these primary texts and the mass of secondary texts that they give rise to; there is certainly no homogeneity in the second category. Legal commentary is very different from religious or scientific commentary. In the case of literature, the distinction almost breaks down. A work like the *Odyssey* gives rise to translations in different languages and different periods, to a work like Joyce's *Ulysses*, all of which, in turn, give rise to an endlessly proliferating mass of commentary. Commentary performs a double, interrelated role. By drawing on the multiple or hidden meanings attributed to the primary texts, it makes new discourse possible; it also says *at last* what was articulated silently in the primary text. Paradoxically, it 'says for the first time what has already been said and tirelessly repeats what was never said'.

> The endless froth of commentary is worked up from within by the dream of masked repetition: on its horizon, there is nothing else, perhaps, but what was at its point of departure, mere recitation. Commentary averts the unpredictable in discourse by giving it its due: it allows us to say something other than the text itself, but on condition that it is the text itself that is spoken and, in a sense, fulfilled. The open multiplicity, the fortuitousness, is transferred, by the principle of commentary, from what might be said to the number, the form, the mask, the circumstances of repetition. The new lies not in what is said, but in the event of its return (OD, 27–8).

Foucault's second 'principle of rarefaction' in discourse is the notion of the 'author', not, of course, the individual who has written a text, but the 'unifying principle in a group of writings, the source of their significations, the focus of their coherence'. In a mass of everyday statements the notion of author does not operate: even such texts as contracts, which require a signature, have no author. But in areas where authorship is usual—literature, philosophy, science—it does not always play the same role. In the Middle Ages, authorial attribution was indispensable in scientific discourse, since it was an indication of truth, of authenticity. Since the seventeenth century, this function has gradually declined in scientific discourse, leaving the proper name as little more than a convenient label on a theory or syndrome. In literature, on the other hand, the reverse process has been at work. We not only pay a great deal of attention to questions of authorship in more recent work but seek the individuality buried in that mass of anonymous work that circulated freely in the Middle Ages.

> For some time now the individual who sits down to write a text that may one day form part of an *oeuvre* assumes the functions of an author: what he does and does not write, his outlines for future works, his everyday conversation, all this interplay of differences is prescribed by the authorial function in the form that he receives it from his period or in the way he modifies that form. . . Commentary limits the unpredictability of discourse to the action of an *identity* that takes the form of *repetition* and the *same*. The authorial

principle limits this unpredictability through the action of an *identity* that takes the form of *individuality* and the *I* (OD, 30–1).

The third of these internal principles of limitation is that of the
'disciplines'. This works in a contrary direction to that of the author,
for it constitutes an anonymous system that is available to anyone
who wishes to use it: a corpus of propositions regarded as true, a set
of rules and definitions, techniques and instruments. But the disciplines also operate in a way quite opposed to that of commentary. For
them, there is no hidden meaning that is presupposed at the outset
and which is to be uncovered yet again, nor an identity that must be
repeated. A discipline is what makes new statements, new propositions possible. But it is not simply all that may be said to be true
about something. For every discipline is made up of errors as well as
truths and these errors are not merely foreign bodies to be ejected in
time from the organism of the discipline, but have often played an
active, necessary part in its history. For a proposition to belong to a
particular discipline it must refer to a specific range of objects, which,
however, changes from one period to another. Thus a proposition
concerning the symbolic or medicinal qualities of a plant was no
longer considered a part of botany by the eighteenth century. To
belong to a discipline, a proposition must also refer to a certain body
of theory. Thus the search for the primitive language, which was an
accepted theoretical concern in the eighteenth century, was inadmiss-
ible in late nineteenth-century philology. The discipline is a principle
of control in the production of discourse. It fixes limits through an
identity that takes the form of a permanent reactivation of rules.

> We are used to regarding an author's fertility, the multiplicity of
> commentaries and the development of a discipline as so many
> infinite resources for the creation of discourses. Perhaps they are,
> but they are also principles of constraint; and perhaps we cannot
> appreciate their positive, multiplicatory role without also consider-
> ing their restrictive, constraining function (OD, 38).

Foucault now analyses a third group of procedures for the control
of discourse. These concern the conditions in which they are communicated, the rules that bind those who communicate them, thus
restricting access to them: in short, a 'rarefaction of the speaking
subjects'. The most obvious of these systems of restriction are what

might be called *'ritual'*: the qualifications required of the speaking subject, the gestures, behaviour, circumstances, and the whole set of signs that must accompany the discourse. Religious, judicial, medical, even political discourses are inseparable from this ritual framework. Then there are the *'societies of discourse'*, whose function is to preserve discourse by producing it in a restricted group. In archaic times, one such group was the caste of bards, which possessed the knowledge of the poems to be recited and which required a long initiation before entry. Such closed societies are rare today, but discourse is still communicated within a structure that, while more diffuse, is nevertheless constricting: one has only to think of the way in which medical discourse is circulated. Even the act of writing implies membership of a loosely organized institution, of which the 'book trade' is only the most obvious aspect. 'Doctrines', whether of a religious, political, or philosophical kind, also form such a procedure of rarefaction. They bind individuals to certain types of enunciation and, consequently, forbid all others, but they also use these types of enunciation to bind individuals together. Lastly, on a broader scale, there are the great cleavages in the *'social appropriation'* of discourse. Education may be the means by which every individual, in a society like ours, gains access to any kind of discourse.

But we know very well that, in its distribution, in what it permits and what it prevents, it follows the lines laid down by social differences, conflicts and struggles. Every educational system is a political means of maintaining or modifying the appropriation of discourses, with the knowledge and power they bring with them (OD, 46).

These procedures for the subjection of discourse do not exist in isolation, of course. An educational system is a ritualization of speech, a means of qualifying the speaking subjects, the constitution of a doctrinal group, however diffuse, a distribution and an appropriation of discourse. At this point, Foucault suggests that certain philosophical themes conform to them by proposing an ideal truth as law of discourse and an immanent rationality as the principle of their expression; they reinforce them by denying the specific reality of discourse. Thus the theme of the *founding subject* makes it possible to elide the material reality of discourse. The subject is seen as the living source that animates through his expression the otherwise dead, empty forms of language.

It is as if our culture's apparent veneration of discourse concealed a profound fear of it, as if all the prohibitions and limitations placed upon it were intended to master a threat. If we are to understand that fear, says Foucault, we have a three-fold task: we have to question our will to truth, restore to discourse its character as event, and abolish the sovereignty of the signifier. This requires a number of methodological principles. First, there is what Foucault calls reversal. What, traditionally, have been regarded as the sources of discourse—author, discipline, will to truth—must be seen as the negative action of a segmentation and rarefaction of discourse. But the existence of these principles of rarefaction does not mean that beneath them lies a great unlimited expanse of discourse waiting to be freed. There is also a principle of discontinuity: discourses must be treated as discontinuous practices that variously intersect, juxtapose, and exclude one another. A principle of specificity: discourse is not a system of significations that exists prior to our intervention and which we have only to decipher. Discourse must be conceived as a violence we do to things or, at least, as a practice we impose on them, in which the events of discourse find their regularity. A principle of exteriority: we must not go from discourse towards some inner core of meaning concealed within it, but proceed from discourse, from its specific emergence and regularity, to its external conditions of possibility, to that which gives rise to the random series of those events and lays down its limits. These four principles might be summed up in four terms, each of which is opposed to another: event to creation, series to unity, regularity to originality, condition of possibility to signification. It is the second series that has dominated the history of ideas in so far as one has always sought the point of creation, the unity of an *oeuvre*, a period or a theme, the mark of individual originality, and the inexhaustible treasure of buried significations.

Foucault then turns to the question of the historical method, reviewing many of the things he said in the opening pages of *L'archéologie du savoir*. The methods practised by, for example, Le Roy Ladurie and the *Annales* school of French historians—the meticulous analysis of such primary sources as official price-lists, title deeds, and parish registers, year by year, even week by week—is not to be seen as a flight from the event itself. It is true that these historians no longer regard events—especially the great 'events' of history, the 'French Revolution', for example—as unitary, unquestionable facts. And if what they reveal is often a series of long-term structures, rather than isolated events, this is because of the *work* they perform on the endless series of minute events that constitutes their material.

> History has long since abandoned its attempts to understand events in terms of cause and effect in the formless unity of some great evolutionary process. . .; but it did this not to rediscover structures that were prior, alien and hostile to the event. It was rather to establish the diverse, intersecting, often divergent, but never autonomous series that enable us to circumscribe the 'locus' of the event, the margins of its unpredictability, the conditions of its emergence (OD, 58).

The key-notions required by historical research are no longer those of consciousness and continuity (with their correlative problems of freedom and causality), nor those of sign and structure, but those of the event and the series (with the related notions of regularity, unpredictability, discontinuity, dependence, transformation).

But if discourse is to be treated as 'sets of discursive events', what is the philosophical or theoretical status of this notion of 'event'? It is neither substance nor accident, neither quality nor process; it does not belong to the order of bodies. Yet it is not immaterial; it occurs in material elements and consists of their relation, coexistence, dispersion, accumulation, selection. The event must be seen, paradoxically, in terms of 'a materialism of the incorporeal'. And what is the status of the 'discontinuous series' in which discursive events are arranged? We are dealing not with a succession of moments in time, nor with the plurality of thinking subjects, but with discontinuities that shatter the moment into a series of different time-scales and disperse the subject into a plurality of possible positions and functions. And if we are to abandon notions of mechanical causality or ideal necessity, we must introduce the category of unpredictability, of chance, into the production of events. These three notions of materiality, discontinuity, and chance will require further theoretical elaboration.

It would be untrue to say that the notion of discourse as instrument and object of power was entirely absent from *L'archéologie du savoir*. Certainly there is nothing in *L'ordre du discours* that contradicts what was said in the earlier book. On the other hand, this theme remained more or less implicit in the *Archaeology* and tended to be associated with the notion of institution. In *L'ordre du discours* a theory of power is introduced for the first time into Foucault's theory of discourse. But much remains to be done, of course, and there is a sense in which this is a transitional piece. Power still tends to be seen in a negative way, as a limitation on discourse. What is not yet made clear is the way in which power actually produces discourse: it is this notion, as elaborated in Foucault's next two major works, that is most radical and far-reaching of all.

However, Foucault's discourse was to lead him not only to a theory of power, but to action, more quickly than he perhaps anticipated. A few weeks after he delivered his inaugural lecture hunger-strikes broke out among France's leftist political prisoners. Not only did they demand the 'special' conditions laid down by the law for political prisoners, but they initiated a movement of solidarity with all other prisoners. For the first time, political prisoners were not content to demand advantages for themselves, but denounced the entire prison system, making common cause with common law prisoners, seeing them as victims of a social system in the same way as other exploited individuals. As a result, Michel Foucault and a small group of intellectuals started the Groupe d'Information sur les Prisons (GIP). With the help of former prisoners, the Group drew up a questionnaire, which it sent out to about a thousand prisoners, former prisoners, prisoners' families, disaffected members of the prison service, lawyers, students, and sympathizers. The GIP set out not to speak for the prisoners, but to make it possible for prisoners themselves to speak about what was happening in the prisons. The spectacular riots that took place in a number of French prisons in 1972 were evidence of the effectiveness of the GIP's activities. At the end of that year, it went into voluntary liquidation, leaving two organizations, the Association for the Defence of Prisoners' Rights and the Prisoners' Action Group. Certainly Foucault's presence in the GIP brought it a certain amount of additional attention in the mass media. For many French people, well used to the politicized intellectual, there was nonetheless something shocking in the spectacle of a Professor of the Collège de France championing the rights not of the deserving poor, but of criminals. The shock was no doubt redoubled when the founders withdrew and handed over the direction of the struggle to the prisoners themselves. For the French, this was the new kind of politics that reached them in 1968 from the United States, based not on administrative areas and the ballot box, but on whatever real situations held people together, their place of residence, work, study, or confinement, their colour, sex, or sexuality.

Meanwhile, during the academic year 1971–72, Foucault had devoted his course at the Collège de France to 'Penal theories and institutions'. He summed up his intentions as follows:

> The working hypothesis will be this: power relations (with the struggles that traverse them or the institutions that maintain them) do not only play with respect to knowledge a facilitating or obstructive role; they are not content merely to encourage or to stimulate it, to distort or to limit it; power and knowledge are not linked together solely by the play of interests or ideologies; the problem is not therefore that of determining how power subjugates knowledge and makes it serve its ends, or how it imprints its mark on knowledge, imposes on it ideological contents and limits. No body of knowledge can be formed without a system of communications, records, accumulation and displacement which is in itself a form of power and which is linked, in its existence and functioning, to the other forms of power. Conversely, no power can be exercised without the extraction, appropriation, distribution or retention of knowledge. On this level, there is not knowledge on the one side and society on the other, or science and the state, but only the fundamental forms of knowledge/power . . . (B3, 283).

In the course of his research, working systematically through medical and legal documents, Foucault stumbled on the case of Pierre Rivière, a twenty-year-old Norman peasant, convicted in 1836 of murdering his pregnant mother, his eighteen-year-old sister, and his seven-year-old brother. The case was unusual enough, but what particularly interested Foucault was the fact that, while awaiting trial, the murderer had written a forty-page account of his life, the relations between his parents, his reasons for committing the murders, the murders themselves and his wanderings around the Normandy countryside up to his arrest. Foucault organized a seminar to study the case and, with the collaboration of ten others, produced in 1973, *Moi, Pierre Rivière, ayant égorgé ma mère, ma soeur et mon frère . . .* (An English translation appeared in the USA in 1975—it is now also available in Great Britain.) The book consisted of an introduction and one short essay by Foucault, six other essays by his various collaborators, and a mass of contemporary documents—statements by doctors and psychiatrists, newspaper reports of the trial, letters, verbatim accounts of the legal proceedings. It was an exceptionally well documented case for that, or any, period. 'To be frank, however,' Foucault remarks, 'it was not this that led us to spend more than a year and a half on these documents. It was simply the beauty of Rivière's memoir' (PR, 11; x). The centre of the book, therefore, its *raison d'être*, is an uncorrected transcription of Rivière's own hand-written story. Foucault and his collaborators had no intention of producing an *interpretation* of Rivière's actions. To do so would have been to fall into one or other of those discourses (medical, legal, psychological, criminological) whose reductive effort they wished to demonstrate. GIP was set up to enable prisoners to speak to one another; this book was published to enable us to read Pierre's own words. Reading them today, one is astonished that his name did not pass into folk legend and criminal history. Yet, before Foucault redis-covered it, it was practically unknown. The process of *erasure* began in Rivière's own time. Even the contemporary transcription of his memoir is a travesty. His lawyer, whose writings later became well known, never referred to the case. Speaking of the 'professional' reactions to Rivière's statements Foucault remarked in an interview: 'What is astonishing is that this text, which left them silent at the time, has left them equally dumb today' (B8, 32). Could it be that it is what Rivière says rather than what he did that is so disturbing?

> I wholly forgot the principles which should have made me respect my mother and my sister and my brother, I regarded my father as being in the power of mad dogs or barbarians against whom I must take up arms, religion forbade such things, but I disregarded its rules, it even seemed to me that God had destined me for this and that I would be executing his justice. I knew the rules of man and the rules of ordered society, but I deemed myself wiser than they, I regarded them as ignoble and shameful (PR, 128–9; 105).

He was determined to save his beloved father from the tyranny of a cruel, domineering wife. His sister and brother had to share her fate because they aided and abetted her. He rails against an 'age of enlightenment' in which women are in command and a nation which, while 'so avid for liberty and glory', obeys women. The Romans, Hurons, and Hottentots, he maintains, had more sensible views on the role of women. He cites an impressive list, culminating in 'our

Lord Jesus Christ', of historical figures who were prepared to sacrifice themselves for others—for he sees his action as a sacrifice that will end in his own death. Though with unimpeachable logic, he points out that whereas there was no need for God to suffer the crucifixion, since he could either have punished or pardoned those who had offended him, 'I can deliver my father only by dying for him'.

> I thought it would be a great glory to me to have thoughts opposed to all my judges, to dispute against the whole world, I conjured up Bonaparte in 1815. I also said to myself: that man sent thousands to their death to satisfy mere caprices, it is not right therefore that I should let a woman live who is disturbing my father's peace and happiness, I thought that an opportunity had come for me to raise myself, that my name would make some noise in the world, that by my death I should cover myself with glory, and that in time to come my ideas would be adopted and I should be vindicated (PR, 132; 108).

Ironically, the memoir in which Rivière had set out to prove the rationality of his actions and thus to assure the death-sentence was used by Paris psychiatrists to prove his insanity ('monomania') and thus rob him of the death he sought. (In fact, he killed himself four years after his sentence had been commuted to life imprisonment.) Foucault analyses at some length the complex relations between the narrative and the deed. Although written after the murder, the memoir was in fact conceived, 'written in my head', before it—or, rather, they were 'consubstantial', conceived inextricably together, discourse as act, act as discourse.

> Pierre Rivière was the subject of the memoir in a dual sense: it was he who remembered, remorselessly remembered it all, and it was he whose memoir summoned the crime, the horrible and glorious crime, to take its place beside so many other crimes. He contrived the engineering of the narrative/murder as both projectile and target, he was propelled by the working of the mechanism into the real murder. And, after all, he was the author of it all in a dual sense; author of the crime and author of the text (PR, 274; 209).

The text did not *express* a desire, which was then *expressed* in action. Desire, text, and action were indissolubly linked beause they were shaped, made possible, therefore, in a sense, *produced* by a particular

133

'discursive practice' made up of Bible stories and history learnt at school, famous murders commemorated in flysheets and broadsheets and, not least, the confessional autobiography, written at the magistrate's request, but, significantly, conceived beforehand. But it is not Rivière's discourse alone that is conceived of in terms of struggle. All those who contributed to the case 'file' took part in

> a strange contest, a confrontation, a power relation, a battle among discourses and through discourses. . . [These discourses] give us a key to the relations of power, domination and conflict within which discourses emerge and function, and hence provide material for a potential analysis of discourse (even of scientific discourses) which may be both tactical and political, and therefore strategic (PR, 12–13; x–xxii).

In 1975, a film was made about Pierre Rivière, based on Foucault's book, in which Foucault himself appears (as one of the judges).

◊ 2 ◊

Society, Power, and Knowledge

During the next year or two, Foucault continued his study of 'penal theories and institutions', publishing in 1975, *Surveiller et punir*, subtitled 'naissance de la prison'. (The English translation, *Discipline and Punish, the Birth of the Prison*, appeared in Britain and the USA in 1977.) In a sense, this book is a return, after the 'interdiscursive' analyses of *Les mots et les choses* and *L'archéologie du savoir*, to the single discourse/institution study as exemplified in *Histoire de la folie* and *Naissance de la clinique*. Like the study of medicine, it charts the 'birth' of an institution and covers roughly the same period of time. For just as the teaching hospital and clinical medicine were created in the early nineteenth century, so too were the prison and penology as we understand them today. Foucault shows how the still largely 'medieval' penal theory and practice of the *ancien régime* gave way in France, after the Revolution, to an institutionalization of imprisonment based on quite different theoretical premises. Between the two there was a transitional period of 'enlightenment', in which reformers tried to discredit the old barbarities and create a new penology based, not on punishment, but on dissuasion by public display. But this book is not just about 'the birth of the prison', or rather, the implications of that event reach far beyond the sphere of penology. The techniques of discipline and observation incorporated in the new prison derive from three centuries of practice in other spheres, notably in education and the army. Moreover, there is an astonishing coincidence between the new prison and other contemporary institutions: hospital, factory, school, and barracks. It is no accident that Jeremy Bentham's famous 'panopticon', a circular building enclosing

135

a central inspection tower, was recommended and implemented for all these institutions. Lastly, it is Foucault's thesis that our own societies are maintained not by army, police, and a centralized, visible state apparatus, but precisely by those techniques of dressage, discipline, and diffused power at work in 'carceral' institutions.

Surveiller et punir opens in spectacular fashion with the full panoply of a *supplice*, a public execution reserved for the greatest of all crimes under the *ancien régime*, regicide. Poor Damiens was not even successful in his attempt to kill Louis XV with a single blow of his penknife, but this hardly mitigated the conditions of his dying:

> The flesh will be torn from his breasts, arms, thighs and calves with red-hot pincers, his right hand, holding the knife with which he committed the said parricide, burnt with sulphur, and, on those places where the flesh will be torn away, poured molten lead, boiling oil, burning resin, wax and sulphur melted together and then his body drawn and quartered by four horses and his limbs and body consumed by fire. . . (SP, 9; DP, 3).

That, in the future tense, was the sentence. The actual execution, related by an eye-witness, is much more gruesome, because inefficient and long drawn-out. Foucault follows this account with extracts from rules drawn up 'for the House of young prisoners in Paris': for example,

> At the first drum-roll, the prisoners must rise and dress in silence, as the supervisor opens the cell doors. At the second drum-roll, they must be dressed and make their bed. At the third, they must line up and proceed to the chapel for morning prayer. There is a five-minute interval between each drum roll. . . (SP, 12; DP, 6).

These two régimes of punishment do not, of course, apply to the same crime. The point is that neither existed at the time of the other: by the 1840s, torture as a public spectacle had long since disappeared and the disciplinary methods exemplified in Faucher's 'borstal' were spreading to a wide range of institutions. Public execution survived for parricides and regicides, but the tortures undergone by Damiens had shrunk, by the execution of Fieschi, the would be assassin of Louis-Philippe, in 1836, to the wearing of a black veil. There was a growing belief, which began long before the change in practice, that to insist on the punishment exceeding the crime in savagery was, in a sense, to repeat the crime. There were also cases where the anger of the populace had turned from the criminal to the executioner, creating occasions of civil disorder. A feeling of shame seems to have spread from the criminal to those charged with the carrying out of the penal process, and punishment became the most hidden part of that process. Attention moves from the execution to the trial and sentence. Those who carry out the penalty become an autonomous sector, working in secret, once the courts have passed sentence. The courts become less and less concerned with punishment, more and more with correction, reclamation, 'cure'. As the sense of shame in punishment grows, 'the psychologists and the minor civil servants of moral orthopaedics proliferate on the wound it leaves' (SP, 16; DP, 10).

The disappearance of public punishment marks not only a decline in the spectacle but a slackening of the hold on the body. Physical pain was no longer a necessary element in punishment. The body was touched as little as possible and then only to reach something other than the body, what might be called the 'soul'. The expiation that was once inflicted on the body must be replaced by a punishment that acts in depth on the heart, the mind, the will. This change was the result not so much of a change of attitude—less cruelty, less pain, more kindness, more 'humanity'—as of a change of objective. Over the two hundred or so years that Europe has been setting up its new penal systems, the judgement of offences has become more and more supplemented, even supplanted, by knowledge of the offender.

A whole set of assessing, diagnostic, prognostic, normative judgements concerning the criminal have become lodged in the framework of penal judgement. . . Throughout the penal procedure and the implementation of the sentence there swarms a whole series of subsidiary authorities. Small-scale legal systems and parallel judges have multiplied around the principal judgement: psychiatric or psychological experts, magistrates concerned with the implementation of sentences, educationalists, members of the prison service, all fragment the legal power to punish (SP, 24, 26; DP, 19, 21).

But this knowledge of the prisoner is no longer confined to determining the criminal's degree of responsibility; it also plays an active part in the implementation of the penalty. The psychiatrist, for example, is called upon to say whether the subject is 'dangerous', how one should be protected from him, whether punishment or treatment would be preferable. Foucault offers this book as

> a correlative history of the modern soul and of a new power to judge; a genealogy of the present scientifico-legal complex from which the power to punish derives its bases, justifications and rules, from which it extends its effects and by which it masks its exorbitant singularity (SP, 27; DP, 23).

Foucault sets out to examine punishment, not just as part of the legal machinery, but as a political tactic, as a technique for the exercise of power. But punitive mechanisms must be regarded not only in negative terms, as repression, but also in terms of their possible positive effects, as part of a complex social function. The shift away from overt punishment of the body to investigation of the criminal's 'soul' can only be understood by seeing the new penal methods and the social sciences that provide the 'knowledge' on which these methods are based as having a common origin. The provenance, the *Herkunft*, of the human sciences is not a pure, disinterested search for knowledge, the fruits of which were then passed on in the 'humanization' of 'carceral' institutions. It is rather that those 'sciences' have a common origin with those institutions. The forms of power at work in such institutions and, increasingly, in society at large are imbued with social and psychological knowledge, but, equally, those forms of knowledge are permeated by power relations.

> Perhaps we should abandon the belief that power makes mad and that, by the same token, the renunciation of power is one of the conditions of knowledge. We should admit rather that power produces knowledge (and not simply by encouraging it because it serves power or by applying it because it is useful); that power and knowledge directly imply one another; that there is no power relation without the correlative constitution of a field of knowledge, nor any knowledge that does not presuppose and constitute at the same time power relations (SP, 32; DP, 27).

Moreover, the entry of the 'soul' on to the scene of penal justice was made possible by the investment of the body by those power relations. Extremes of violence inflicted on the body may have diminished or disappeared, but they have been replaced by complex, subtle forms of correction and training that are always directed at the body.

> The body is also directly involved in a political field; power relations have an immediate hold upon it; they invest it, mark it, train it, torture it, force it to carry out tasks, to perform ceremonies, to emit signs. The political investment of the body is bound up, in accordance with complex reciprocal relations, with its economic use; it is largely as a force of production that the body is invested with relations of power and domination; but, on the other hand, its constitution as labour power is possible only if it is caught up in a system of subjection (in which need is also a political instrument meticulously prepared, calculated and used); the body becomes a useful force only if it is both a productive body and a subjected body. This subjection is not only obtained by the instruments of violence or ideology; it can also be direct, physical, pitting force against force, bearing on material elements, and yet without involving violence; it may be calculated, organized, technically thought out; it may be subtle, make use neither of weapons nor of terror and yet remain of a physical order. That is to say, there may be a 'knowledge' of the body that is not exactly the science of its functioning, and a mastery of its forces that is more than the ability to conquer them: this knowledge and this mastery constitute what might be called the political technology of the body (sp, 30–1; DP, 25–6).

But this power is exercised rather than possessed; it is not the 'privilege' of a dominant class, which exercises it actively upon a passive, dominated class. It is rather exercised through and by the dominated. Indeed, it is perhaps unhelpful to think in terms of 'classes' in this way, for power is not unitary and its exercise binary. Power in that sense does not exist: what exists is an infinitely complex network of 'micro-powers', of power relations that permeate every aspect of social life. For that reason, 'power' cannot be overthrown and acquired once and for all by the destruction of institutions and the seizure of the state apparatuses. Because 'power' is multiple and ubiquitous, the struggle against it must be localized. Equally, however, because it is a network and not a collection of isolated points, each localized struggle induces effects on the entire network. Struggle cannot be totalized—a single, centralized, hierarchized organization setting out to seize a single, centralized, hierarchized power; but it can be *serial*, that is, in terms of *horizontal* links between one point of struggle and another.

This 'micro-physics of power' is operated, then, through the 'soul', on the body. The 'soul' is to be understood here not in the Christian sense of a soul born in sin and subject to punishment, but as the creation of methods of punishment, supervision, and constraint.

> It is the element in which are articulated the effects of a certain type of power and the reference of a certain type of knowledge, the machinery by which the power relations give rise to a possible corpus of knowledge, and knowledge extends and reinforces the effects of this power. On this reality-reference, various concepts have been constructed and domains of analysis carved out: psyche, subjectivity, personality, consciousness, etc.; on it have been built scientific techniques and discourses, and the moral claims of humanism. . . The soul is the effect and instrument of a political anatomy; the soul is the prison of the body (SP, 34; DP, 29–30).

In the penal system of the *ancien régime*—Foucault's analysis is centred at this point on France, which was typical of the rest of Europe, England excepted—torture was not an uncontrolled expression of anger, but a technique whereby minutely calibrated amounts of pain could be administered to the criminal's body, an organized ritual in which that body was marked by the power of the sovereign. The public display of punishment and its results was a means of publishing the truth of the crime. Up to that point, the criminal procedure had remained secret, hidden not only from the public, but from the accused himself, who was aware neither of the charge, nor of the evidence. Knowledge was the absolute privilege of the prosecution. The judges met the accused only once, in order to question him before passing sentence. All power, including the right to punish, proceeded from the sovereign; it was not to be shared with his subjects. The sole purpose of the legal process was the establishment of guilt. The perfect proof was the confession. The only sure way of extracting a confession was torture. This kind of 'judicial' torture was called in French '*la question*'. (The public torture that preceded execution was called '*la supplice*'.) It is Foucault's belief that the motivation and techniques for scientific investigation (*enquête*) have more than an etymological connection with those of judicial torture; not only was torture conducted with scientific rigour, but science itself has been, not so much a disinterested unveiling of the truth, as its extraction by a kind of torture. In the penalty of the *ancien régime* there were degrees of proof: full proof, approximate or semi-proof and distant proof or clues. These were governed by precise rules: thus a full proof might lead to any sentence, a semi-proof to any of the heavy penalties except death, while mere clues could lead only to the issuing of a writ, a fine, or a deferment for further inquiry. Moreover, they could be combined according to prescribed arithmetical rules: two semi-proofs could make a complete proof, several clues could add up to a semi-proof, but never to a full proof, etc. But a penalty based on the extraction of proof by judicial torture had one curious aspect: if after applying the correct procedures of torture the accused did not confess the magistrate was forced to drop the charges. This meant that judicial torture was applied only when the authorities were reasonably certain of obtaining a confession of guilt.

If the function of judicial torture was to extract the truth, that of the public execution was to manifest it. 'It added to the conviction the signature of the convicted man. A successful public execution justified justice, in that it published the truth of the crime in the very body of the man to be executed' (SP, 48; DP, 44). The execution was often carried out at the very place where the crime had been committed. Murderers would carry the instruments of their crimes. Other criminals might be punished symbolically: the tongues of blasphemers were pierced, the impure burnt. But the public execution was a political as well as a judicial ritual. A crime attacked not only its immediate victim, but the person of the sovereign, for the law represented the will of the sovereign. The intervention of the sovereign was not, therefore, an arbitration between two subjects, but a direct response by the sovereign to the injury inflicted upon him. All crime was treason. But the public execution was a political spectacle in another sense: in it the main character was the people, whose real and immediate presence was required for the performance. The people was not only a witness of the spectacle, it also took part in it, insulting, sometimes attacking, the condemned man. But this participation had another side:

> If the crowd gathered round the scaffold, it was not simply to witness the sufferings of the condemned man or to excite the anger

of the executioner: it was also to hear an individual who had nothing more to lose curse the judges, the laws, the government and religion. The public execution allowed the luxury of these momentary saturnalia, when nothing remained to prohibit or to punish. Under the protection of imminent death, the criminal could say everything and the crowd cheered. . . In these executions, which ought to show only the terrorizing power of the prince, there was a whole aspect of the carnival, in which rules were inverted, authority mocked and criminals transformed into heroes (SP, 64; DP, 60–1).

Increasingly, as the Revolution approached, the people tended to sympathize with the criminal, especially those convicted of offences against property. The transformation of criminal into hero continued after the execution in a whole popular literature of broadsides, broadsheets, and songs in which, in the most ambiguous terms, the criminal was at once execrated and exalted. This literature largely died out with the old order.

They disappeared as a whole new literature of crime developed: a literature in which crime is glorified, because it is one of the fine arts, because it can be the work only of exceptional natures, because it reveals the monstrousness of the strong and powerful, because villainy is yet another mode of privilege: from the adventure story to de Quincey, or from the *Castle of Otranto* to Baudelaire, there is a whole aesthetic rewriting of crime, which is also the appropriation of criminality in acceptable forms. . . By his cunning, his tricks, his sharp-wittedness, the criminal represented in this literature has made himself impervious to suspicion; and the struggle between two pure minds—the murderer and the detective—will constitute the essential form of the confrontation. We are far removed indeed from those accounts of the life and misdeeds of the criminal in which he admitted his crimes, and which recounted in detail the tortures of his execution: we have moved from the exposition of the facts or the confession to the slow process of discovery; from the execution to the investigation; from the physical confrontation to the intellectual struggle between criminal and investigator. It was not only the broadsheets that disappeared with the birth of a literature of crime; the glory of the rustic malefactor and his sombre transformation into a hero by the process of torture and execution went with them.

The man of the people was now too simple to be the protagonist of subtle truths. In this new genre, there were no more popular heroes or great executions; the criminal was wicked, of course, but he was also intelligent; and although he was punished, he did not have to suffer. The literature of crime transposes to another social class the spectacle that had surrounded the criminal. Meanwhile the newspapers took over the task of recounting the grey, unheroic details of everyday crime and punishment. The split was complete; the people was robbed of its old pride in its crimes; the great murders had become the quiet game of the well behaved (SP, 72; DP, 68–9).

In the second half of the eighteenth century protests against the legal system in general and public executions in particular began to mount not only among the philosophical spokesman of the Enlightenment, but also from lawyers, politicians, and popular petitions. The spectacle of the scaffold was seen more and more as a potential occasion for a confrontation between the violence of the king and the violence of the people. In this violence tyranny confronts rebellion: each calls forth the other. Instead of taking revenge, justice should punish. This call for more lenient punishment was first formulated in terms of an optimistic philosophy of 'nature'. No criminal was so vile that he did not possess his share of 'human nature'.

> The day was to come, in the nineteenth century, when this 'man', discovered in the criminal, would become the target of penal intervention, the object that it claimed to correct and transform, the domain of a whole series of 'criminological' sciences and strange 'penitentiary' practices (SP, 76; DP, 74).

For the moment, however, this element of humanity in the criminal was not the object of investigation, but a sacred core that must not be outraged. Punishment should act primarily as a deterrent: it should, therefore, slightly exceed the crime. The massive excess of punishment in the *supplice* proceeded from the unlimited power of the king and was, therefore, tyrannical. Certainly, there were appeals for more 'humane' methods, especially from well-known men of letters, but the main body of the criticism came from inside the legal profession itself and it was from there that reforms were initiated after the Revolution. What the reformers wanted above all was not a more humane, but a more efficient system. The inefficiency of the old system was due to a number of factors: legal offices could be inherited or sold; the income of the judges was proportionate to the heaviness of the sentences; many persons were 'above the law'; there was a mass of overlapping juridical systems—the ecclesiastical courts, the courts of the nobility, several different, and conflicting, royal courts, the semi-juridical powers of the king's representatives, etc. What was required was a simplification and rationalization of the entire structure—and this in the interest of crime prevention. This represented

an effort to adjust the mechanisms of power that frame the everyday lives of individuals; an adaption and a refinement of the machinery that assumes responsibility for and places under surveillance their everyday behaviour, their identity, their activity, their apparently unimportant gestures; another policy for that multiplicity of bodies and forces that constitutes a population. What was emerging no doubt was not so much a new respect for the humanity of the condemned—torture was still frequent in the execution of even minor criminals—as a tendency towards a more finely tuned justice, towards a closer penal mapping of the social body (SP, 80; DP, 77–8).

But there were more material, less ideological reasons why the reformers called for and eventually obtained a finer, more systematic hold on illegalities. The whole century had seen a shift from 'a criminality of blood,' to 'a criminality of fraud'. The growth in population, the increase in wealth, the greater value placed on personal property, the expansion of commerce and industry, with enormous capital sums invested in machinery and stored merchandise, all these factors had led to an unprecedented spread of crime against property. The losses sustained through these crimes could be contained only by a more efficient system of prevention and conviction.

It is this 'economic' rationality that must calculate the penalty and prescribe the appropriate techniques. 'Humanity' is the respectable name given to this economy and to its meticulous calculations. 'Where punishment is concerned, the minimum is ordered by humanity and counselled by policy' (SP, 94; DP, 92).

What distinguishes crimes against property from other crimes is the high incidence of repetition. Penalties must be conceived, therefore, not in relation to the crime itself, but with a view to its possible repetition. As in the old order, example has a role to play, but it is employed differently. In the old *supplice*, example was the answer to the crime: it showed the crime and it manifested the sovereign power that mastered it. In a penalty calculated according to its own effects example must refer back to the crime, but in the most discreet way possible, and indicate the intervention of power with the greatest possible economy. 'The example is no longer a ritual that manifests; it is a sign that serves as an obstacle.' The penal philosophy of the reformers may be summed up as follows: 1) the penalty must suggest a little more interest in avoiding the penalty than in risking the crime; 2) dissuasion must act on the mind of the potential criminal—he must have a clear notion of the outcome of his act; 3) the penalty must have its most intense effects on those who have not committed the crime; 4) the potential criminal must be convinced that the crime will be detected and punished—hence the call for a thorough policing of society; 5) the verification of crime must obey the general criteria for all truth—the truth of the crime will be accepted only when completely proven; 6) crimes must be clearly set out in a code accessible to all and, since penalities do not have the same effect on all, account must be taken of the nature of the criminal himself, the presumable degree of his wickedness, the intrinsic quality of his will—this last concern was to be the site on which a proliferating mass of social and psychological sciences was to intervene in penal practice. These principles owe their theoretical coherence to the theory of interests, representations, and signs to be found in the writings of the *Idéologues*. They constitute

a sort of general recipe for the exercise of power over men; the 'mind' as a surface of inscription for power, with semiology as its tool; the submission of bodies through the control of ideas; the analysis of representations as a principle in the politics of bodies that was much more effective than the ritual anatomy of torture and execution. The thought of the *Idéologues* was not only a theory of the individual in society; it developed as a technology of subtle, effective, economic powers, in opposition to the sumptuous expenditure of the power of the sovereign. Let us hear once more what Servan has to say: the ideas of crime and punishment must be strongly linked and 'follow one another without interruption. . . When you have thus formed a chain of ideas in the heads of your citizens, you will then be able to pride yourself on guiding them and being their masters. A stupid despot may constrain his slaves with iron chains; but a true politician binds them even more strongly by the chains of their own ideas; it is at the stable point of reason that he secures the end of the chain; this link is all the stronger in that we do not know of what it is made and we believe it to be our own work; despair and time eat away the bonds of iron and steel, but they are powerless against the habitual union of ideas, they can only tighten it still more; and on the soft fibres of the brain is founded the unshakeable base of the soundest of Empires' (SP, 105; DP, 102–3).

The art of punishing must rest on a whole technology of representation. Punishment must fit the crime, not only in degree, but in kind: it must conform as closely as possible to the offence. The very thought of a crime should summon up with it its appropriate penalty. Vermeil suggested that those who abuse public liberty should be deprived of their own; financial crime should be punished by fines, theft by confiscation, murder by death, etc. Others were concerned that society, which had inherited the role of the king as the affronted party, should be recompensed for crimes committed against it. Public works were often suggested for this purpose: the convict not only paid the penalty by his labour, his presence on the public highway served as a sign to everyone of the consequences of crime. It was proposed that places where prisoners worked should be open to the public; children should be taken there and so learn the lessons of crime and punishment. The idea of a uniform penalty, modulated according to the gravity of the crime was banished. Imprisonment was envisaged as only one among other penalties, to be used only when appropriate. In fact, it was not at all well regarded by the reformers: it was associated in people's minds with the abuses of the *ancien régime*, it was expensive, it bred idleness, it served as a place of initiation into further crime. Yet, within a few years, detention became the general form of punishment. In the penal code of 1810, it occupied, between death and fines, almost the whole field of possible punishments.

A great prison structure was planned, whose different levels would correspond exactly to the levels of the centralized administration. The scaffold, where the body of the tortured criminal had been exposed to the ritually manifested force of the sovereign, the punitive theatre in which the representation of punishment was permanently available to the social body, was replaced by a great enclosed, complex and hierarchized structure that was integrated into the very body of the state apparatus. A quite different materiality, a quite different physics of power, a quite different way of investing men's bodies had emerged. During the Restoration and the July Monarchy, there were, apart from a few exceptional moments, between 40,000 and 43,000 prisoners in French gaols (approximately one prisoner per 600 inhabitants). The high wall, no longer the wall that surrounds and protects, no longer the wall that stands for power and wealth, but the meticulously sealed wall, uncrossable in either direction, closed in upon the now mysterious work of punishment, was to become, near at hand, sometimes even at the very centre of the cities of the nineteenth century, the monotonous figure, at once material and symbolic, of the power to punish. . . The diversity, so solemnly promised, was reduced in the end to this grey, uniform penalty. Indeed, at the time, there were deputies who expressed surprise that, instead of establishing a natural relation between offences and penalties, a quite different plan had been adopted: 'So that if I have betrayed my country, I go to prison; if I have killed my father, I go to prison; every imaginable offence is punished in the same uniform way. One might as well see a physician who has the same remedy for all ills' (SP, 117–19; DP, 115–17).

How, then, did the conversion to the prison occur so swiftly and so completely? First, a number of 'model' prisons had been founded during the eighteenth century in the Low Countries, in England, and in America. The reputation of those countries for efficiency and humanitarian institutions did much to counter the association of prisons with the old order. And, indeed, these 'reformatories' were very different institutions from anything that had existed in France. There was even a certain convergence between their methods and those of the French reformers. They were directed towards the future; they too were intended not to efface the crime, but to transform the criminal. Punishment must bring with it a certain corrective technique: it must be adjusted therefore to the individual inmate. The prisoners were subjected to a regular and extremely full programme of activity and kept under constant supervision. A file was kept on each individual, his progress charted and rewarded. Where the methods differed from those proposed by the *Idéologues* was in the approach to the individual, the way in which punishment was used to control him, the means used to transform him. The difference lay in the technology of the penalty, not in its aims: it operated on the soul through the body, rather than on the body through the soul.

As for the instruments used, these are no longer complexes of representation, reinforced and circulated, but forms of coercion, schemata of constraint, applied and repeated. Exercises, not signs: time-tables, compulsory movements, regular activities, solitary meditation, work in common, silence, application, respect, good habits. And, ultimately, what one is trying to restore in this technique of correction is not so much the juridical subject, who is caught up in the fundamental interests of the social pact, but the obedient subject, the individual subjected to habits, rules, orders, an authority that is exercised continually around him and upon him, and which he must allow to function automatically in him (SP, 131–2; DP, 128–9).

At the end of the eighteenth century, then, one was confronted by three ways of organizing the power to punish. The first, based on monarchical authority, was still in force. The second, based on the theories of the *Idéologues*, seemed with the Revolution on the point of being implemented. In the end, it was the third, the prison, that was to prevail.

We have, then, the sovereign and his force, the social body, and the administrative apparatus; mark, sign, trace; ceremony, representation, exercise; the vanquished enemy, the juridical subject in the process of rehabilitation, the individual subjected to immediate coercion; the tortured body, the soul with its manipulated representations, the body subjected to training (SP, 134; DP, 131).

The eighteenth century saw a great increase in attention paid to the body as object and target of power, as an instrument that could be trained and manipulated, whose forces could be extracted and increased.

The great book of Man-the-Machine was written simultaneously on two registers: the anatomico-metaphysical register, of which

Descartes wrote the first pages and which the physicians and philosophers continued, and the technico-political register, which was constituted by a whole set of regulations and by empirical and calculated methods relating to the army, the school and the hospital, for controlling or correcting the operations of the body (SP, 138; DP, 136).

These registers were quite distinct: an intelligible body and a useful body. Yet, in practice, they frequently overlapped. It was, after all, a short step from the body understood as a machine to the use of that machine. Automata were not only a means of illustrating the functions of an organism; they suggested how organisms could be treated as automata. To achieve this, however, detailed methods of *dressage*, of training, were required. The body was docile, but it needed to be trained. This notion of the docility of the body was not entirely new, of course. It was familiar to the Christian tradition of asceticism, especially in its monastic form. What was new was the scale at which the disciplinary techniques operated: the body was treated not as a unit, but as a mechanism made up of separately usable parts. It differed from the ascetic tradition, too, in that its purpose was an increase in utility rather than in renunciation. The human body was being subjected to a machinery of power that broke it down and rearranged its parts. This 'political anatomy' was also a 'mechanism of power'. It increased the forces of the body in economic terms of utility and diminished them in political terms of obedience. 'Discipline,' says Foucault, 'is a political anatomy of detail.' This itself, of course, requires detailed demonstration, which, as always, is amply provided, but unexpectedly clear collaboration is to be found in the period. There is Napoleon's 'world of detail. . . the most important of all that I flatter myself that I have discovered'; Marshall de Saxe's advocacy of attention to detail ('It is not enough to have a liking for architecture. One must also know stone-cutting'); and La Salle's 'great hymn' to 'small things' ('Yes, little things; but great motives, great feelings, great fervour, great ardour, and consequently great merits, great treasures, great rewards').

The meticulousness of the regulations, the fussiness of the inspections, the supervision of the smallest fragment of life and of the body will soon provide, in the context of the school, the barracks, the hospital or the workshop, a laicized content, an economic or technical rationality for this mystical calculus of the infinitesimal and the infinite. . . . A meticulous observation of detail and at the same time a political awareness of these small things, for the control and use of men, emerge through the Classical age, bearing with them a whole set of techniques, a whole corpus of methods and knowledge, descriptions, plans and data. And from such trifles, no doubt, the man of modern humanism was born (SP, 142–3; DP, 140–1).

Discipline requires and developed a number of conditions for its implementation. Foucault arranges these under four heads. First, it is cellular: the space in which individuals are subjected to discipline is divided and sub-divided into more or less self-contained units. The monastery and the monastic cell were the original models: it soon spread to educational institutions, barracks, factories, and prisons. In the schools, the boarders not only slept in cells under constant supervision, but their day-time activities were dictated by a cellular system of grading according to age and ability. The old method of teaching, whereby the pupils of all ages and ability were placed under the authority of one master, who attended to each pupil in turn, was replaced by the class system, which made possible the supervision of each individual and the simultaneous work of all. The educational space functioned like a learning machine that also supervised, hierarchized, rewarded and punished. Barracks evolved their own cellular structure: the old unruly mass of soldiers, which presented a constant threat of looting, violence, and desertion, were turned into a controlled, disciplined body under strict supervision. Curiously, the hospitals owed their new organization to the armed forces: it was the naval hospital at Rochfort that pioneered methods of segregation, regulation, and strict control. Supervision of supplies and expenditure led to techniques of medical observation: patients were registered, their progress monitored, later came the isolation of contagious patients in separate beds. Discipline gave birth to a medically useful space. The earliest factories were founded explicitly on the monastic model; the working day even began with prayers. The aim was to maximize output and to reduce the incidence of theft, interruptions of work, disturbances, and the formation of secret associations. With the advance of industrialization, the productive machinery added its own requirements.

Second, the disciplines initiated a control of activity. The chief mechanism for this was the time-table. This, too, was of monastic origin: it clearly derived from the regular division of the monk's day into set tasks and a set rhythm of activities. It soon spread to schools, workshops, and hospitals. But regularity and rhythm were applied not only to the individual's general activities, but also to the very movements of the body. La Salle describes at length exactly what position each part of the pupil's body must assume in relation to every other part in the act of handwriting. Similarly, military manuals break down the apparently simple action of loading a rifle into a series of minute acts performed by various parts of the body. The factory worker had to train his body to become an articulated extension of the machine he was operating.

Third, discipline was imposed upon the body in a temporal sense: the process of training could be broken down into stages with a view to the development of ever greater skills. The procedure used was that of 'exercise'. It, too, orginated in the tradition of 'spiritual exercises' and was first transferred to the teaching of children by a religious order.

> In its mystical or ascetic form, exercise was a way of ordering earthly time for the conquest of salvation. It was gradually, in the history of the West, to change direction while preserving certain of its characteristics; it served to economize the time of life, to accumulate it in a useful form and to exercise power over men through the mediation of time arranged in this way. Exercise, having become an element in the political technology of the body and of duration, does not culminate in a beyond, but tends towards a subjection that has never reached its limit (SP, 164; DP, 162).

Fourth, in order to obtain the combination of forces, it arranges 'tactics'. The individual body becomes an element that may be placed, moved, combined with others. The bravery or strength of the soldier is no longer of prime concern; what matters is that he perform precisely the role accorded him in the overall strategy. This carefully arranged combination of forces requires a precise, economical system of command. It is not only the soldier who receives a well-understood set of signals; the teaching of children is also best conducted in this way, in silence punctuated only by bells, the clapping of hands, or that ingenious wooden device used by the Brothers of the Christian Schools to reduce the teacher's speech to an absolute minimum.

These four disciplinary procedures combined to produce the dream, and something of the reality, of a totally rational, totally efficient, totally controlled society.

> Historians of ideas usually attribute the dream of a perfect society to the philosophers and jurists of the eighteenth century; but there was also a military dream of society; its fundamental reference was not to the state of nature, but to the meticulously subordinated cogs of a machine, not to the primal social contract, but to permanent coercions, not to fundamental rights, but to indefinitely progressive forms of training, not to the general will, but to automatic docility.

> 'Discipline must be made national,' said Guibert. 'The state that I depict will have a simple, reliable, easily controlled administration. It will resemble those huge machines, which by quite uncomplicated means produce great effects; the strength of this state will spring from its own strength, its prosperity from its own prosperity. Time, which destroys all, will increase its power. It will disprove that vulgar prejudice by which we are made to imagine that empires are subjected to an imperious law of decline and ruin' (SP, 171; DP, 169).

Discipline 'makes' individuals; it is the specific technique of a power that regards individuals both as objects and instruments of its exercise. This power is not triumphant, excessive, omnipotent, but modest, suspicious, calculating. It operates through hierarchical observation, normalizing judgement, and their combination in the examination. The telescope, the lens, and the light beam introduced a major technology into physics and cosmology; 'the minor techniques of multiple and intersecting observations', of eyes that must see without being seen, were the means of establishing a new knowledge of man. The military camp was one of the earliest forms of such 'observatories', but its principles are at work in the design of hospitals, asylums, prisons, schools, and working-class housing estates. A new kind of architecture was required: one that would make it possible for those on the inside to be kept under continuous observation. The perfect disciplinary apparatus would make it possible for a single gaze to see everything constantly. It was precisely these requirements that were met by Bentham's 'panopticon'. The inmate of each cell is in full view of the central observer, himself unseen. The inmate never knows when he is being observed and, therefore, behaves at all times as if he is. A state of conscious and permanent visibility assures the automatic functioning of power. The massive architecture of the old prisons, in which prisoners were kept crammed together in darkness, could be replaced by a light structure in which the inmates were separated and permanently on view. But the panopticon was intended not only for prison: it was readily adaptable to any enclosed institution.

> It makes it possible to draw up differences: among patients, to observe the symptoms of each individual, without the proximity of beds, the circulation of miasmas, the effects of contagion confusing the clinical tables; among schoolchildren, it makes it possible to observe performances (without there being any imitation or copying), to map aptitudes, to assess characters, to draw up rigorous classifications and, in relation to normal development, to distinguish 'laziness and stubborness' from 'incurable imbecility'; among workers, it makes it possible to note the aptitude of each worker, compare the time he takes to perform a task, and if they are paid by the day to calculate their wages (SP, 205; DP, 203).

The panopticon is not just a 'dream building' it is also, says Foucault, the diagram of a mechanism of power reduced to an ideal form. The unitary, centralized point of observation was not always the most practical. In factories, especially, what was required was a breaking down of surveillance into smaller elements, a relayed form of observation. As the machinery of production became larger and more complex, as the number of workers and the division of labour increased, supervision became more necessary and more difficult. Authority had to be devolved, subdivided. Similarly, in schools, pupils were selected to act as 'officers' whose task it was to observe the others and report all cases of bad behaviour. Hierarchized, continuous surveillance became an integrated system, a multiple, automatic, anonymous power; for, although it rests on individuals, it functions as a network, a piece of machinery.

These disciplinary systems employ a micro-penality that operates in areas that the legal system has left unattended.

The workshop, the school, the army were subject to a whole micro-penality of time (latenesses, absences, interruptions of tasks), of activity (inattention, negligence, lack of zeal), of behaviour (impoliteness, disobedience), of speech (idle chatter, insolence), of the body ('incorrect' attitudes, irregular gestures, lack of cleanliness), of sexuality (impurity, indecency). At the same time, by way of punishment, a whole series of procedures was used, from light physical punishment to minor deprivations and petty humiliations. It was a question both of making the slightest departures from correct behaviour subject to punishment, and of giving a punitive function to apparently indifferent elements of the disciplinary apparatus: so that, if necessary, everything might serve to punish the slightest thing; each subject finds himself caught in a punishable, punishing universality (SP, 180–1; DP,178).

But the system not only punishes, it also awards. All behaviour can be assessed in terms of good and bad works. A penal accountancy, constantly brought up to date, can provide a balance-sheet on each individual. By comparing one individual with another, by a continuous assessment of each individual, discipline exercises a normalizing judgement. A coercive, centralized Normality is imposed on education: in France the teachers' training colleges are called '*écoles normales*' (and, in Britain, the classes of the old 'elementary' schools were called 'standards'). The medical profession and hospital system were organized in order to operate general norms of health. Industrial processes were designed to produce standardized products. Normalization functions perfectly within a system of formal equality, for not only does it impose homogeneity, it also individualizes, by making it possible to measure gaps, by providing a measure of differentiation.

The techniques of hierarchical observation and normalizing judgement combine in the examination.

It is a normalizing gaze, a surveillance that makes it possible to qualify, to classify and to punish. It establishes over individuals a visibility through which one differentiates them and judges them. That is why, in all the mechanisms of discipline, the examination is highly ritualized. In it are combined the ceremony of power and the form of the experiment, the deployment of force and the establishment of truth. At the heart of the procedures of discipline, it manifests the subjection of those who are perceived as objects and the objectification of those who are subjected. The superimposition of the power relations and knowledge relations assumes in the examination all its visible brilliance (SP, 186–7; DP, 184–5).

It was through the examination that the medical profession gradually took charge of the hospital. In the seventeenth century the physician made infrequent visits to the hospital from the outside; he took little part in its administration. The visit became more regular, more rigorous, more extended. Resident physicans were eventually appointed, followed by trained nurses. The medical began to gain over the religious. This transformation paved the way for the development of anatomo-clinical medicine at the end of the eighteenth century. Similarly, the school became an apparatus of continuous examination that duplicated the operating of teaching. The examination not only tested the knowledge imparted to the pupil, it also provided the teacher with a knowledge of the pupil. Moreover, the knowledge extracted from the various forms of examination was committed to writing in the form of reports and files. Each individual became a 'case', which is at once an object for knowledge and a site for the exercise of power: the individual as he may be described, judged, measured, compared with others in his very individuality and the individual who has to be trained or corrected, classified, normalized, or excluded. Hitherto only the great had been written about. The chronicle of a man's deeds formed part of the rituals of his power.

The disciplinary methods reversed this relation, lowered the threshold of describable individuality and made of this description a means of control and a method of domination. It is no longer a monument for future memory, but a document for possible use. And this new describability is all the more marked in that the disciplinary framework is a strict one: the child, the patient, the madman, the prisoner were to become, with increasing ease from the eighteenth century and according to a curve which is that of the mechanisms of discipline, the object of individual descriptions and biographical accounts. The turning of real lives into writing is no longer a procedure of heroicization; it functions as a procedure of objectification and subjection. The carefully collated life of mental patients or delinquents belongs, as did the chronicle of kings or the adventures of the great popular bandits, to a certain political function of writing; but in a quite different technique of power. . .

The disciplines mark the moment when the reversal of the political axis of individualization—as one might call it—takes place. In certain societies, of which the feudal régime is only one example, it may be said that individualization is greatest where sovereignty is exercised and in the higher echelons of power. The more one possesses power or privilege, the more one is marked as an individual, by rituals, written accounts or visual reproductions. The 'name' and the genealogy that situate one within a kinship group, the performance of deeds that demonstrate superior strength and which are immortalized in literary accounts, the ceremonies that mark the power relations in their very ordering, the monuments or donations that bring survival after death, the ostentation and excess of expenditure, the multiple intersecting links of allegiance and suzerainty, all these are procedures of an 'ascending' individualization. In a disciplinary régime, on the other hand, individualization is 'descending'; as power becomes more anonymous and more functional, those on whom it is exercised tend to be more strongly individualized; it is exercised by surveillance rather than ceremonies, by observation rather than commemorative accounts, by comparative measures that have the 'norm' as reference rather than genealogies giving ancestors as points of reference; by 'gaps' rather than by deeds. In a system of discipline, the child is more individualized than the adult, the patient more than the healthy man, the madman and the delinquent more than the normal and the non-delinquent. . . All the sciences, analyses or practices employing the root 'psycho-' have their origin in this historical reversal of the procedures of individualization. The moment that saw the transition from historico-ritual mechanisms for the formation of individuality to the scientifico-disciplinary mechanisms, when the normal took over from the ancestral, and measurement from status, thus substituting for the individuality of the memorable man that of the calculable man, that moment when the sciences of man became possible is the moment when a new technology of power and a new political anatomy of the body were implemented. And if from the early Middle Ages to the present day the 'adventure' is an account of individuality, the passage from the epic to the novel, from the noble deed to the secret singularity, from long exile to the internal search for childhood, from combats to phantasies, it is also inscribed in the formation of a disciplinary society (SP, 193–5; DP, 191–3).

The economic take-off of Western Europe began with the tech-niques that made possible the accumulation of capital; methods for the accumulation of men made possible a political take-off, as the traditional, ritual, costly, violent forms of power were superseded by a subtle, calculated technology of subjection. The two processes are interdependent: economic expansion provided the means of sustain-ing and using the increase in population, while the disciplinary tech-niques accelerated the accumulation of capital. The process by which the bourgeoisie became the politically dominant class in the eigh-teenth century was masked by the establishment of a coded, formally egalitarian constitution, supported by a system of representative government. But this 'Enlightenment' politics had its dark underside in the ever-proliferating network of disciplinary mechanisms. While the first was based on the notion of the freely negotiated contract, the second ensured the submission of forces and bodies. Foucault is perhaps the first 'political theorist' of modern times to draw out the full implications of these techniques. Bentham's panopticon has been regarded as little more than a folly, 'a bizzare little utopia', a 'perverse dream'. Contemporaries were less self-deluding: the German penologist Julius called it 'an event in the history of the human mind'. Compared with the steam-engine or Amici's microscope it may seem of little account. Yet in a way it is much more. The empirical sciences used the inquisitorial model to extract information from the world and to establish 'facts'; the sciences of man have emerged from similarly 'ignoble' origins, from 'the petty, malicious, minutiae of the disciplines'.

The public execution was the logical culmination of a procedure governed by the Inquisition. The practice of placing individuals under 'observation' is a natural extension of a justice imbued with disciplinary methods and examination procedures. Is it surprising that the cellular prison, with its regular chronologies, forced labour, its authorities of surveillance and registration, its experts in normality, who continue and multiply the functions of the judge, should have become the modern instrument of penality? Is it sur-prising that prisons resemble factories, schools, barracks, hospi-tals, which all resemble prisons? (SP, 228–9; DP, 227–8).

The final section of the book is devoted exclusively to the prison itself, to the theory and practice of that 'complete and austere institution' from its modern development at the beginning of the nineteenth century. It traces the controversies that centred on such questions as whether or not prisoners should be isolated from one another, if so which categories of prisoner and for how long; whether prisoners should work and, if so, whether they should be paid; the extent to which the prison authorities should have the power to reduce or increase the legal penalty either in quantity or quality. It shows that dissatisfaction with the prison as an institution and the movement to reform it are not recent phenomena, but as old as the prison itself. Moreover, the same questions have arisen and the same answers have been paraded, one way or another, whenever the prison is in question: prisons do not diminish the crime rate, detention causes recidivism, the prison creates, even encourages, the organization of a milieu of habitual criminals, the prison indirectly produces criminals by throwing the prisoner's family into destitution. Proposals for reform invariably amount to the same set of principles: penal detention must have as its essential function the transformation of the individual's behaviour; convicts must be segregated according to the gravity of their offence, age, mental attitude, the techniques of correction to be used, the stages of their transformation; it must be possible to alter penalties according to the individuality of the convict and his response to imprisonment; work must be one of the essential elements in the transformation and progressive socialization of convicts; the education of the prisoner is in the interests of society and an obligation to the prisoner himself; the prison régime must, at least in part, be administered by staff possessing the moral qualities and specialized training of educators; imprisonment must be followed by measures of supervision and assistance until the rehabilitation of the former prisoner is complete.

But one should not think of the prison in terms of inception, 'failure', and 'reform', of three successive stages.

One should think rather of a simultaneous system that historically has been superimposed on the juridical deprivation of liberty; a fourfold system comprising: the additional, disciplinary element of the prison—the element of 'super-power'; the production of an objectivity, a technique, a penitentiary 'rationality'—the element of auxiliary knowledge; the *de facto* reintroduction, if not actual increase, of a criminality that the prison ought to destroy—the element of inverted efficiency; lastly, the repetition of a 'reform' that is isomorphic, despite its 'idealism', with the disciplinary functioning of the prison—the element of utopian duplication. It is this complex ensemble that constitutes the 'carceral system', not only the institution of the prison, with its walls, its staff, its regulations and its violence. The carceral system combines in a single figure discourses and architectures, coercive regulations and scientific propositions, real social effects and invincible utopias, programmes for correcting delinquents and mechanisms that reinforce delinquency (SP, 276; DP, 271).

Foucault then asks what may seem a surprising question: 'Is not the supposed failure part of the functioning of the prison?' He explains the point with another question:

> Is it not to be included among those effects of power that discipline and the auxiliary technology of imprisonment have induced in the apparatus of justice, and in society in general, and which may be grouped together under the name of 'carceral system'? If the prison-institution has survived for so long, with such immobility, if the principle of penal detention has never seriously been questioned, it is no doubt because this carceral system was deeply rooted and carried out certain very precise functions (SP, 276; DP, 271).

The prison, and the legal system generally, is to be understood as a means not of eliminating crime, but rather of differentiating between types of crime, types of criminal, setting one potential source of social instability against another, using one against another. In the eighteenth and early nineteenth centuries there was a wide range of popular illegalities that made little distinction between political and non-political offences. There was a sense in which whole sections of the population were in a permanent state of subdued rebellion: they may have feared, but they certainly did not respect the law. The law was no longer seen as an expression of the King, even of God, but quite clearly as an instrument of the new rich class. In the countryside, the liquidation of the aristocracy had freed the land for commercialization, for the benefit of the post-Revolution bourgeoisie. (In England, the change was less violent because the process had begun much earlier; it reached a head with the enclosures.)

In the towns, the law forbade workers' coalitions, while allowing
employers to form cartels and to introduce more machines, lower
wages, longer working hours, and stricter factory regulations. For the
most part, the workers who suffered these conditions were peasants
who had been forced to leave the land by the actions of the landowners. Illegalities begun in the country were continued in the town,
with others added:

> from the most violent such as machine-breaking, or the most last-
> ing such as the formation of associations, to the most everyday,
> such as absenteeism, abandoning work, vagabondage, pilfering
> raw materials, deception as to the quantity and quality of the work
> completed. A whole series of illegalities was inscribed in struggles
> in which those struggling know that they were confronting both
> the law and the class that had imposed it (SP, 279; DP, 274).

For many sections of the population offences against property were
not regarded as crimes and people did not regard those who committed them as criminals. On the contrary, it was difficult to separate
such acts from a certain political outlook and a certain social struggle.
Legislators, philanthropists, and investigators into working-class life
certainly had what one can only call a 'great fear' of the people, who
were believed to be seditious and criminal as a whole. In the course of
the century, penal theory began to reflect these changed conditions:
crime was not a matter of individual choice for or against a tendency
to be found in all men; it was committed almost exclusively by a
certain social class, by those at the bottom of society. It is therefore
hypocritical or naive to believe that the law was made for all in the
name of all: rather it was made by the few and made to bear upon the
many. What prison and its attendant disciplinary mechanisms has
achieved over the last century and a half is the creation of an autonomous sub-class of delinquents, or habitual offenders, drawn largely
from, but no longer belonging to, the working class. By concentrating
the illegalities that threatened to infect the mass of the population in
one, relatively small group, it was possible to contain them.

> For the observation that prison fails to eliminate crime, one should
> perhaps substitute the hypothesis that prison has succeeded
> extremely well in producing delinquency, a specific type, a politi-
> cally or economically less dangerous—and, on occasion,

usable—form of illegality; in producing delinquents, in an apparently marginal, but in fact centrally supervised milieu; in producing the delinquent, as a pathologized subject. . . The carceral system substituted the 'delinquent' for the offender, and also superimposed upon juridical practice a whole horizon of possible knowledge. Now this process that constitutes deliquency as an object of knowledge is one with the political operation that dissociates illegalities and isolates delinquency from them. The prison is the hinge of these two mechanisms; it enables them to reinforce one another perpetually, to objectify the delinquency behind the offence, to solidify delinquency in the movement of illegalities. So successful has the prison been that, after a century and a half of 'failures', the prison still exists, producing the same results, and there is the greatest reluctance to dispense with it (SP, 282; DP, 277).

The establishment of a class of delinquents as a kind of enclosed illegality has a number of advantages. It is possible to supervise it (by locating individuals, infiltrating the group, organizing mutual informing). It may be diverted to forms of illegalities that are politically harmless and economically negligible. This concentrated, supervised, and disarmed illegality is directly useful. Penal colonies were an essential element in the expansion of colonization. It is useful in controlling and supervising such semi-clandestine activities as prostitution, arms trafficking or, more recently, the circulation of drugs. The danger is contained, the profits are extracted and public morality satisfied. In the nineteenth century delinquents were widely used in the infiltration of political parties and workers' associations, in breaking strikes and quelling riots. At times they seemed to form a kind of standby army at the disposal of the state: they played an important role in Louis Napoleon's seizure of power. But, above all, delinquency provided a justification and a means for the general surveillance of the population. Much of this policing was carried out, at its lowest level, by a mass of informers drawn from the criminal body itself. Later, this function of providing information about the population was taken up by statisticians and sociologists, psychiatrists and social workers.

Crime produced the prison; the prison the delinquent class; the existence of a delinquent class an excuse for the policing of the entire population. This policing led to the extraction and recording of information about groups and individuals; the human sciences gained a terrain and a patron; crime came to be seen as a departure from the Norm, a sickness to be understood if not cured; this provided a justification for the 'examination' of the entire population. The exercise of power over the population and the accumulation of knowledge about it are two sides of a single process: not power and knowledge, but power-knowledge.

The judges of normality are present everywhere. We are in the society of the teacher-judge, the doctor-judge, the educator-judge, the 'social worker'-judge; it is on them that the universal reign of the normative is based; and each individual, wherever he may find himself, subjects to it his body, his gestures, his behaviour, his aptitudes, his achievements. The carceral network, in its compact or disseminated forms, with its systems of insertion, distribution, surveillance, observation, has been the greatest support, in modern society, of the normalizing power. The carceral texture of society assures both the real capture of the body and its perpetual observation; it is, by its very nature, the apparatus of punishment that conforms most completely to the new economy of power and the instrument for the formation of knowledge that this very economy needs. Its panoptic functioning enables it to play this double role. By virtue of its methods of fixing, dividing, recording, it has been one of the simplest, crudest, also most concrete, but perhaps most indispensable conditions for the development of this immense activity of examination that has objectified human behaviour. If, after the age of 'inquisitorial' justice, we have entered the age of 'examinatory' justice, if, in an even more general way, the method of examination has been able to spread so widely through society, and to give rise in part to the sciences of man, one of the great instruments for this has been the multiplicity and close overlapping of the various mechanisms of incarceration. I am not saying that the human sciences emerged from the prison. But, if they have been able to be formed and to produce so many profound changes in the *episteme*, it is because they have been conveyed by a specific and new modality of power: a certain policy of the body, a certain way of rendering the accumulation of men docile and useful. This policy required the involvement of definite relations of knowledge in relations of power; it called for a technique of overlapping subjection and objectification; it brought with it new procedures of individualization. The carceral network constituted one of the armatures of this power-knowledge that has made the human sciences historically possible. Knowable man (soul, individuality, consciousness, conduct, whatever it is called) is the object-effect of this analytical investment, of this domination-observation (SP, 311–12; DP, 304–5).

◇ 3 ◇

Sexuality, Power, and Knowledge

It was only a matter of time, I suppose, before Foucault devoted a full-length book to the subject of sexuality. It had been promised some fifteen years earlier in the Preface to the first edition of *Histoire de la folie* and again offered as a possible field of inquiry in *L'archéologie du savoir*. In 1963, for a special number of *Critique* devoted to the memory of Georges Bataille, Foucault wrote 'Préface à la transgression', which foreshadows many of the dominant notions to be found in *La volonté de savoir*.

We like to believe that sexuality has regained, in contemporary experience, its full truth as a process of nature, a truth which has long been lingering in the shadows and hiding under various disguises—until now, that is, when our positive awareness allows us to decipher it so that it may at last emerge in the clear light of language. Yet, never did sexuality enjoy a more immediately natural understanding and never did it know a greater 'felicity of expression' than in the Christian world of fallen bodies and sin. The proof is its whole tradition of mysticism and spirituality which was incapable of dividing the continuous forms of desire, of rapture, of penetration, of ecstacy, of that outpouring that leaves us spent: all of these experiences seem to lead without interruption or limit, right to the heart of a divine love of which they were both the outpouring and source returning upon itself. . . We have not in the least liberated sexuality, though we have, to be more exact, carried it to its limits: the limit of consciousness, because it ultimately dictates the only possible reading of our unconscious; the

164

limit of the law, since it seems the sole substance of universal taboos; the limit of language, since it traces that line of foam showing just how fast speech may advance upon the sands of silence (B1, 751; LCP, 29–30).

Yet when *La volonté de savoir* appeared in 1976 even those accustomed to Foucault's reversals of the received wisdom were taken aback. What was promised was nothing less than a 'history of sexuality', of which this slim volume was merely the introduction. Of course, no one who did know Foucault's work would have been misled into expecting some kind of encyclopaedia erotica, though some of the titles to come might have tempted the unwary browser: *The Flesh and the Body; The Children's Crusade; Woman, the Mother and the Hysteric; The Perverts; Population and Races*. It would, of course, be no more a 'history of sexuality' than *Histoire de la folie* was a 'history of madness'. Anyway, this first, very Foucaldian title, *The Will to Knowledge*, should have warned us. (The translation, which appeared in 1978 in the United States and the following year in Britain, rejects the original title in favour of *The History of Sexuality, Volume 1: An Introduction*. In this case, I felt I had no alternative but to retranslate the passages I wished to quote. However, for those who wish to refer to the published translation, I have provided page references to it.) The title could have been given to any of Foucault's books, yet what, specifically, has a 'will to knowledge' to do with sexuality? Then one remembers the Garden of Eden and the Tree of Knowledge—and their survival in such expressions as 'carnal knowledge'. But Foucault is referring not so much to carnal knowledge as to knowledge of—and therefore a power over—bodies. In *Surveiller et punir* he was at pains to show that power was not simply repressive, negative; it was also positive, productive of knowledge:

> We must cease once and for all to describe the effects of power in negative terms: it 'excludes', it 'represses', it 'censors', it 'abstracts', it 'masks', it 'conceals'. In fact power produces; it produces reality; it produces domains of objects and rituals of truth. The individual and the knowledge that may be gained of him belong to this production (SP, 196; DP, 194).

What he is asking us to consider in this book is a similar thesis: that the relation of power to sex is not essentially repressive, that it is rather productive of an ever-proliferating discourse on sexuality. The book opens, however, with a dazzling summary of the received view, which an inattentive reader, missing the implication of the French conditional tense and the odd 'it seems' or 'we are told', might take for Foucault's own.

> For a long time now, it seems, we have been subjected to a Victorian régime. The imperial prude is still emblazoned on our sexuality, stiff-backed, tight-lipped, hypocritical.
>
> In the early seventeenth century, we are told, there still existed a certain frankness about sexual matters. Sex had no need of secrecy; parts were named without too much disguise and the words spoken without undue reticence; there was a tolerant familiarity with the illicit. The codes governing what was coarse, obscene or indecent were lax compared with those of the nineteenth century. It was a time of straightforward gestures and speech without shame, when official morality was openly flouted, anatomies displayed and conjoined at will, when knowing children, listening to the bawdy laughter of their elders, neither felt nor caused embarrassment, when bodies strutted about in their pride.
>
> But the daylight failed, dusk fell and we were plunged, it seems, into the monotonous nights of the Victorian bourgeoisie. Sexuality was carefully locked away. It moved into the home. The conjugal family confiscated it, absorbing it whole and entire into the serious function of reproduction. One did not speak of sex. The legitimate, procreating couple laid down the law, imposed itself as model, enforced the norm; it alone possessed the truth of sex, reserving to itself the right to speak of it or to keep it secret. Throughout the entirety of social space, sexuality was recognized in one place, and one alone, that ultilitarian, fertile heart of every home, the parents' bedroom. The rest had to fade away; correct behaviour decreed that bodies did not touch, decent words ensured the purity of conversation (VS, 9–10; HS, 3–4).

For the Victorians, then—and this includes the 'Continentals', the fog of puritan prudery having spread across the Channel, the Queen reigning not only over Britain and the Empire, but also, like her earlier predecessors, over France—sex that was not directed towards procreation, and transfigured by it, was not only illicit, but silenced, reduced to non-existence. A few concessions had to be made: if one could not stamp out unlawful sex entirely, it should at least be contained, placed in special, enclosed places: the brothel and the lunatic asylum. There the prostitute and her client, the hysteric and her psychiatrist could act, or, at least, speak out all that was forbidden beyond their walls. In the course of the present century, it is said, we have begun painfully to free ourselves from sexual taboos. Freud is usually cited as one of the early heroes in this process. Yet a more extreme version of the repressive thesis would even consign Freud to the repressive side, condemning his bourgeois conformism, the tendency of psychoanalysis to normalize. Freud may be an improvement on what went before,

> but with such circumspection, such medical prudence, such a scientific guarantee of innocuousness, and so many precautions in order to contain everything, with no fear of 'overflow', in that safest and most discreet of spaces, between couch and discourse: more profitable whispering on a bed (vs, 11; hs, 5).

The consulting room is altogether too reminiscent of the prostitute's bedroom: a safety valve that allows the machinery of repression to go on working.

This view of sexuality, that from the mid-seventeenth century power has acted upon sex in an essentially repressive way, seems so unquestionable, says Foucault, because it is made to coincide with the rise of the bourgeoisie and the advent of capitalism.

> The inglorious chronicle of sex and its petty tribulations is transposed into the ceremonious history of the modes of production; its futility vanishes. A principle of explanation emerges from this very fact: if sex is so rigorously repressed, it is because it is incompatible with a situation in which everything is being put to work. At a time when labour capacity was being systematically exploited, how could this capacity be allowed to dissipate itself in pleasurable pursuits, except those—reduced to a minimum—that enabled it to reproduce itself? (vs, 12–13; hs, 5–6).

What is being attacked here is not so much Marxism, which, traditionally, has regarded the individual as being outside its area of concern, nor psychoanalysis, which, equally, has disregarded social relations, but rather *freudo-marxisme*, a certain unsystematic 'New Left' amalgam. Sexual freedom, knowledge about sex and the right to speak of it, have become a cause, a cause identified in some minds with that of the people and thus belonging to the future. If sex is repressed, doomed to prohibition, non-existence, and silence, merely to speak of it takes on the proportions of a deliberate act of transgression; a blow is struck against power in the name of a future freedom.

> Some of the ancient functions of prophecy are revived in it. Tomorrow sex will be good once more. This denunciation of repression makes it possible to bring together, without anyone noticing, concepts that a fear of ridicule or a cynical view of history prevents most of us from putting side by side: revolution and pleasure. What sustains our desperate eagerness to speak of sex in terms of repression is no doubt the opportunity it affords us to speak out against the powers that be, to tell the truth and to promise true ecstasy; to link together enlightenment, liberation and the enjoyment of new pleasures; to speak at one and the same time of the thirst for knowledge, a determination to change the law and the hoped for garden of earthly delights. Perhaps this also explains the commercial value we place not only on everything that is said about sex, but also on the mere fact of lending an ear to those who would rid themselves of the effects of its repression. Ours is, after all, the only civilization in which officials are paid to listen to all and sundry confide the secrets of their sexual life; as if the urge to talk about sex and the interest it is hoped to arouse in it had far exceeded the possibility of being heard, some individuals have even offered their ears for hire (vs, 14; hs, 7).

But more important than such economic implications is the existence of a new sexual evangelism in which the revelation of the truth, the stripping bare of old hypocrisies, the promises of immediate fulfilment and future bliss are mingled together. This lyrical religiosity, which for a long time accompanied so much revolutionary thinking, seems in the past few decades to have spread to the subject of sex. Foucault sums up the question that occurred to him at the outset thus:

> Briefly, my aim is to examine the case of a society which, for more than a century, has loudly castigated itself for its hypocrisy, talked endlessly of its own silence, persisted in recounting in great detail the things of which it does not speak, denounced the power it

exercises and promised to free itself from the very laws that made it function. I would like to explore not only these discourses, but also the will that sustains them and the strategic intention that supports them. The question I would like to ask is not, Why are we repressed? but rather, Why do we say, with such passion, such resentment against our recent past, against our present and against ourselves, that we are repressed? By what spiral have we come to declare that sex is denied, to show so openly that we hide it, to say that we silence it, while, all the time, expressing ourselves in the most explicit words, striving to reveal it in its darkest reality, affirming it in the positivity of its power and its effects? (VS, 16; HS, 8–9).

The main argument against such doubts is put by Foucault himself. The 'repressive hypothesis' is so widely accepted that it seems historically self-evident. Sex is the subject of so much debate because this repression is so deeply rooted in our thinking, in our deepest feelings. It is only to be expected that the effects of sexual liberation should take so long to manifest themselves. Foucault responds with three questions: 1) Is it so self-evident that sex itself has been repressed to a unique degree since the seventeenth century? 2) Is the machinery of power that operates in capitalist societies essentially repressive? 3) Does the liberationist movement constitute a true opposition to the machinery of power and the repression it operates or does it, on the contrary, form part of the same historical network that it condemns? However, his purpose is not to erect an inverted, symmetrical version of the repressive hypothesis. He is not saying that sex, far from being repressed in bourgeois society, has enjoyed unprecedented freedom, that power in societies like ours is more tolerant than repressive, etc. His aim is not so much to disprove the repressive hypothesis as to situate it in 'a general economy of discourse on sex' in modern society. A new set of questions arises: Why has sexuality become such a subject for discussion? What exactly has been said about it? What have been the effects in terms of power of this discourse on sex? What connections exist between this discourse, its power effects, and the pleasure on which they operate? What knowledge did it give rise to? What, in short, is the 'régime of power-knowledge-pleasure' that sustains this sexual discourse? We should be examining how power flows through the channels formed by discourse to reach, penetrate, and control individuals right down to their most private pleasures, using the negative methods of refusal and prohibition, but also, in a positive way, excitation and intensification—what Foucault calls 'the polymorphous techniques of power'. It is a question not of deciding whether this discourse produced by power and this power produced by discourse tend to reveal or conceal the truth about sex, but rather of locating the 'will to knowledge' that serves power and discourse as both object and instrument of their action. Foucault does not deny the fact of repression; what he rejects is a view of power as monolithic, centralized, and repressive. Repression is rather one effect, among others, of a complex set of mechanisms concerned with the production of discourse (and silence), power (and prohibition), knowledge (and error). An initial examination of the material along these lines suggested that sexual discourse has been subjected not to a process of restriction, but rather to an increasing stimulation; that the techniques of power that have operated on sexuality have obeyed a principle not of rigorous selection, but of polymorphous dissemination; that the will to knowledge has not been obstructed by taboos, but has striven to found a science of sexuality.

Certainly, with the advent of the Classical period, a purification of the authorized vocabulary took place. A new, stricter code governed what could be said, where, in what circumstances, and to whom. Yet at the level of discourse proper the reverse was the case: rather a proliferation of discourse on sex, an incitement to discourse by the organs of power themselves. Thus the practice of confession in the Catholic Church underwent a marked change after the Council of Trent. Again a superficial restriction was accompanied by an actual increase. The questions asked and the answers expected became less explicit; the degree of detail considered necessary to a true confession in the Middle Ages, was now regarded as unseemly. The dialogue between penitent and confessor became more veiled, more circumlocutory. On the other hand, the single annual confession was now thought to be quite inadequate. Moreover, an ever greater attention was paid to sins against the flesh than to others. A subtle process of self-examination was imposed on Christians with a view to locating and categorizing every sin of thought, word, and deed. The flesh became the root of all evil, but it was in the soul that sin had its first stirrings, in the slightest thought, imagining, memory.

Under cover of a language that had been carefully expurgated so that it was no longer directly named, sex was taken charge of, tracked down as it were, by a discourse that claimed to allow it no obscurity, no respite. (vs, 29; hs, 20).

This technique for transforming sex into discourse was not new. It had long been a part of the monastic, ascetic tradition: the seventeenth century merely made it a rule, or at least an ideal, for all Catholics. The task is endless, for the more one tries to track down impure thoughts the more one is besieged by them. What is ostensibly a mechanism of restriction is in fact a mechanism of production: the penitent is obliged not only to confess to every sin, but to transform his every desire into discourse. Foucault sees a direct line of descent from the Catholic examination of conscience to the 'scandalous' literature of later centuries. Sade's injunction in *The 120 Days of Sodom* to recount 'the most numerous and searching details' bears a striking resemblance to the instructions of the directors of conscience: 'Tell everything, not only consummated acts, but sensual touchings, all impure looks, all obscene remarks . . . all consenting thoughts'. A similar desire to transform a lifetime's sexual activity into words motivated the anonymous author of *My Secret Life* at the end of the nineteenth century. He may seem to us to be one of Steven Marcus's 'other Victorians', a rebel against the puritanism of his time and a precursor of a later, more enlightened age; he may equally well be seen as a representative figure in a long, uninterrupted tradition of talking about sex.

Yet this technique was not confined to Christian spirituality and erotic literature. From the mid-eighteenth century the secular power, too, became increasingly concerned with sex. It did not take easily to talking about sexual matters: a new language, a new mode of discourse, based not only on morality, but also on reason had to be developed. How could one speak seriously of a subject that aroused only disgust or ridicule? How could one tell the truth about it and avoid both hypocrisy and scandal? This rise of a scientific interest in sex was not, however, a disinterested pursuit of knowledge. Sex entered the public domain with the population problem: population as wealth and manpower, population balanced between its own growth and the resources it could produce. Governments saw that they were dealing not simply with 'subjects', or even with 'the people', but also with a 'population', possessing its own phenomena: birth and death rates, life expectancy, fertility, health, diet, etc. At the centre of this economic and political problem of population was sex: it was necessary to analyse the birthrate, the age of marriage, legitimate and illegitimate births, the precocity and frequency of sexual relations, the nature and extent of contraceptive practices, etc. The increase in population was no longer an unquestioned good; what was now needed was a subtle calculation of needs.

> The state must know what is happening with its citizens' sex and the use they make of it, but each individual must also be capable of controlling the use he makes of it. Between the state and the individual, sex became an issue and a public issue no less; it became invested by a whole network of discourses, new forms of knowledge, analyses and exhortations (vs, 37; hs, 26).

With the nineteenth century, society increasingly developed mechanisms for policing the individual's behaviour. The school was one of the most important sites for the play of power-knowledge; the sexuality of schoolchildren was of paramount interest to all those concerned with education, from the architects who designed the buildings to the teachers who taught in them. The distribution of the pupils in a classroom, the planning of recreation, the shape of the dormitories (with or without partitions, with or without curtains), the rules for bedtime and sleep periods—all this was directed at the child's sexuality. A whole learned literature proliferated around the schoolboy and his sex. Before long other kinds of discourse were turning to sex. Medicine, first in the study of 'nervous disorders', then in psychiatry, sought the origin of mental illness in sexual excesses, onanism, frustration, 'frauds against procreation', sexual perversions. The law, which had once concerned itself only with the more blatantly 'unnatural' crimes, now extended its interest to all kinds of petty offences, minor acts of indecency, insignificant perversions. In the last hundred years, a whole mass of social controls has grown up, screening the sexuality of its citizens of all ages, in every form of relationship, warning, protecting, and condemning, calling for diagnoses, piling up reports, organizing therapies. Sex has become an area fraught with innumerable dangers, known and unknown; everyone must be aware of it; everyone must speak of it.

Sex was driven out of hiding and forced to lead a discursive existence. From the singular imperialism that compels everyone to transform his sexuality into a permanent discourse, to the multiple mechanisms which, in the areas of economy, pedagogy, medicine and justice, incite, extract, distribute and institutionalize sexual discourse, our civilization has demanded and organized an immense prolixity. Perhaps no other type of society has ever accumulated—and in such a relatively short time—such a quantity of discourse on sex. It may well be that we talk about sex more than anything else . . . that where sex is concerned, the most long-winded, the most impatient of societies is our own (vs, 45–6; hs, 33).

It would be wrong, however, to suppose that what has occurred is a mere quantitative increase in sexual discourse. Increase there certainly has been, but there has also been a dispersion of centres from which discourse emanates and a diversification of their forms. This has been paralleled by a dispersion and diversification of 'sexualities', what Foucault calls 'a multiple implantation of "perversions"'. Up to the end of the eighteenth century, sexual practices were governed—apart from custom and accepted beliefs—by three major codes: canon law, Christian pastoral teaching, and civil law. All three were concerned with the distinction between the lawful and the unlawful. All were centred on marital relations: their obligations, their insufficient or excessive fulfilment, the actions and gestures that were lawful or unlawful, the times when a sexual act was not permitted, the degree of violence tolerated. Marital sexuality was besieged by prohibitions and recommendations; it was discussed far more than any other form of sexuality. These other forms were, of course, condemned as unlawful and 'contrary to nature', but they did not receive the attention given to marital relations. With the discursive explosion of the late eighteenth and nineteenth centuries, however, the reverse trend set in. Marital relations continued to serve as the standard, but they became ever more veiled in privacy. 'Debauchery' (extra-marital relations), which had been one of the most common causes of confinement, was now rarely prosecuted. Correspondingly, 'the rest' became the object of unprecedented interest. A new conception of the 'unnatural' began to appear, distinguished for the first time from the merely 'unlawful' (adultery or rape, for example), which was condemned less and less.

An entire sub-race was born, different—despite certain resemblances—from the libertines of the past. From the end of the eighteenth century to our own, they circulated in the interstices of society; they were always hounded, but not always by laws; were often locked up, but not always in prisons; were sick perhaps, but scandalous, dangerous victims, prey to a strange evil that also bore the name of vice and sometimes crime. They were prematurely aroused children, precocious little girls, ambiguous schoolboys, dubious servants and educators, cruel or maniacal husbands, solitary collectors, street idlers with strange impulses; they haunted the borstals, reformatories, the courts and the asylums; they carried their shame to the doctors and their sickness to the judges. This was the numberless family of perverts who consorted with criminals and were akin to madmen. In the course of this century they were given such labels as 'moral insanity', 'genital neurosis', 'aberration of the genetic instinct', 'degeneracy', or 'psychologically unbalanced' (vs, 55–6; hs, 40).

The fact that such peripheral sexualities had come out into the light of day may suggest a relaxation of the moral code. Certainly sexual offences were punished less and less severely in the nineteenth century as the law deferred more and more to medicine. Yet the proliferation of mechanisms for study and observation, stemming from or working with medicine, may also be seen as a form of tightening control. This new persecution of peripheral sexualities brought with it an incorporation of the perversions into scientific discourse and a specification of individuals according to ever-changing taxonomies of deviation, sporting ever more outlandish Graeco-Latin names (mixoscopophiles, gynecomasts, sexoaesthetic inverts . . .). The old legal systems, civil and canonical, were concerned exclusively with acts; the new, medically permeated order invented species and sub-species of pervert. Sodomy had been a sin and a crime, and its perpetrator was treated as no more than simply that—a citizen who had committed that particular crime. In the nineteenth century the homosexual became a member of a species, with a case history, a particular type of childhood, mode of life, even anatomy. What qualified him was not so much a type of sexual relation as a certain quality of sexual sensibility, a certain way of inverting the masculine and feminine in oneself. The sexuality of

children was a favourite target: teachers and doctors combated mas-
turbation like an epidemic. Yet, in a sense, the child's 'vice' was not so
much an enemy as a support. One can only conclude from the
extraordinary effort that went into the hopeless task of eliminating it
that what was required of it was its endless proliferation rather than
its disappearance. Using the child's sexuality as a support, power
could advance its tentacles ever more widely, more deeply, more
thoroughly. Later, medicine and its epigones even made their entry
into marital relations, thus reviving the attention that had once been
lavished on them by the Church. A whole new organic, functional, or
mental pathology was derived from 'incomplete' sexual practices; a
careful classification of all forms of related pleasures was worked out
and incorporated in notions of 'development' and 'instinctual disturbances'. Medicine had taken over the management of sex.

This new form of power required a closer relationship between
agent and patient; it proceeded by examination, observation, interrogation. The medical report, the psychiatric investigation, the
school report, and family controls all seem to share a negative attitude
to 'abnormal' or unproductive sexualities; in fact, they function as
dual mechanisms of pleasure and power.

> The pleasure that comes from exercising a power that questions,
> observes, watches, spies, searches out, palpates, brings to light;
> and, on the other hand, the pleasure that is aroused at having to
> evade, flee, mislead or travesty this power. . . Capture and seduc-
> tion, confrontation and mutual reinforcement; parents and chil-
> dren, adult and adolescent, teacher and pupils, doctors and
> patients, the psychiatrist with his hysteric and his perverts, all have
> played this game continually since the nineteenth century. These
> appeals, these evasions, these circular incitements have traced
> around sexes and bodies not closed frontiers, but *perpetual spirals of
> power and pleasure* (vs, 62; hs, 45).

Modern society is perverse, not because it has tried to repress sex and
succeeded only in producing deformed expressions of the sexual
instinct, but because of the type of power it has brought to bear on the
body. Far from limiting sexuality, it has extended its various forms,
penetrating it with its power. It has acted by multiplication. These
multiple sexualities—those associated with a particular age (with
infancy or childhood), those that become fixated on some particular

form (gerontophilia, fetishism), those that permeate social relationships (doctor and patient, teacher and pupil), those identified with
certain places (the home, the school, the prison)— all correspond to
precise procedures of power. They are extracted from people's
bodies, from the infinite possibilities of their pleasures, and frozen
into a particular rigid stance.

A proliferation of sexualities through the extension of power; an
increase of the power to which each of these local sexualities gives a
surface of intervention: this concatenation, particularly since the
nineteenth century, has been secured and relayed by the countless
economic interests which, with the help of medicine, psychiatry,
prostitution and pornography, have connected up with this analytical division of pleasure and this increase of the power that
controls it. Pleasure and power do not cancel each other out; nor do
they turn against one another; they pursue, overlap and reinforce
one another. They are linked together by complex, positive
mechanisms of excitation and incitement (vs, 66–7; hs, 48).

There have been two great procedures, says Foucault, for producing the truth about sex: the *ars erotica*, as developed in China, Japan,
India, the Muslim world, etc., and our own *scientia sexualis*. In the 'art
of love', truth is extracted from pleasure itself; pleasure is considered
in relation neither to an absolute law of the permitted and the forbidden, nor to a criterion of utility, but first and foremost to itself, in
terms of its intensity and duration, its effect on the body and soul.
This knowledge is kept secret, handed down from master to disciple;
only in this way is its efficacy preserved. Our own civilization possesses no such *ars erotica*; it is, however, alone in producing a *scientia
sexualis*, procedures for telling the truth about sex that are based on a
form of power-knowledge, namely the confession, that is strictly
opposed to an art of initiation. Both are invested with a power
structure, but of opposite kinds. In the initiatory tradition, the revelation of truth comes from above, from the master, who passes it on to the
disciple. In the Western confessional tradition, truth rises from
below, from the penitent, offender, or patient and is received and
used by the authority figure. In Greece, truth and sex were linked, in
the form of pedagogy-paederasty, by the transmission of a precious
knowledge from one body to another: sex was a medium for truth. In
our tradition, truth serves as a medium for sex and its manifestations.

Since the Middle Ages, at least, Western societies have developed the confession as one of the main rituals for the production of truth: the Lateran Council of 1215 laid down the confessional techniques to be used in the sacrament of penance and in the legal processes confession became an increasingly important element.

> The confession has spread its effects far and wide. It plays a part in law, medicine, education, family relationships and sexual relations, in ordinary, everyday matters and in the most solemn rites; one confesses one's crimes, one confesses one's sins, one confesses one's thoughts and desires, one confesses to one's past and to one's dreams, one confesses to one's childhood, one confesses one's illnesses and troubles; one sets about telling, with the greatest precision, what is most difficult to tell; one confesses in public and in private, to one's parents, to one's teachers, to one's doctor, to those one loves; one confesses to oneself, in pleasure and in pain, things that it would be impossible to tell anyone else, the things people write books about. One confesses—or one is forced to confess. When it is not spontaneous or dictated by some internal imperative, it is extracted; it is driven out of the soul, or drawn out of the body. Since the Middle Ages, torture has accompanied it like a shadow and supported it when it began to falter: the dark twins. Like the most vulnerable of creatures, the bloodiest of powers have need of confession. Western man has become a confessing animal (vs, 79; hs, 59).

Literature, too, has passed from a stage where deeds were recounted to one where souls are laid bare. Confession is so all-pervasive that we no longer see it as the effect of a power that constrains us; instead, we see it as liberating, truth as belonging not to power, but to our freedom. Yet this extension of confessional techniques has been nothing less than

> an immense labour to which the West has submitted generations in order to produce—while other forms of work ensured the accumulation of capital—men's subjection: their constitution as 'subjects' in both senses of the word (vs, 81; hs, 60).

This 'immense labour' has culminated in an ever widening network of 'human' and 'social' sciences. Yet this entry of sexuality into scientific discourse in the nineteenth century was not easily accomplished. There was the fundamental theoretical problem to be faced—one that

177

had confronted clinical medicine and prevented it, unlike physiology for example, from becoming a science—namely, how a science could be based on individuals. Was it possible to constitute a science of the subject? What was the validity of introspection? Could lived experience be used as evidence? There was also a more pressing, more immediate problem: scientists were clearly embarrassed by this 'discourse from below'. Foucault cites telling evidence of alternating tactics of stimulation and censorship practised at La Salpetrière by no less a figure than Charcot. Yet sex did become an object of scientific discourse and practice. Indispensable in this process was the old confessional mechanism. Soon this led to an all-pervasive sexualization of illness. The slightest sexual defect or deviation was thought to possess untold consequences in terms of health and sanity. Contrarywise, there was scarcely an illness of mind or body that was not attributed to some sexual cause. Yet the workings of sex remained largely hidden, not only from the scientist or doctor, but also from the subject or patient himself. Its truth could only emerge, therefore, in two stages: first, in the form, blind to itself, in which the patient offered it and, secondly, in the form of interpretation, given back to the patient by the specialist. The work of producing the truth could only take place within the dual relationship; only in this way would it be scientifically validated. Furthermore, this confession-interpretation had a therapeutic effect; spoken in time, to a qualified-interpreter, or 'analyst', the truth could heal.

> We demand that sex speak the truth (but, since it is itself the secret and is denied access to itself, we reserve to ourselves the task of telling the truth of its truth, revealed and deciphered at last), and we demand that it tell us our truth, or rather, the deeply buried truth of that truth about ourselves that we think we possess in our immediate consciousness. We tell it its truth by deciphering what it tells us about that truth; it tells us our own by yielding up that part of it that escaped us. It is from this interplay that, slowly, over several centuries, a knowledge of the subject has been constituted; a knowledge not so much of his form, as of that which divides him, determines him perhaps, but above all keeps him ignorant of himself. Unlikely as this may seem, it should not surprise us when we think of the long history of Christian and judicial confession, of the displacements and transformations this form of knowledge-power,

so crucial in the West, has undergone: the project of a science of the subject has gravitated, in ever-diminishing circles, around the question of sex. Causality in the subject, the unconscious of the subject, the truth of the subject in the other who knows, the knowledge within him of what he does not know himself, all this could be deployed in discourse on sex. Not, however, by reason of some natural property inherent in sex itself, but by virtue of the tactics of power immanent in this discourse (vs, 93–4; hs, 69–70).

This clear, if not explicit, reference to psychoanalysis is as good an example as any of Foucault's genealogical approach. He does not engage in a confrontation with psychoanalysis: at this point, he does not even mention it by name. He does not counter its claim to truth with another truth of comparable status. He does not criticize it for its lack of scientific foundation, its cultural Euro-centrism, its paternalism, its patriarchalism, its class basis, its financial scandals, its endemic paranoia; or rather, he would see all these things as unsurprising, if not inevitable, characteristics of an institution and a practice with that particular genealogy. Its 'truth' and its 'knowledge' are rooted not in transcendence, but in history. They are weapons in which a society manages itself; positive mechanisms that act, in Foucault's electronic imagery, as 'producers of knowledge, multipliers of discourse, inductors of pleasure and generators of power'.

Foucault describes his aim in this series of books as that of transcribing into history Diderot's tale *Les bijoux indiscrets*. In this story the 'curious sultan' is given a ring whose stone possesses the extraordinary power of making the sexual organs it encounters speak. Foucault sees his task as making this magic ring, which is so indiscreet when it comes to making others speak, speak in turn of its own mechanism. What is needed is a history of this will to truth. Why is it that we ask so much of sex over and above the pleasure it affords? Relatively recently, geneticists discovered that life was not simply an organization that happened to be equipped with a capacity to reproduce itself, but that the reproductive mechanism was of the very essence of biology, of life itself. Yet, centuries ago, 'theoreticians and practitioners of the flesh' had realized that man was 'the child of an imperious and intelligible sex. Sex, the reason for everything.' Then why has the task of discovering this difficult truth finally turned into an attempt to banish prohibitions and to set our sexuality free?

Was the labour, then, so arduous that we needed this promise, dangled before our eyes? Or had this knowledge become so costly—in political, economic and ethical terms—that if everyone were to be subjected to it, we had to be assured, paradoxically enough, that in it we would find our liberation? (vs, 105; hs, 80).

Foucault's aim is to produce not so much a 'theory' of power as an 'analytics' of power. That is to say, he is not prepared to engage in theoretical battle with adverse forces on a field of their choosing, but rather, in the spirit of the genealogical method, to stand back from the battlefield and to relate the conflict to a wider context, which can only be that of a *wirkliche Historie*, a history without illusions. However, before proceeding, Foucault feels compelled to make one theoretical clarification. He is well aware, he says, that a body of psychoanalytic thinking—the reference is clearly to Lacan and his followers, though they are not named—has abandoned the notion of a rebellious natural energy that wells up from below and encounters a superior, repressive authority. Or rather, with the aid of linguistic mechanisms, they have been able to produce a more subtle, more complicated account of the relations between desire and power. According to this view, desire is not repressed in some secondary stage since it is power—in the form of Law—that constitutes desire and the lack from which desire springs. Where there is desire, there is power in its midst. To the Lacanians, Foucault seems to be saying, it may seem as if I have set up the weaker, outdated theory of repression only to knock it down, while ignoring the real threat posed by the new, stronger interpretation of desire as product of Law. Yet, Foucault points out, what distinguishes the two psychoanalytic theories is not the way in which they conceive of power, but rather the way in which they conceive of the 'drives'. Each has recourse to a representation of power that Foucault calls 'juridico-discursive'. Depending on the use to which it is put and the position accorded desire, it leads to two contrary results: either to a promise of 'liberation', if power is conceived as affecting desire only from the ouside, or, if it is seen as constitutive of desire itself, to the belief that one can never be free. This representation of power is not confined to discourse on sex; it permeates the whole of our political thinking and is deeply rooted in the history of the West. The way it is seen to operate on sex is, however, exemplary. It rejects any relation between power and sex that is not negative; it operates exclusively by rejection, exclusion, refusal, or concealment—in short, by limit and lack. Its aim is that sex should disappear. To achieve that aim it issues threats: renounce yourself or be suppressed, do not appear if you do not want to disappear, your existence will be tolerated only on my terms which—by a logic both paradoxical and circular— consists of silence, non-appearance, non-existence.

> One must not speak of that which is forbidden until it is annulled in reality; that which is non-existent has no right to appear, even in the order of speech, where its non-existence is declared; that which must be silenced is banished from reality as that which is forbidden above all else (vs, 111; hs, 84).

Power lays down the laws by which sex functions and by which its workings are to be interpreted. It operates on the individual subject and his sex through his very acquisition of language; language is the means by which the individual is initiated into society; as he acquires it he encounters the Law. The Law tells him what he desires by forbidding it. The pure form of power is that of the legislator; its relation to sex is of a juridico-discursive type. Power operates on sex in the same way at all levels.

> From the state to the family, from prince to father, from the courts to the small change of everyday punishments, from the agencies of social domination to the constitutive structures of the subject himself, one finds a general form of power that varies only in scale (vs, 112; hs, 84–5).

In all cases, there is a legislative power on one side and an obedient subject on the other.

Why is it that this unitary, juridical conception of power is so widely accepted when it appears to ignore all that is positive, productive, and differentiated in it? The reason, Foucault suggests, is that power is tolerable only when a good deal of its workings are concealed. Its efficacy is proportional to the degree of that concealment. For power, secrecy is not an abuse, but a necessity; and this not only for its greater efficiency, but also for its acceptance. Would people acquiesce in it so readily if they did not see it as an external limit on their desire, one that nonetheless left intact some measure of freedom. The conception of power as mere limitation of liberty is, in our society at least, the means of its acceptability. Foucault suggests a historical reason for this. The more or less centralizing monarchies that grew up during the Middle Ages brought a measure of order and peace to the mass of warring forces that preceded them, by a system of delimited territory and hierarchized authority. That authority was embodied in the sovereign and his law: the law bound the subjects to keep the peace and the sovereign passed judgement and punished accordingly—*pax et justitia*. The law was not merely a weapon manipulated by monarchs: it was the very mode in which the monarchical system was manifested and gained acceptance. From the Middle Ages the exercise of power has always been formulated in terms of law. Of course, there are times—one thinks especially of early seventeenth-century England or late eighteenth-century France— when monarchical authority was identified with arbitrary rule, with the exercise of power above the Law. But despite attempts to free law from monarchical rule and politics from the juridical, the representation of power is still caught up in this system. Whatever criticism the eighteenth-century jurists made of monarchy in the name of law, they never questioned the principle that power must be formulated in terms of law and exercised within the law—a principle that had been established and developed by the monarchy. The nineteenth century saw a more radical critique of political institutions; not only did real power operate outside the rule of law, but the legal system itself was a form of violence, a weapon used to reinforce political and economic inequalities. But even this critique was based on the postulate that power should be exercised according to a fundamental right.

> Despite differences of objective from one period to another the representation of power has remained haunted by monarchy. In political thought and analysis we have still not cut off the head of the king. Hence the importance still accorded in the theory of power to the problems of right and violence, law and illegality, will and liberty and, above all, the state and sovereignty (even if sovereignty is no longer embodied in the person of the sovereign, but in a collective being). To conceive of power in these terms is to do so from within a historical form—juridical monarchy—that is peculiar to our own societies. Peculiar and, after all, transitory. For, although many of its forms have survived and will continue to do so, it has been gradually penetrated by quite new mechanisms of

power that are probably irreducible to the representation of law (vs, 117; hs, 88–9).

As Foucault demonstrated at length in *Surveiller et punir*, it is these micro-mechanisms of power that, since the late eighteenth century, have played an increasing part in the management of people's lives through direct action on their bodies: they operate not through a code of law, but through a technology of normalization, not by punishment, but by control, at levels and in forms that go beyond the state and its machinery. As the action of these mechanisms has increased there has been a corresponding decline in the capacity of the juridical to serve power as a channel or a system of representation. Paradoxically, this movement was ushered in, during the years following the French Revolution, by unprecedented activity in the drawing up of new political constitutions and legal codes. Moreover, this juridical representation is still dominant in much of our thinking about power and its workings, including the relations between power and sex. Whether one sees desire as alien to power, as existing prior to the law, or as constituted by the law, one still conceives of it in relation to a power that is juridical and discursive—a power that finds its central point in the enunciation of the law. We must free ourselves from this image of power as law and sovereignty, says Foucault, if we are to understand how power actually operates in our technologically advanced societies. Foucault has two aims in this proposed series of studies: to show that sex—an area where, above all others, power seems to function in terms of prohibition—is not, in fact, subjected to power in this way and, second, to formulate an alternative theory of power, 'another grid for deciphering history'. 'We must at the same time conceive of sex without the law and power without the king.'

By 'power', Foucault does not mean 'Power', in the sense of a unified state apparatus whose task it is to ensure the subjection of the citizens of a particular society. Nor does he mean a general system of domination exerted by one group over another, the effect of which spreads to the whole of society . Power should be understood as 'the multiplicity of power relations' at work in a particular area. These power relations are the object of an unceasing struggle in which they are transformed, strengthened and, sometimes, reversed. The condition of possibility or intelligibility of power is to be found not in some primary, central point, in a single source of sovereignty from which secondary forms emanate. Power is ubiquitous, not because it is able to assemble everything under its invincible unity, but because it is produced at every moment, at every point, or rather in every relation of one point with another.

> Power is everywhere: not because it embraces everything, but because it comes from everywhere. . . One should probably be a nominalist in this matter: power is not an institution, nor a structure, nor a possession. It is the name we give to a complex strategic situation in a particular society (vs, 123; HS, 93).

Power, then, is not something that can be acquired, seized, or shared. It is exercised from innumerable points, in a set of unequal, shifting relations. Power comes as much from below as from above. Power relations do not exist outside other types of relation (those found in economic processes, in the diffusion of knowledge, in sexual relations), but are immanent in them. They are the immediate effects of the divisions, inequalities, and imbalances to be found in them and, by a movement of return, the internal conditions of these differences. They do not belong to some superstructure, with a simple role of prohibition or mediation; they play a directly productive role. They are not governed by a total, binary opposition between dominators and dominated, which is then reproduced from top to bottom in ever smaller groupings, but are formed and operate in places of work, families, institutions, groups of all kinds, etc., and serve as the supports for the broad effects of division that run through the whole of society. These 'effects of division' form a general line of force that traverses local confrontations and links them together; in turn, the local confrontations reverberate back through the series thus created to effect new alignments, new convergences, new conflicts. The intelligibility of power relations is not to be found in terms of causality, of events at one level causing or explaining events at another, but rather in a series of aims and objectives. However, these are not attributable to an individual subject, not even to a ruling caste, but arise in an apparently anonymous way from the local situations in which they first appear. Where there is power, there is resistance, not in the sense of an external, contrary force, but by the very fact of its existence. Power relations depend on a multiplicity of points of resistance, which serve at once as adversary, target, support, foothold. Just as there is no centre of power, there is no centre of revolt, from which secondary rebellions derive, no unified class that is the seat of rebellion. There is a plurality of resistances, each a special case, distributed in an irregular way in time and space. Sometimes a broad series of resistances converges to bring about a major upheaval, a 'revolution', but, like power, and inextricably linked with it, resistance usually takes the form of innumerable, mobile, transitory points.

Our approach to the problem of the relations between sex and power should not, therefore, be dominated by a notion of the state structure and its needs. We must look for the most immediate, most local power relations at work in a particular type of discourse, that concerning, for example, the child's body, women's sexuality, birth control. We must examine how the power relations gave rise to such discourses and how the discourses have been used by them; what resistances the exercise of these power relations has given rise to and in what way these have altered their overall configuration; in what ways these power relations were linked together to form what seems like an overall strategy. Foucault proposes four principles or rules that guide the type of research he is undertaking.

(1) *Rule of immanence.* One cannot separate knowledge of sexuality and the power exercised within it. Sexuality does not belong to a free, disinterested branch of science upon which power imposes its economic or ideological requirements. Sexuality became an area accessible to knowledge when power relations established it as a possible object; equally, power was able to invest sexuality because certain techniques of knowledge, certain procedures of discourse, were able to penetrate it; this is to be seen not so much in terms of a dialectical process, in which the one has priority over the other, but rather as two aspects of a single process. We must begin with 'local centres' of power-knowledge.

(2) *Rule of continuous variations.* We must not treat the power at work in sexuality in terms of those who possess it (men, adults, parents, doctors) and those who are deprived of it (women, adolescents, children, patients), nor the knowledge of sexuality in terms of those who have a right to it and those kept in ignorance. Power-knowledge relations are not given forms of distribution, but 'matrices of transformation'.

(3) *Rule of double conditioning.* No 'local centre' of power-knowledge could function without a series of successive links based

on particular relations that converged to form an overall strategy. Conversely, no strategy could ensure overall effects that was not based on particular relations that provided it with points of application. This process should be seen, not in terms of different levels (microscopic, macroscopic), nor as a mere difference of scale, but rather as the double conditioning of a strategy by specific tactics and of tactics by an overall strategy. Thus the father is not the 'representative' of the state, nor the state a projection of the father on a different scale. The family does not reproduce society; society does not imitate the family. The family has, by its very specificity, served as a base for such overall strategies as the Malthusian policy of birth control, policies for encouraging population growth, the medicalization of sex and the pyschiatricization of its non-genital forms.

(4) *Rule of the tactical polyvalence of discourses*. Discourse follows the same principle of distribution as power and knowledge. It does not operate in a uniform, stable way; there is not an accepted discourse and an excluded discourse, a discourse of the dominant and a discourse of the dominated. It is made up of a multiplicity of elements that intersect in a complex, unstable way, as instruments and effects of power, but also as points of resistance. Discourse transmits, produces, and reinforces power; it also undermines, exposes and even blocks it. Similarly, an absence of discourse provides a site for both power and resistance to it.

In short, this new conception of power replaces law with objective, prohibition with tactics, sovereignty with a mobile multiplicity of power relations, from which overall but shifting strategies emerge. The model is military, rather than legal.

> And this not out of speculative choice or theoretical preference, but because it is one of the fundamental features of Western societies that the power relations, which for so long had found expression in war, in all forms of war, were gradually invested in the order of political power (vs, 135; hs, 102).

There is not, therefore, a single overall strategy, affecting in a uniform way all manifestations of sexuality throughout society. The view, for example, that society has reduced sex to its reproductive function and its adult, heterosexual form within the family cannot account for the multiplicity of objective and means implemented in sexual policies concerning the two sexes, different ages, and various social classes. Foucault elicits four great strategies that have emerged in Western society since the late eighteenth century. The *'hystericiza- tion' of the female body* is a process whereby the woman's body is seen as an organism saturated with sexuality, integrated into the field of medical practice, and linked to the social body, through the regula- tion of birth and the woman's role in the family as biological and moral guardian of her children. The Mother, with its negative image of the 'nervous woman', is the most visible form of this process. *The 'pedagogicization' of children's sexuality* is based on the assumption that all children indulge in sexual activity, or are likely to; that this activity is inappropriate, both 'natural' and 'unnatural', and therefore a source of danger, physical and moral, individual and social. Children are 'borderline' sexual beings. Parents, priests, teachers, doctors and, later, psychologists took charge of this dangerous and endangered sexuality. *A socialization of procreation* operated through policies designed to increase or decrease the birth rate. *A 'psychiatrization' of perverse pleasure*: all deviations from genital heterosexuality were catalogued and analysed as so many anomalies for which a corrective technology was developed and applied. But these strategies should not be conceived of in negative terms, as part of a struggle against sexuality, or of an effort to control it, but positively as a means of producing sexuality.

> Sexuality is the name that may be given to a set of interlocking historical mechanisms; not some reality below the surface on which it is difficult to get a hold, but a great surface network on which the stimulation of bodies, the intensification of pleasures, the incitement to discourse, the formation of sciences, the strength- ening of controls and resistances are linked together in accordance with a few great strategies of knowledge and power (vs, 139; hs, 105–6).

In every known society sexual relations have given rise to a *machin- ery of alliance*, a system governing marriages and kinship relations, the transfer of names and possessions. This machinery, with all its con- straints, has gradually declined in importance as economic processes and political structures called for other, more flexible instruments and supports. Since the late eighteenth century, Western societies have superimposed upon it another mechanism, a *machinery of sexuality*. It, too, operates upon the sexual partners, but in a quite different way. The machinery of alliance works through a system of rules prescribing the permitted and the forbidden; the machinery of sexuality uses mobile, polymorphous, contingent techniques of power. One of the functions of alliance is to reproduce a set of relations and maintain the law that governs them; sexuality engenders a permanent extension of the domains and forms of control. Alliance is clearly articulated upon the economy, owing to its role in the circulation of wealth; sexuality is linked to the economy by innumerable, subtle relays, but principally through the body, which produces and consumes. Alliance has a homeostatic function in society; hence its closeness to the legal system and, also, the importance it places on 'reproduction'. The function of sexuality, on the other hand, is not to reproduce but to proliferate, to invent, to annex, to penetrate bodies in an ever more detailed way and to control populations in an ever more extended way. The machinery of sexuality arose out of the machinery of alliance. Indeed, it is in the family, at the heart of the alliance machinery that the principal elements of the sexuality machinery have been developed (the female body, infantile sexuality, birth control and, to a lesser degree, the specification of perverts). The modern family must not be seen as a social, economic, and political structure of alliance that excludes or limits sexuality. On the contrary, it has provided sexuality with a permanent support. It has made possible the production of a sexuality quite different in nature from the alliance, while allowing the systems of alliance to be permeated by a whole new tactics of power.

The superimposition in the family of the sexuality machinery on the machinery of alliance explains a number of facts: that, since the eighteenth century, the family has become the place where above all others our strongest feelings of love and affection have arisen and been fostered. As a result, sexuality, too, is first expressed in the family: sex is born 'incestuous'. Of course, the incest prohibition has existed in most societies where the alliance machinery predominates; but in our own type of society, where the family is the most active site of sexuality, incest occupies a central place, constantly solicited and refused. If, for the last hundred years or so, the West has paid so much attention to the incest prohibition, seeing it as a necessary, universal step in the establishment of any culture, the reason, Foucault suggests, is that we found in this a means of defending

188

ourselves, not against incestuous desires, but against the extension of this machinery of sexuality, whose disadvantages—as well as advantages—are that it ignores the laws of alliance. By stressing the universality of this law of laws, we made sure that the sexuality machinery, whose strange effects, including the emotional intensification of family life, was beginning to be felt and exploited, was subjected, in the last resort, to the old system of alliance. If one declares that the incest prohibition is the threshold of all culture, sexuality is placed under the authority of law.

The process that has taken place in Western society may be summed up thus: the machinery of sexuality first developed on the fringe of the family (in the confessional and school), then became centred on the family itself, a more tightly organized, more intense family than earlier. Parents and spouses become the principal agents within the family of a sexuality machinery which, outside it, rests on doctors, teachers and, later, psychiatrists and which, within it, leads to the 'psychologization' or 'psychiatrization' of relations of alliance with a cast of new characters, the nervous woman, the frigid wife, the indifferent mother or the mother besieged by murderous obsessions, the impotent, sadistic, or perverse husband, the hysterical or neurasthenic daughter, the precocious, listless child, the young homosexual who rejects marriage or who neglects his wife. These are the mixed figures of a deviant alliance and an abnormal sexuality; they bring the disorder of the second into the order of the first, while ensuring the authority of the first over the second.

It was in this area that psychoanalysis came to birth. Much of the initial hostility directed at psychoanalysis may be attributed to the fact that it refused to take the part of the patient's spouse or family, to accept their interpretation of events, to carry out their instructions. Instead, it carried to its limit a practice established by such psychiatrists as Charcot of treating the patient's sexuality in confidence, depriving the family of information about it. Furthermore, in its analysis of that sexuality, which it approached directly without benefit of the neurological model, it brought into question the patient's family relationships. In this way, psychoanalysis, which seemed to place the avowal of sexuality outside the sovereignty of the family, rediscovered at the very heart of this sexuality, as the principle of its formation and the key to its interpretation, the old law of alliance, of marriage, kinship, and incest. Thus at the precise moment when the machinery of sexuality seemed to be effacing the alliance machinery, it was brought back in a new, but no less secure way, under the old jurisdiction. Sexuality could hardly seem to be alien to the law when it was constituted by it. The machinery of sexuality grew out of the machinery of alliance, but far from superseding it, it is now its principal guarantee of survival.

In a chapter devoted to the history of the sexuality machinery Foucault returns to his attack on the 'repressive' theory. He points out that if the purpose of sexual repression was a more intensive use of the labour force, one would expect that the machinery of repression would have been directed above all at the working class, in particular the young, adult male. In fact, the contrary was the case. The most rigorous techniques, from the examination of conscience to psychoanalysis, were applied to the more economically privileged and politically powerful.

> The bourgeoisie began by considering that its own sex was something important, a fragile treasure, a secret that had to be discovered at all costs. It should not be forgotten that the first figure to be invested by the machinery of sexuality, one of the first to be 'sexualized', was the 'idle' woman. She inhabited the fringes of 'society', in which she always had to appear as a value, and of the family, where she was assigned a new set of marital and parental obligations. Thus there emerged the 'nervous' woman, the woman afflicted with 'vapours'; in this figure, the hystericization of women found its anchorage point. As for the adolescent wasting his future substance in secret pleasures, the onanistic child who was of such concern to doctors and teachers from the end of the eighteenth century to the end of the nineteenth, this was not the child of the people, the future worker who had to be taught the disciplines of the body, but rather the schoolboy, the child surrounded by servants, tutors and governesses, who was in danger of compromising not so much his physical strength as his intellectual capacity, his moral duties and his obligation to preserve a healthy line of descent for his family and his social class (vs, 159–60; hs, 120–1).

When the religious authorities, in the Catholic and especially in the Protestant countries, with the Evangelicals and Methodists, spread this 'moralizing' concern to wider sections of the population it was in a much simplified form. It was, in its origin and in its fullest expression, a mechanism that the bourgeoisie applied above all to itself. Was it, then, a new form of that puritan asceticism that historians have linked with the Reformation and the rise of capitalism? What is involved is certainly not a renunciation of pleasure nor a rejection of the flesh, but, on the contrary, an intensification of the body, a concern for health, a desire to increase vitality. It suggests the self-affirmation of a class, rather than the enslavement of another. What is at work, Foucault suggests, is an attempt by the bourgeoisie to find its own way of distinguishing itself. The aristocracy had done this through the notion of 'blood', of alliances between ancient lineages. The bourgeoisie's 'blood' was its sexuality. The nineteenth-century bourgeoisie became obsessed with biological, medical, eugenic doctrines of all kinds. Genealogy became important, not for its age, name, or title, but for its health, its freedom from any taint of mental instability, physical disability, paralysis, consumption, venereal disease, or immoral living. The value placed on the body and its sexuality was bound up with the establishment in society of bourgeois hegemony. By the end of the century and the beginning of our own, many of these preoccupations had taken on the 'racist' overtones that we recognize so clearly today. As the bourgeoisie was able to identify its fortunes more and more with the nation state, its concern with its own inherited and carefully preserved health was extended to the national 'races'.

What we are witnessing here is what Foucault calls the 'entry of life into history', that is, the entry of phenomena proper to the life of the human species into the order of knowledge and power. For the first time in history biology is reflected in politics: it is no longer simply a question of biological events—epidemics or famines—affecting social life, but for the first time life has come under the partial control of knowledge and the intervention of power.

> For thousands of years man remained what he was for Aristotle: a living animal who was more and more capable of a political existence; modern man is an animal in whose politics his life as a living being is in question (vs, 188; hs, 143).

Previously, the relation between life and politics had been conceived not in biological, but in legal terms. The sovereign enjoyed the right of life and death over his subjects. In this form of society, power operated essentially by deduction: the right to appropriate a proportion of the subject's wealth, produce, goods, services, labour, blood. In the final analysis, power could deprive of life. Since the seventeenth century, this mode of deduction played a less dominant role in the exercise of power. Other functions—incitement, reinforcement, control, surveillance, organization—increased in importance. Death, which had been based on the sovereign's right to defend himself and be defended, became the reverse side of the right of society as a whole to maintain and develop its livelihood.

> Yet never have wars been more bloody than those waged since the nineteenth century. . . never have régimes involved their own populations in such holocausts. But this formidable power of death. . . now presents itself as the counterpart of power that acts positively upon life, which undertakes to administer it, to increase it, to multiply it, to exert over it precise controls and general regulations. Wars are no longer waged in the name of a sovereign who must be defended; they are waged on behalf of the existence of all; whole populations are incited to kill one another in the name of their need to live. Massacres have become vital. . . But the existence in question is no longer the juridical existence of sovereignty; it is the biological existence of a population (vs, 179–80; hs, 136–7).

Since the seventeenth century this new form of power over life has operated in two principal ways. In the first, the body has been treated like a machine, its capacities extended, its performance improved, its power extracted. The increase of its utility and docility, its integration into efficient, economical systems of control, were ensured by the disciplines described at length in *Surveiller et punir*. What resulted was a political anatomy of the human body. The second, which developed about a century later, about the mid-eighteenth century, was centred on the body as species, as a living organism subject to such biologico-environmental factors as birth- and death-rates, health levels, life expectancies. These factors were operated by a series of regulatory controls: a bio-politics of the population. The disciplines of the body and the regulations of the population are the two poles of the organization of power over life. This two-sided technology—anatomical and biological—characterizes a power whose main function was not to inhibit vital functions or to kill, but to penetrate life in an ever more thorough manner. The law, with its ultimate weapon of death, receded in favour of the norm, whose task was to ensure the continuous, regulated functioning of the mechanisms of life. Rather than a division between loyal subjects and enemies of the sovereign, the norm effects a graduated, measuring, hierarchizing system of distributed power-knowledge. A normalizing society is the historical effect of a technology of power centred on the body as mechanism and organism. Hence the importance assumed by sex as a political issue. It forms a hinge between the two axes of the political technology of life: the disciplines of the body and the regulation of populations. It gives rise to minute surveillances, unceasing controls, meticulous spatial arrangements, endless medical and psychological examinations—a whole micro-power over the body. But it also gives rise to measures on a massive scale, statistical calculations, interventions in societies as a whole. Sex provides access both to the life of the body and to the life of the species.

Through these new procedures of power, developed in the eighteenth and expanded in the nineteenth century, our societies moved from what Foucault calls a 'symbolics of blood' to an 'analytics of sexuality': from law, death, transgression, sovereignty to norm, life, knowledge, the disciplines and regulations. The one has not, of course, entirely superseded the other. Foucault makes an interesting analysis of racism and psychoanalysis as two examples, at opposite extremes, of the reappearance of the 'symbolics of blood' in the 'analytics of sexuality'. In its modern 'biologizing', statist form, racism has made full use both of overall policies of social regulation and of the micro-policies of corporal discipline available to modern societies, but it has done so with a view to justifying some mythical concern for the purity of the nation's blood and the triumph of the race. Nazism was possibly the most naive and, by that very fact, the most cunning combination of phantasies about the blood and the paroxisms of a disciplinary power (vs, 197; HS, 149). At the opposite extreme, though exactly contemporary with the modern racialisms, psychoanalysis may be seen as a theoretical attempt to bring sexuality back under the system of law, sovereignty, and the symbolic order. By basing one of its most fundamental concepts— the Oedipus complex—on the law of alliance, the incest prohibition, and the Father-Sovereign, psychoanalysis is essentially backward-looking. 'The sexuality machinery must be conceived in terms of techniques of power that are contemporary with it' (vs, 198; HS, 150).

Finally, in response to an imaginary question, Foucault poses the problem of the relative positions to be accorded the notions of sexuality, which he has examined at length, and sex, of which he has said little. The reason for this, says Foucault, is that sex, as such, as a real, unitary entity corresponding to the definitions proposed for it in discourse, does not exist. Far from being the initial reality from which sexuality derives as a secondary effect, the reverse is the case. Sex is really no more than 'an ideal point made necessary by the machinery of sexuality and its functioning'. It is this machinery that has produced a 'theory of sex'—a theory that carries out a number of functions on behalf of the machinery of sexuality. First, it has made it possible to group together under an artificial unity anatomical elements, biological functions, modes of behaviour, sensations, pleasures and allowed this fictional unity to function as causal principle, ubiquitous meaning, secret to be discovered, or, to use linguistic terms, 'a single signifier and a universal signified'. Second, by presenting itself in this unitary way as both anatomy and lack, function and latency, instinct and meaning, it has linked a knowledge of human sexuality to the biological knowledge of reproduction. Third, this unitary notion of 'sex' has reduced the real, multiple, heterogeneous nature of sexuality and thus concealed its true relation of total confrontation with an equally single, universal conception of power and law.

> A history of sexuality should not, therefore, be referred to sex as if to a higher authority. Rather we must show how 'sex' is historically dependent on sexuality. We must not place sex on the side of reality and sexuality on the side of confused ideas and illusions. Sexuality is a very real historical figure; it is what gave rise to the notion of sex, as a speculative element necessary to its own functioning. We must not think that by saying yes to sex, we are saying no to power; on the contrary, we are following a course laid down by the general machinery of sexuality. It is from the notion of sex that we must free ourselves if, by a tactical reversal of the various mechanisms of sexuality, we wish to counter the grip of power with bodies, pleasures, skills, in their multiplicity and capacity for resistance. Against the machinery of sexuality the strong point of the counter-attack should not be sex-desire, but the body and its pleasures (vs, 206–8; hs, 157).

◇

Conclusion

This is no time for conclusions. It is curious enough to write about an author who could well produce more books than he has already done, without drawing conclusions about his *oeuvre*. Perhaps this book should be published in instalments, a new chapter despatched to subscribers as each new Foucault appears. In this way it could pursue its own provisional, parallel, parasitic existence. But Foucault is resistant to conclusions for another reason: his unpredictability. With each book he never fails to astonish. A conclusion, then, only because this book must end here; and, if end it must have, it cannot but be open-ended.

Foucault begins where all truly original minds begin, in the present. Such minds are not ahead of their times; it is the rest of us who are dragging our feet. His passion is to seek out the new, that which is coming to birth in the present—a present that most of us are unable to see because we see it through the eyes of the past, or through the eyes of a 'future' that is a projection of the past, which amounts to the same thing. Foucault's interest in the past is guided by that passion: there is nothing of the antiquarian about it. 'Why am I writing this history of the prison?', he asks in *Surveiller et punir*. 'Simply because I am interested in the past? No, if one means by that writing a history of the past in terms of the present. Yes, if one means writing the history of the present' (SP, 35; DP, 31). This is the key to the coherence of all Foucault's work since 1961—*Maladie mentale et personnalité* of 1954 being a false start, in approach if not in area. It also explains Foucault's early rejection of an academic career in philosophy, his exile and his silence. When *Histoire de la folie* was published in 1961, Foucault was thirty-five. He could already have been the respected author of three or four works of philosophy. He chose silence until such time as he could hear the voice of the present.

During that period of waiting Foucault sensed that Western civilization was undergoing one of its periodic mutations. Years later, in the Preface to *Les mots et les choses* Foucault wrote:

> In attempting to uncover the deepest strata of Western culture, I am restoring to our silent and apparently immobile soil its rifts, its instability, its flaws; and it is the same ground that is once more stirring under our feet (MC, 16; OT, xxiv).

Shortly afterwards, in an interview, Foucault even placed a date on it. The interviewer had just pointed out that when Foucault's attention moved from the Classical period to the nineteenth century there was a distinct change of tone. Foucault's reply is illuminating.

> When one is dealing with the Classical period, one has only to describe it. When it comes to the modern period, however, which began about 1790–1810 and *lasted until 1950* [my italics], the problem is to free oneself from it. The apparently polemical character derives from the fact that one has to dig out a whole mass of discourse that has accumulated under one's feet. One may uncover with gentle movements the latent configurations of earlier periods; but when it is a matter of determining the system of discourse on which we are still living, when we have to question the words that are still echoing in our ears, which become confused with those we are trying to formulate, the archaeologist, like the Nietzschean philosopher, is forced to take a hammer to it (B4, 206).

Just as the epistemic configurations of the Classical period were inaccessible to analysis until they began to crumble and others to emerge, 'about 1790–1810', so we have been unable to question our own epistemic presuppositions until very recently indeed, 'until 1950'. (The actual date should not concern us too much: it is mentioned in the context of an unprepared interview and Foucault never refers to it again. Perhaps it owes something to symmetry—the Classical period also lasted about a century and a half.) What is important is that it coincides with Foucault's working life; that his life's work has been an attempt to catch what the present was telling him over the din of the past still echoing in his ears.

Such a postion bears a superficial resemblance to that of the dominant philosophical movement of his youth. What may broadly be termed 'existentialism' and 'phenomenology' had a similar commitment to the present, a similar desire to escape the tyranny of history and the past. But the resemblance ends there. Existentialism sought to escape a restrictive ethical inheritance in the free 'authentic' exercise of individual choice. Phenomenology placed acquired knowledge 'in parenthesis' and tried to return to a pure, unprejudiced apprehension of the world by the individual consciousness. Both were philosophies of the subject, while rejecting a unitary notion of 'man'. For a French philosophy student of the late 1940s and early 1950s the only other system of thought with any pretension of speaking to present realities was Marxism, at the time almost exclusively in the hands of doctrinaire Communist Party ideologues. Most French intellectuals of the time managed to combine a general theoretical allegiance to existentialism/phenomenology, which precluded full acceptance of Marxism, with tacit support, in practice, of the Party. By the mid-fifties, Foucault had outgrown this particular combination of options; he had not yet worked out a coherent alternative. In 1954, Foucault left Paris for Sweden.

The impasse that afflicted Foucault at this time was shared by a number of French left-wing intellectuals. In the next few years it was to affect the entire French Left. In post-war French intellectual life two years stand out as major turning-points. The second, which I have referred to more than once in connection with Foucault, was, of course, 1968. The first was 1956. That year saw the scandalous revelations of Khruschev's 'secret report', to the Twentieth Congress of the Soviet Party; the election of a new centre-left government in France, which, with the support of the CP, stepped up military action against the Algerian 'rebels' and, then, engineered the Anglo-French attack on Egypt; the Soviet invasion of Hungary and the forcible establishment there of a subservient régime, which also gained the support of the CP. In the next few years, the Communists toed the 'patriotic' line on the Algerian question, while remaining more 'Stalinist' than perhaps any other Communist Party in the world. Membership of the Party dropped dramatically, especially among intellectuals. Many of those who remained formed a kind of internal opposition, demanding that democratic centralism be democratic as well as centralist, the creative application of Marxism as an analytical tool rather than its imposition as a body of doctrine, a consistently revolutionary policy rather than an opportunistic dependence on short-term tactics. These modest enough demands were not, of course, implemented. They were not even permitted as a matter for discussion. Their promulgation brought expulsion—and the Party suffered further defections. Meanwhile the atrocities of the Stalin era were dismissed as unfortunate effects of 'the cult of the personality of the general secretary' or 'violations of socialist legality'. In other words they were the result of human error or weakness—ultimately *moral* failings. No serious attempt was made to account for them in *historical* terms. Marxism, apparently, found it easier to analyse capitalist societies than 'socialist' ones—with good reason. The accession of de Gaulle, with the political stability and economic advance that followed, still further reduced the support given to the CP by electorate and intellectuals alike.

During the late fifties and early sixties this ever-widening disillusion with politics was also accompanied, among intellectuals, by what can only be called a flight from history. In the opinion-forming centres of Parisian academic life, pre-eminently in the École Normale Supérieure, new voices were being heard. Some of these—Lacan, Lévi-Strauss—were relatively old voices, but they were now gaining an audience well beyond the confines of their disciplines. Not, of course, that one can attribute 'a flight from history' to these voices themselves, let alone a concerted polemic against history. There was no reason, for example, why Lacan, a psychoanalyst, should concern himself with history at all. Lévi-Strauss, though studying social forms, was concerned, as an ethnologist, with societies unaffected by history in the European sense. The 'flight from history' is to be attributed to their audiences: to the fact that students, whose thinking had previously been dominated by certain political and historical notions, were flocking, in unprecedented numbers, to lectures in subjects that could not properly be concerned with history, but which nevertheless seemed to propose important truths about human life.

What was new about this movement away from history was that, unlike existentialism and phenomenology, it did not return to the *subject* as ground of its validity. This, in the case of a psychoanalyst at least, may seem paradoxical. But the philosophical concept of the subject must not be confused with the psychological concept of the psyche or the biological concept of the individual. What Lacan did, it

Conclusion

might be said, was to take the Freudian concept of the psyche and show that it cannot be assimilated to the philosophical notion of a unitary, founding subject. The ego was all too readily identified as the true centre of the psyche, as a kind of knowing responsible subject. Lacan showed that, on the contrary, the ego could be seen as a kind of convenient illusion, an 'imaginary' construct, composed of projections and introjections. All three Freudian topographies—the divisions between conscious and unconscious, between id, ego, and super-ego, and between Eros and Thanatos, the life drives and the death drives—were not so much expressions of the contrary forces within a unitary psyche as an indication of a deeply riven psyche, a psyche without unity or centre. The most important fact about man's psychical life was that what *seemed* most peculiarly his own was illusory and that what was most real about it was not his, but Other, alien to his conscious self. None of this is inconsistent with Freud's own teaching, though, until Lacan, most post-Freud psychoanalysis tended, especially in America, to move in the opposite direction, to so-called 'ego psychology', to the analysis, not so much of unconscious motivation, as of the ego, the inter-personal relations that the individual forged in social life. Lacan's return to the unconscious as the heart of Freudian doctrine was facilitated by his introduction of linguistic concepts—though, even here, there were sound Freudian precedents, in *The Interpretation of Dreams* and the hitherto little noticed *Jokes and their Relation to the Unconscious*.

Structural linguistics begins with a realization that languages are systems that operate more or less independently of their expressive or representational function. A sentence expressive of a desire is not a perfect, original copy of that desire. All its elements, words, may be used by any of the users of the language to which they belong. They are not the exclusive possession of the speaker; their range of meanings is circumscribed by shared usage. Were this not so, of course, language would lose its primary function of communication. Moreover, the rules that govern the ways in which these elements may be combined are far more rigid than speakers usually realize and go well beyond the more obvious rules of grammar—well beyond, indeed, the requirements of communication. We can understand children and foreigners even when they use our language ungrammatically. Languages operate autonomously; but they also operate arbitrarily. Sentence structure does not reflect any prior structure in thought: the same meaning is expressed in a different order of words in different languages. Moreover, except in rare cases of onomatopoeia, there is no necessary connection between the sound of a word and the object it represents. Nor do the objects of the world have a self-evident identity or individuality outside the words that denote them. Even in closely related languages, words in one language often do not correspond exactly to words in another. Saussure stressed this arbitrary nature of language, its separation from things, by restoring the old notion of words as signs. The sign consisted of a signifier, the sound or printed letters that signified the sign, and a signified, the concept that it signified. The object represented by the sign he called the 'referent', which lay outside the linguist's area of concern. In the 1930s, Roman Jakobson and the 'Prague Circle' extended Saussure's theories, applying them in particular to folk tales and works of literature. Jakobson revived the old rhetorical system of tropes or figures of speech, laying particular stress on metaphor (one thing standing for another) and metonymy (the part standing for the whole).

From Saussure Lacan took the concept of the linguistic sign and from Jakobson the use of metaphor and metonymy, assimilating the first to Freud's 'condensation' and the second to 'displacement'. Not only could dreams be analysed like works of literature, the unconscious itself was 'structured like a language'. The world did not enter the unconscious directly, or in images, but through language, through signifiers, which usually had no more than an arbitrary relation to their referents, to the real objects. Dreams were often an elaborate form of punning. The human subject was a linguistic construct, alienated at its very source because, not only did the language that made it up come from outside itself and could not, therefore, be an adequate expression of its desire, but language was the bearer of society's prohibitions, of the super-ego, and was therefore a bar to the subject's desire. About the same time, Lévi-Strauss, who had met Jakobson in America during World War II, was introducing linguistic concepts into social anthropology. As early as 1949, he laid out many of the principles that were to become, fifteen or twenty years later, the stock-in-trade of Structuralism. One of his most famous statements is also one of his earliest: 'any culture may be looked upon as an ensemble of symbolic systems, in the front rank of which are to be found language, marriage, laws, economic relations, art, science and religion' (*Les Structures élémentaires de la parenté*, Paris, 1949—trans-

Conclusion

lated, *twenty years later* as *The Elementary Structures of Kinship*, 1969).
Significantly, language is placed first in the 'front rank' and the
rest—*even economic relations*—are analysed as linguistic systems.
Barthes, whose earliest concern was to take up Brecht's attack on the
Soviet cultural doctrine of Socialist Realism and produce a Marxist
defence of modernism in art, soon began to incorporate linguistic
concepts into his work—directly from the linguists themselves and,
later, in their transformed Lacanian version.

In this period of practical and theoretical doldrums for the CP, a
Communist philosopher, Louis Althusser, set about a major rethink-
ing of Marxist theory. It is important to stress that Althusser is a
philosopher, not a historian or economist. His output has been relatively small and devoted to a very narrow area: the analysis of Marxist
theory, solely in terms of what he sees as its philosophical, *scientific*,
validity. History and the real world are almost totally absent from his
pages: they are peopled entirely by concepts, the old terms of Marxism (infrastructure, superstructure, mode of production, relations of
production, contradiction, state apparatus, etc), jostling side by side
with a whole set of terms imported from Freud (overdetermination,
condensation, displacement, denegation, fetishism) and neologisms
(decentred structure, structure in dominance, dislocation). Perhaps
Althusser's most significant contribution to Marxist theory was the
use of the concept of an 'epistemological break', a term used earlier in
the history of science by Gaston Bachelard and Georges Canguilhem.
It indicated the point at which a body of theory throws off the
'ideological' distortions of its pre-history and becomes truly scientific.
In particular, Althusser applied this break to Marx's own works, thus
stressing a discontinuity between the 'young' and the 'mature' Marx.
Althusser's work was the most daring reformulation of Marxist
theory, from within the Party, since Gramsci (whose originality
owed much to his isolation from Party colleagues in the safe custody
of a Fascist prison cell). Arguably, one would have to go much further
back for precedents. For it was one thing for the unquestioned leaders
of states and parties (Lenin, Mao) to make major redefinitions of
theory; it was quite another for an ordinary Party member, with no
official status in the Party apparatus, to do so. Not, of course, that his
activity would have been tolerated in any of the 'socialist' states, then
or now, and his relations with the French party have always been
strained. There are no doubt many reasons why those relations have

not so far reached the point of resignation or expulsion. On Althusser's part, there is no doubt a personal commitment, an emotional investment, that is impregnable to intellectual persuasion, but, on the intellectual level alone, Althusser's position would become meaningless and irrelevant, in its own terms, outside the Party. For Althusser is a convinced Leninist; for him there can be no questioning of the role of the Party, leading and directing the revolutionary struggle. Indeed, his theoretical enterprise had two practical aims: to recall the Party leadership to the true Leninist middle way, away from what many saw as its right-wing deviation, and to undermine the attraction, especially for the young, of that 'left-wing Communism' characterized by the Father of the Revolution as an 'infantile disorder'. (Though what, those disorderly children might ask, is a Revolution doing with a father?) The Party's toleration of Althusser is no less complicated. Althusser's loyalty was such that he never made any public criticism of the Party or the Soviet Union. He has rarely stepped outside his theoretical activity, and that activity has been carried out at such an exalted level of abstraction that only Althusserians are capable of practising it. Certainly no Party ideologist could compete with Althusser on his home ground. The Party chose therefore to ignore him. But attacks were made, often from behind the scenes. Althusser has always been ready to accept criticism and, if necessary, to 'rectify' his 'errors'. At one stage he condemned his earlier work as 'theoreticist'. Yet his influence, radiating outwards from the École Normale Supérieure, has been immense. For a whole generation of France's most gifted teachers, a knowledge of Marxism has been an indispensable part of their intellectual equipment. Althusser has done for Marxism what Lacan did for psychoanalysis at about the same time in the same place. Indeed, it would not be an exaggeration to say that the new toleration of psychoanalysis by Marxists and the formation of what can only be called Freudo-Marxism owe their existence to relations of mutual respect established by these two men and their followers in and around the École Normale.

Given the cross-fertilization that had been taking place between the work of Lévi-Strauss, Barthes, Lacan, and Althusser; their common 'anti-humanism', 'anti-subjectivism', and 'anti-historicism'; their shared conviction of the scientificity of their work; the crucial role played by structural linguistics in the work of all of them except Althusser; the sudden upsurge of interest in linguistics itself—given

Conclusion

all this, it was only a matter of time before rumours were spreading of a new movement known as Structuralism. Structuralism is the extension of the linguistic model to other areas than language. It approaches its object—a myth, a work of literature, a social system—with an initial act of isolation. Such questions as the intentions of a creative subject, the functional origins of a system, the effects of external factors on the object, or of the object on its environment are set aside as irrelevant. The isolated object is then analysed in terms of a 'combinatory', that is, a system of relations between elements in which it is the relations, rather than the elements, that are significant. In its pure form Structuralism did little more than that, but many soon came to realize the limitations of such a method. The 'world', even 'history', could be smuggled back into the sealed-off system by expanding analysis into interpretation. The interpretative concepts used were usually psychoanalytical, sometimes Marxist, or both. The structure formed, like a dream, a manifest content, which concealed a latent content. It was not permitted to use a work of literature to psychoanalyse its author, but it was quite permissible—in some quarters obligatory—to psychoanalyse the work itself. Before long, everything from dreams to advertisements, from novels to women's fashions, from cities to restaurant menus was being subjected to structural analysis. Everything was a sign; everything was in metaphoric or metonymic relation with something else. Linguistics was a *science*, because language was a sign system that existed independently of individual utterances. Individual utterances should, therefore, be analysed, not, in terms of meaning or expression, but as exempla of that system. Other sign systems—and everything under the sun belonged to some sign system—could be studied in the same way. Semiology, the science of sign-systems, was launched. What 'Structuralism' represented in short, was a simultaneous rejection, in the name of science, of the two earlier antagonistic philosophies based respectively on the subject and on history.

Meanwhile, Sartre was pursuing an exactly reverse course. Not only through his major philosophical work, *L'Être et le Néant (Being and Nothingness)*, but also through plays, novels, essays, and journalism, Sartre had become, in the late 1940s, the unchallenged leader of French intellectual life. Sartrean existentialism, with its more refined sister philosophy, phenomenology, dominated the thinking of the French intelligentsia. Sartre was probably more responsible than anyone for preventing widespread adherence to Marxism among intellectuals, despite their broad support of the CP as the Party of the Working Class. Then, by the mid-1950s, Sartre had come to believe that what he saw as the philosophically untenable nature of certain Marxist formulations had blinded him to the fundamental correctness of the Marxist interpretation of history. In his monumental—and uncompleted—*Critique de la Raison dialectique*, he set out to restate historical materialism in terms of his own philosophical position: history and the subject. Yet when this work was published in 1960, it was regarded by most of its potential audience as an indigestible anachronism. The French intelligentsia was not interested in a marriage between existentialism and Marxism: it had moved on to quite different concerns. Not surprisingly, Sartre became one of the bitterest opponents of the new Structuralism.

By the early 1960s, then, the pattern of intellectual allegiances in France was beginning to look something like this. Sartre had taken the previously antagonistic positions and fused them into a new synthesis. Structuralism had emerged out of a rejection of both positions. Within the broad Structuralist umbrella, Lévi-Strauss represented its purest expression. With the introduction of linguistic concepts Lacan had moved towards it and away from his earlier interest in Heidegger, Husserl, and Sartre. Althusser, as a Marxist, remained, of course, on the side of history, but it was a singularly generalized, disembodied history, one in which 'structures' seemed to be of more interest than 'events'. Further along that line, now much closer to Structuralism than Marxism, stood Barthes. But—and this is the whole point of this brief, necessarily schematic digression into French intellectual history—where does Foucault stand in all this? Like the Structuralists he rejected both the philosophy of the subject and a history based on such notions as causality, contradiction, teleology—which was why he was taken to be one of them and found such difficulty in extricating himself from their embrace. But, equally, he rejected the form that the Structuralists' rejection took. They had rejected nineteenth-century subjectivism and historicism only to fall back into a nineteenth-century scientism of Truth and Objectivity. However, at this point in time, we are speaking of the author of *Les mots et les choses*. For the Foucault writing *Histoire de la folie* in the late fifties, the situation was not yet so clear. 'Structuralism' had not yet emerged as a movement: it was not yet something one felt impelled

Conclusion

either to accept or to reject. At this time, no doubt, Foucault felt varying degrees of sympathy for the figures who were later to emerge at the head of this journalists' invention. But the problems that exercised his mind at this time were not ones to which their work had any particular relevance. If philosophy and that all too human science, psychology, had failed to provide a ground in which he could begin to answer the questions that they had aroused in him, the reason might be more than a personal impasse. That impasse—that sense of a widening gap between the apprehension of the present and the truth that they promised—might be symptomatic of what he later came to call an epistemic mutation. Foucault was in a position analogous with that of thinkers living around, say, 1650 or 1800. Philosophy and psychology did not possess truth because they possessed a history. The search for their origins led him, as we have seen, to a common source, the establishment of reason as sole, undisputed ruler of the mind. The way forward, as I suggested in my Introduction, was to go back. This meant a return to history. It would, of course, have to be a new kind of history. But how was such a history to be conducted? Nietzsche living at the end of German Idealist philosophy and in the immediate wake of Hegel, had faced a similar problem: his answer had been a new *wirkliche Historie*, which he called genealogy. It was not a question of history taking over 'the legislative and critical power of philosophy' as a certain nineteenth-century historicism had attempted to do. The history he envisaged would play the role of a kind of 'internal ethnology of our culture and our rationality' (B4, 205).

It would ill behove an analyst of Foucault's thought to impose on the succession of his books any such notions as causal development, underlying unity, common origin. On the other hand, Foucault is not, despite the latest edition of the Petit Larousse, 'author of a philosophy of history based on discontinuity'. One's task is to recognize coherences and differences where they occur. The coherence of Foucault's works does not extend to a Foucault 'system'. This is why, if one is to write about his work at all, one can only do so chronologically, taking each book in turn. In a sense, each book arrives as a fresh start in a new world: methodology has to be adapted, new concepts forged. I have respected this elementary periodization in my chapter divisions. I have also recognized something of a mutation in Foucault's work in my broader division of the book into two parts.

But, above all, the deepest discontinuity occurs with *Histoire de la folie*, not only in relation to whatever Foucault had written previously, but also in relation to his own period. This book constitutes the first, essential stage in a radically new analysis of Western civilization since the Renaissance. Foucault's philosophical quest led him to psychology, the science of the mind, which led him to madness, the limit of the mind, which led him in turn to reason, to the will to knowledge and truth. To put it crudely—something Foucault himself never does —modern rationalism and science have the same ignoble origins as the lunatic asylum. *Histoire de la folie*, is, of course, a long detailed account of the changes that have occurred in Western Europe's view and treatment of insanity over a period of some three hundred years. But it is also, inseparably linked with this, the genealogy and therefore a relativization, an ethnology, of Western Reason, Knowledge, and Truth. Yet, astonishingly, or perhaps one should say significantly, this second aspect was largely ignored during the first few years of the book's life. Those who welcomed the book were usually engaged in literary or artistic activities, those with a more subtle, if confused, notion of 'truth'. The self-confident guardians of truth—academic historians, philosophers, sociologists, psychiatrists—remained silent. The book was ignored by the more or less Marxist journals. How could a work concerned with an experience that lay beyond the limits of reason, outside the productive processes of society, be of interest to them? In England, or rather in one small, untypical part of it, the book was received enthusiastically. Two as yet little known psychotherapists, R. D. Laing and David Cooper, knew exactly, from their own experience, what Foucault was talking about. At a theoretical level, too, it had a lasting effect on the two men. It enabled them to move away from the Sartrean existentialist psychology within which they had been striving to formulate the fruits of that experience. Laing published the English translation, *Madness and Civilization*, in his series 'Studies in Existentialism and Phenomenology'—no doubt to Foucault's mingled gratification and amusement—and Cooper provided an introduction. As the reputations of Laing and Cooper grew in the late 1960s the effect of their work began to be felt in France: a new 'movement', 'anti-psychiatry', was born. By this time *Histoire de la folie* was being given a great deal more attention than ever before. Foucault regularly received abusive letters from members of the psychiatric profession and, in 1969, a group of 'distinguished' psychiatrists met in Toulouse to sit in judgement on him. Foucault, it was said, not only questioned the methods, the intentions, and the object of psychiatry, he was committing 'psychiatricide'; he was criticized for using the 'vulgar', 'inaccurate' term 'madness', rather than the correct categories of 'mental disorder'; Foucault's description of madness as an *'absence d'oeuvre'* was accused of being too 'nihilistic'; Foucault was attacked for making no reference to the vast literature of psychiatry and for ignoring 'recent improvements' in the treatment of the mentally disturbed (Foucault's account ends in the first decade of the nineteenth century). Some gentler voices suggested that, in spite of all its faults, Foucault's work was a 'salutary' reminder of the often unsavoury pre-history of their science. Such responses are not what one expects of 'men of science'; they are more reminiscent of those of mid-nineteenth-century churchmen to *The Origin of the Species*. They, too, saw the revelation of origins as a threat.

> It is essential to the possibility of a positive science of man that there should be, at its most distant point, that region of madness in which and from which human existence falls into objectivity. In its essential enigma, madness lies awake, forever promised to some form of knowledge that will encompass it entirely, but forever eluding capture since it is madness itself that originally gave objective knowledge a hold on man. The possibility for man of being mad and the possibility of being an object were joined together at the end of the eighteenth century, and this encounter gave birth at one and the same time (it is not a case of coincidence here) to the postulates of positive psychiatry and to the themes of an objective science of man. . . Positivism was not only a theoretical project, but the stigmatum of alienated existence. The status of object will be imposed from the outset on any individual recognized as insane; insanity will be inscribed as a secret truth at the heart of all objective knowledge of man (HF, 482).

Histoire de la folie is not simply the first volume in Foucault's archaeology of Western culture, in the sense that it might just as easily have been the second or third. Nor has it been superseded by a later, more developed theory. It provides the very foundations of Foucault's whole enterprise: the writing of the later books is inconceivable except by the author of *Histoire de la folie*. Similarly, the full extent of the book's originality can really only be measured retrospectively, in the light of the later work. It is quite clear, for example at so many points in the book, that Foucault knew exactly what his future achievement was to be. One can sense the exhilaration and trepidation in the first Preface. One can only guess at what the writing must have cost him, yet this study was to be only the first, 'and no doubt easiest', of a long investigation carried out 'under the sun of Nietzsche's great search'.

Nietzsche may have provided the inspiration; he could not provide what is nowadays called the 'methodology'. There was no discipline, with its institutions, journals, internal controversies, conceptual apparatus, methods of work, within which Foucault could carry out the task he had set himself. Indeed, there was a sense in which, like Nietzsche's, his work would have to be carried on outside, even against, the existing academic frameworks. Not only would he have to create his own mode of analysis, his own operational concepts, even his own vocabulary; he would also have to create his own audience. His books would have to be addressed to the general educated public; it was a public of a kind that existed nowhere else in the world, but unlike a few thousand specialized students it was not a captive one. Foucault did conquer that audience and, through it, in the less rigid period after 1968, he was to win his academic audience as well. But before his election to the Collège de France, his writing and his teaching were quite separate activities; one did not deliver sections of *Histoire de la folie* or *Les mots et les choses* in a philosophy lecture hall. If his books could be classified as anything it was as 'history of ideas', but no such academic discipline existed in France at the time. In any case, that amorphous hold-all was shot through with all the theoretical preconceptions that he was striving to escape from. There were historians in France, those associated with the *Annales* journal, who shared his distaste for that kind of history. But their example was little help in the areas in which he wished to work: for one thing, their research tended to be concentrated on very short periods of time. Something of a model was to be found in Georges Dumézil's accounts of the societies of early Europe, in which myths, art, religion, law, institutions, political, social, and economic systems were all analysed in terms of a cultural totality, a 'combinatory', in which each element was related to every other and in which only the overall structure was dominant. There were obvious difficulties in this model for anyone trying to adapt it to the analysis of recent

European cultures over a long period of time: it was ill-equipped for dealing with change and transformation. Foucault's notion of the *episteme*, the underlying set of rules governing the production of discourses in any single period, may be seen as an attempt to reconcile change with the notion of a cultural totality. Of course, it would be quite incorrect to see Foucault's periods—the Renaissance, Classical, modern—or *epistemei* as 'cultural totalities' of the Dumézil kind, which simply followed one another in complete discontinuity and for no apparent reason. Indeed, it was an inability to appreciate this that led to much of the categorizing of Foucault—especially after *Les mots et les choses*—as a Structuralist.

Traces of Dumézil's example remain in *Histoire de la folie*, but they should not be exaggerated. They are more a matter of terminology than anything else. However, Foucault has himself made criticisms of the use he made of certain concepts. In particular he admits that he tended to see madness as 'a free, wild, voluble condition that reason had succeeded in taming and silencing'. (This purely negative, repressive concept of power has, of course, been attacked in his last two books.) Because madness lay on the other side of the division that had established the modern sciences and because, in its *'absence d'oeuvre'*, it lay outside the real labours of history, Foucault had tended to suggest that it was a permanent, unchanging, 'singular experience'. Like death, it marked the extinction—and therefore the limit—of the subject of science and history. This suggestion was to be found more explicitly in the 1961 Preface than in the detailed analyses of the book itself—this, undoubtedly, is one reason for Foucault's suppression of this Preface in the second edition of 1972.

If *Histoire de la folie* was largely ignored by Marxist intellectuals (Louis Althusser being one of the few to recognize its importance), *Les mots et les choses* aroused their furious attention. In moving from the Other to the Same, from the birth of reason to the productions of reason, from the 'tragic' to history, Foucault had invaded their area of operations. They found plenty to object to, both in detail and in the general theoretical postulates. To begin with there was the problem of style: how was one to take seriously a work that began with a laugh and a ridiculous Chinese (pre-Revolutionary) encyclopaedia. Unlike Marx himself, one of the wittiest of polemicists, Marxists are not noted, in the performance of their public duties, either for their elegance of expression or their sense of humour. The prospect of

Marxist critics trying to get a grip on *Les mots et les choses* was rather like that of a policeman attempting to arrest a particularly outrageous drag-queen. Of course, their attentions would not have been required if the book had not been so phenomenally successful. The ever-resourceful Enemy—Idealism—was once more abroad. The forces of progress must be mobilized for another battle in 'the class struggle in the realm of theory': Structuralism, the latest of the fiend's disguises— others had been psychoanalysis, logical positivism, existentialism and 'modernism' in the arts—had to be stripped away and destroyed.

Les mots et les choses set out to examine the continuities and transformations in European thought from the Renaissance to the present. It chose to concentrate on the three essential areas concerned respectively with living beings, language, and wealth, their relations with the philosophy of each period and their extension into the 'human sciences' that emerged in the nineteenth century. From a Marxist point of view, therefore, it covered the whole of the 'bourgeois' period from the rise of capitalism, through its mercantilist to its industrial stage, from the rise of the bourgeoisie to its final ascendency. Furthermore, it concerned those areas of human thought most permeable to 'ideology', that is to say, to the distorted representation of reality, and to the shaping power of the 'mode of production'. Yet, not only did Foucault deliberately exclude any reference to social, economic, or political considerations, the continuity of that discourse was broken down into three clearly defined periods bearing names drawn, not from the 'science' of historical materialism, but from art history. No reasons were given for the sudden mutation from one such *episteme* to another. Human thought followed its own unpredictable laws: it was a clear case of Idealism.

Of course, Foucault had no wish to deny the role of what he later called 'non-discursive formations' in the production of thought. The reverse is the case: *all* Foucault's work, before and after this book, is concerned precisely with this problem. But for Foucault it was a *problem* and not one to which a solution had been found.

> I realized that things were more complicated than I had thought in the first two books, that the discursive domains did not always obey structures shared with the practical and institutional domains associated with them, that, on the contrary, they obeyed structures

Conclusion

that they shared with other epistemological domains, that a kind of isomorphism existed between discourses at a given period (B4, 195–6).

Marxists invariably cite their theory of that problem—the relations between 'base' and 'superstructure'. They make ritual criticisms of attempts to reduce the latter to the former and stress the 'relative autonomy' of superstructural phenomena. Yet little attempt is ever made to analyse the functioning of that 'relative autonomy'. In concrete instances, the productions of individuals are related not to a complex, mobile ensemble of interlocking discursive and non-discursive formations but, almost invariably, to that individual as a founding subject, to his class affiliations, and to his experience of the 'contradictions' within his society. Thus Racine is, 'in the final analysis', a 'representative' of the *noblesse de robe* (Goldmann) or Shakespeare 'represents' a nascent, post-bourgeois 'humanism' (Lear's diatribes against 'authority') within what is, 'objectively', a 'reactionary', feudal view of politics ('Take but degree away . . .') a view expressed by Marx himself, developed by Lukàcs, and repeated by every Marxist who approaches the subject. Given the theoretical and practical poverty of Marxism in this area, it was understandable that Foucault should feel that there might be something to be gained, by a sort of controlled experiment, in deliberately *excluding* the so-called 'explanatory' factors. What he hoped to discover by this special mode of analysis was how, at the purely discursive level, different discourses appeared over certain periods of time to be governed by a common underlying set of rules and then, in a matter of a few years, undergo profound transformations. In any case, as Foucault himself admitted, it would have been quite beyond his means to cover so long a span of time and operate at the non-discursive level as well.

For the Marxists, then, Foucault could now be dismissed as an 'idealist'. It was a new kind of idealism, one not founded on the notion of a constitutive subject: all the more reason to expose it, since Marxism, too, saw the subject as a secondary effect of processes outside himself. But Foucault was more dangerous for another reason: not only did he carry out an analysis of Western culture with no mention of the 'science' that, alone, was capable of such an analysis, but at the end of that analysis, Foucault makes a few brief references to Marx, the founder of that 'science', placing him very firmly in the framework of nineteenth-century thought. For Foucault, it seemed, Marx was not the originator of a whole new world of social, economic, and political analysis, but a figure circumscribed by his time and now superseded. And as if that were not enough, Foucault had managed, by reference to his *epistemei*, to make Ricardo the occasion of a deeper break in economic theory than Marx himself. For Marxists, accustomed to seeing Ricardo as a transitional figure between the Classical economics of Adam Smith and the new socialist economics of Marx, this was not a matter open to discussion. Foucault maintained that by freeing labour from its role as a measure of value and making it, in the productive process itself, prior to all exchange, Ricardo had made the fundamental break with Classical economics. In relation to that break, Marx's introduction into economics of the political notion of class was a secondary phenomenon; the differences between nineteenth-century 'bourgeois' and 'socialist' economic theories was an internal dispute within the post-Classical *episteme*, 'storms in a children's paddling pool'. The stock Marxist response to Foucault's denial of Marx's continuing relevance is to brand Foucault's analysis as pre-Marxist. Foucault's conclusion is the result of a respectful, detailed analysis of the relation of Marx's economic theory to the discourse in which it appears and of the relation of that discourse to other contemporary discourses. The Marxist judgement on Foucault is a typical example of tautological dogmatism. Since no Marxist can contemplate the prospect of a post-Marxist, to say that someone is pre-Marxist is simply to say that he is non-Marxist—and no one would deny that Foucault was that. Yet nowhere, except in the minds of Marxists, is it inscribed that the 'dialectic' is an ineradicable law of nature. If, at the end of the nineteenth century, Nietzsche set light to 'the intermingled promises of the dialectic and anthropology', then those who attempt to rethink history after Nietzsche must be post-Marxist.

> Is it not necessary to draw a line between those who believe that we can continue to situate our present discontinuities within the historical and transcendental tradition of the nineteenth century and those who are making a great effort to liberate themselves, once and for all, from this conceptual framework? (B2; LCP, 120).

Foucault's relation to 'theory' is often misunderstood. Foucault does not have a theory of history, which he then sets about 'proving'. The mass of detailed analysis he brings to bear in his work is not

Conclusion

material to support a theory, in the sense that this analysis would be 'invalidated' if the theory were proved 'false'. Foucault has always worked in quite the reverse way. In approaching a new area—and almost every book of his does this—he certainly has a number of prejudices and presuppositions deriving from his previous work and from the opinions of others in that field. However, he is not only on his guard against these 'given' theoretical notions, he subjects them, in the course of his detailed analysis, to the most rigorous scrutiny. What finally emerges is not theory, in the sense of a general statement of the truth as Foucault see it, but rather a tentative hypothesis, an invitation to discussion, which, more often than not is startlingly at odds with received opinion. For Foucault, theory does not enjoy the same status as detailed analysis, to which it is secondary, subservient. *Histoire de la folie* is not superseded or invalidated, therefore, when Foucault criticizes the conceptualization of 'madness' to be found in that book. Nor is the value of *Les mots et les choses* in any way diminished because it left a number of theoretical loose-ends and occasions of misunderstanding. However, Foucault regarded these shortcomings as sufficiently important to require full and detailed elucidation. *L'archéologie du savoir* reverses Foucault's usual practice: it is his only full-length book devoted primarily to theoretical and methodological problems—though even here, in the way it extends the concrete analyses of the previous book, it is not a matter of *pure* theory.

In a sense, the crux of *L'archéologie du savoir* is the elucidation by replacement of the concept, central to *Les mots et les choses*, of the *episteme*. The misunderstandings that this concept gave rise to are largely the result of inattentive or unsympathetic reading. Certainly there is nothing in Foucault's immensely subtle and detailed analysis of epistemological changes to warrant the crude distortions they give rise to. I have already discussed the charge that Foucault's discourses floated in some disembodied state, unconnected to social, economic, and political realities. Another charge is that Foucault interrupted the chronological flow of ideas, breaking it into unitary, self-contained 'periods', each determined by a quite different underlying *'episteme'*. In fact, Foucault's 'periods' are not operational concepts, but short-hand references to a number of related changes in various disciplines. Foucault never suggested that all intellectual activity during, say the 'Classical' period, was determined by the *episteme* shared by the three disciplines analysed. The 'Classical *episteme*' that emerged in *Les mots et les choses* was precisely, and no more than, the underlying system of those three disciplines. Were one to extend the comparison to other disciplines, the *episteme* would alter accordingly. Clearly, one cannot speak of a Classical physics or Classical mathematics in the sense used by Foucault. Again, not all disciplines undergo transformations at the same time: change is affected in a staggered way. Nor is change so total: one has only to consider Foucault's analysis of the transitional stages between the Classical and modern disciplines.

It was pointed out by the Althusserian Dominique Lecourt, that the concept of the *episteme* was scarcely referred to in *L'archéologie du savoir*, which, nevertheless, purported to be a theoretical reconsideration of the book in which that concept had a leading role. Lecourt concluded from this that Foucault had realized his error, but was unwilling to admit it; 'the thick growth of new words' was an elaborate cover to hide that fact. But *Les mots et les choses* was not a demonstration of some 'theory of the *episteme*'; there could be no question therefore, of 'error'. If the term *episteme* began to cause more trouble than it was worth, then Foucault was quite willing to jettison it in favour of something else. Of course, no Althusserian can be expected to understand such a light-hearted attitude to theory: for Althusser and his disciples there is no more glorious activity than 'theoretical practice'. By careful selection and omission, Lecourt manages to produce a quite distorted, not to say dishonest, account of Foucault's book. His 'theoreticism' is so invincible that it blinds him to the true nature of Foucault's activity. He even makes the astonishing statement that the 'category of practice' is 'foreign' to Foucault's earlier works. What Lecourt is referring to is Foucault's notion of 'discursive practice' as 'a set of anonymous historically determinate rules imposed on every speaking subject, rules which are not universally valid but always have a specified domain of validity' (B9, 202). These rules form a 'regularity' that 'orders every discursive formation'. Lecourt has correctly grasped Foucault's notion. How, then, could he say that such a category is 'foreign to Foucault's earlier works'. *Les mots et les choses* is about little else, while *Naissance de la clinique* is a sustained analysis of the relations between a discursive practice and its corresponding non-discursive practice. Clearly, for a 'theoreticist' like Lecourt, the word *is* the concept: if the word is new to Foucault, so must the concept be. Lecourt's whole analysis of *L'archéologie du savoir*—or rather of a few terms used by Foucault in that book—is based on the following 'argument', each stage of which is no more than a doctrinal assertion: 1) historical materialism is 'a constituted and living science'; 2) any attempt to cover the same ground as historical materialism must be pre-scientific, 'ideological'; 3) an ideology cannot continue its parallel course indefinitely—its 'internal contradictions' must sooner or later become apparent; 4) at that point the ideology would attempt to overcome these contradictions by the use of the concepts of the parallel 'science', but 'in displacement'. In other words, Foucault has tried to solve the problems created by his refusal of Marxism by adopting Marxist concepts in disguise. This leads to the absurd conclusion that Foucault's concept of knowledge (*savoir*) is a displacement of Althusser's 'ideology', whereas it is clearly a means of avoiding the Althusserian distinction between 'science' and 'ideology'. It comes as no surprise, therefore, when Lecourt raises the old objection that Foucault 'describes', but does not 'explain'.

> If my interpretation is correct, the task of the 'archaeology' is in fact to constitute the theory of the 'discursive' instance insofar as it is structured by relations invested in institutions and historically determinate relations. This task is only carried out by Foucault in the form of a description; he says so himself: 'the time for theory has not yet arrived' (B9, 198).

Whether his interpretation is 'correct' or not, it is certainly not Foucault's—why else would Foucault say 'the time for theory has not yet arrived'. But it cannot be 'correct' either, for the whole archaeological enterprise is profoundly anti-theoretical: at no point does Foucault show the slightest desire to produce a theory to account for the 'structuring' of discursive formations by 'relations invested in institutions', etc. To use his own distinction, he is striving to write a 'general' not a 'total' history.

Immediately after the passage quoted, Lecourt adds his ritual obeissance: 'for my part, I think that the time for theory was inaugurated by Marx, *at least in its most general principles*, a long time ago' (my italics). Principles so general, it seems, that they have not advanced even Marxists very far along the road to explanation. What kind of relations exist, Lecourt asks a few pages later, between discourse and non-discursive practices? Any Marxist can answer that, he replies, by reference to 'the classical schema of the infrastructure and the superstructure'. But such an answer, we are surprised to learn, though 'fundamentally correct', is surely inadequate.

> For it is still descriptive: even if it has the inestimable advantage of 'showing' what is the *materialist* order of determination; even if it has a well-tried polemical value against all the idealist conceptions of history for which it is ideas that conduct the world; even if, for these decisive reasons, it has to be resolutely defended as a theoretical acquisition of Marxism, insofar as it enables us to draw a line of demarcation between the two 'camps' in philosophy, between our enemies and ourselves—it must still be recognized that it does not give us the means to think the mechanism that links ideology . . . to the mode of production (B9, 208–9).

Even if, after a century or more, it has got no further towards an explanation than Foucault after eight years! Such an admission is a rare grace in these tedious, obtuse pages. Foucault is even praised for making it 'imperative on us to think theoretically' the mechanism that he has described, but, Lecourt continues impenitently, 'we know that only historical materialism can resolve this problem'. I would prefer to say that only historical materialism, by virtue of its intrinsic metaphysics of causality, would seek such an 'explanation'. The 'descriptions' that Foucault offers, with all their wealth of detail, do constitute as much of an explanation as is usual in most scientific discourse:

> It's fifty years since it was realized that the tasks of description were essential in such areas as history, ethnology and language. After all, since Galileo and Newton, mathematics has not functioned as an explanation of nature, but as the description of a process. So I don't see why non-formal disciplines like history should be criticized for undertaking the primary tasks of description (B4, 194).

It is curious that the magical 'explanations' in terms of the 'classical Marxist schema' that have satisfied Marxists for a century should now, upon a reading of Foucault, be themselves demoted to the status of 'description'. (In fact, they are not even that; they are simply theoretical assertions.) Such dissatisfaction could only be indicative of a decline in the efficacy of the old Marxist magic. It is not Foucault who should 'trust himself' to the false 'certainties' of historical materialism, but Lecourt who should trust himself to the real uncertainties of post-Marxist thought.

The notion of discourse as 'event', of knowledge as power, which began to emerge in *L'archéologie du savoir*, was given a fuller, more developed analysis in *L'ordre du discours*. In *Surveiller et punir* and *La volonté de savoir* what has emerged is nothing less than a radically new analysis of the history of our west European societies. This 'political anatomy'—anatomy of the body politic in terms of an anatomy of the politicization of the body—is presented with Foucault's usual modesty as 'another grid for deciphering history'.

> When I think of the mechanics of power, I think of its capillary form of existence, of the extent to which power seeps into the very grain of individuals, reaches right into their bodies, permeates their gestures, their posture, what they say, how they learn to live and work with other people (B8, 28).

Such a notion is nowhere to be found in the Marxist tradition. Indeed, it *could* not be found there. Marx, for all his research into historical and economic facts, remained a philosopher, invincibly a European, more particularly German 'idealist' philosopher. Marx could only think history and economics from within metaphysics. All philosophy belonging to that tradition is ultimately 'idealist'; 'materialism' is a philosopher's attempt, doomed in advance, to escape idealism and reach the real world. Without the ennobling action of the dialectic, shaping it and giving it meaning, investing it with the causal reasoning of philosophy, the real world of facts would be unworthy of a Marxist's attention. Not that 'facts', or the 'real' world for that matter are self-evident, transparent. They certainly require analysis: they are, indeed, the unrecognized effects of earlier analyses. 'Facts' are both the material and the instruments of historical analysis, but they do not require the *interpretation* of philosophers. The Marxist tradition has maintained its contempt for facts, especially the facts of its own history. As ever, Soviet Communism has produced the most grotesque version of this contempt. Facts are weapons: they can get into the wrong hands. But other Marxists, those who are as appalled as anyone else by the horrors of the Soviet state, share this dangerous contempt for mere fact, this yearning for meaning, for purpose, for the *truth* beneath. Not for them the 'fetishism of the fact'; yet they are quite capable of taking such 'events' as 'the French Revolution' or 'the rise of the bourgeoisie' as unquestionable historical givens. For them ordinary *wirkliche* history is merely the servant of the great movements of History—a relation not dissimilar to that between 'masses' and 'vanguard'. Marxists are closer to Plato than they think, or deserve to be: a nightmare version of *The Republic*, the Soviet state is also run by a caste of 'philosophers'. In the last resort, Mind cares only for Mind. To become a true materialist, the philosopher must cease to be a philosopher. Nietzsche, the classical philologist, never became a philosopher; he also prevented Foucault from becoming one. The power-body conjunction, the basis for a true materialism, is clearly expressed in Nietzsche, in *The Genealogy of Morals,* in *The Gay Science,* in *Dawn*. Not, of course, that Foucault simply repeats what is found in Nietzsche. Nietzsche does not offer a systematic analysis, but a series of insights, scattered over a variety of different texts, often themselves in the form of aphorisms. It requires a particularly *active* form of reading, of the kind practised by Foucault, for these insights to be appropriated. That is why, despite the fact that Nietzsche had been with Foucault from the beginning, it was not until *Surveiller et punir,* which he has called 'my first book', that his analysis of history really comes of age.

Foucault's 'political anatomy' constitutes a radical break with all previous conceptions of power, whether of the 'right' or of the 'left'. To begin with, power is not a possession, won by one class that strives to retain it against its acquisition by another. Power is not the prerogative of the 'bourgeoisie'; the 'working class' has no historical mission in acquiring it. Power, as such, does not exist, but in challenging existing notions of how societies operate, one is forced, in the first instance, to employ the same word. Power is an effect of the operation of social relationships, between groups and between individuals. It is not unitary: it has no essence. There are as many forms of power as there are types of relationship. Every group and every individual exercises power and is subjected to it. There are certain categories of person—children, prisoners, the 'insane'—whose ability to exercise power is severely limited, but few members of these groups do not find some means of exercising power, if only on each other. Power is not, therefore, to be identified with the state, a central apparatus that can be seized. The state is rather an overall strategy and effect, a composite result made up of a multiplicity of centres and mechanisms, so many states within states with complex networks of common citizenship. Factories, housing estates, hospitals, schools, families, are among the more evident, more formalized of such 'micro-powers'. It is the task of a political anatomy to analyse the operation of these 'micro-powers', the relations that are made between them and their relations with the strategic aims of the state apparatus. Power is not to be seen as subordinate to some other factor. It does not exist simply to enforce economic exploitation: it does not play the role of superstructure to an economic infrastructure. Power is already present at the very inception of the mode of production: it constitutes its very structure. Power has no finality: political transformations are not the result of some necessity, some immanent rationality, but responses to particular problems, combining not in a totalized, centralized manner, but by serial repercussion. Power is not simply repressive; it is also productive. It is here that the role of the body becomes crucial. Power subjects bodies not to render them passive, but to render them active. The forces of the body are trained and developed with a view to making them productive. The power of the body corresponds to the exercise of power over it. Hence the possibility of a reversal of that power.

This notion of the training of the body to productive ends brings with it what Foucault calls the 'soul'. A political anatomy is also a genealogy of modern morality. Here, too, Nietzsche provides the starting-point. The hold exercised by power over the body is also a hold over the 'soul', for the more power renders the body productive, the more forces there are to control and direct. This difficulty is overcome by the action of the disciplinary mechanisms: 'discipline increases the forces of the body (in economic terms of utility) and diminishes the same forces (in political terms of obedience). . . It dissociates power from the body' (SP, 140; DP, 138). This 'dissociation' is the creation of a soul. The soul is a part of the body set against itself: 'the soul is the effect and instrument of a political anatomy; the soul is the prison of the body' (SP, 24; DP, 30). To the extent that man has a soul, power does not need to be applied from the outside; it penetrates his body, occupies it, animates it, gives it 'meaning'. The soul mobilizes the body, gives it consciousness and conscience. The soul is both the result of the political investment of the body and an instrument of its mastery. As François Ewald observes, in his remarkable essay on *Surveiller et punir*, we should reconsider the matter/mind opposition. It is time we abandoned the opposition between materialism and idealism. The question of the primacy of being or thought no longer has any meaning in the light of Foucault's political anatomy.

This political anatomy also forces us to reconsider the relations between knowledge and power. Knowledge derives not from some subject of knowledge, but from the power relations that invest it. Knowledge does not 'reflect' power relations; it is not a distorted expression of them; it is immanent in them. 'Power produces knowledge. . . Power and knowledge directly imply one another. . . There is no power relation without the correlative constitution of a field of knowledge, nor any knowledge that does not presuppose and constitute at the same time power relations' (SP, 32; DP, 27). Power and knowledge are two sides of the same process. Knowledge cannot be neutral, pure. All knowledge is political not because it may have political consequences or be politically useful, but because knowledge has its conditions of possibility in power relations. No science can create its own conditions of possibility: these are to be found in transformations of power relations. Political anatomy deprives science of its own foundations. It shows that the techniques of power, production, and knowledge have a common matrix. Political anatomy does not itself produce knowledge: it retraces its genealogy. In doing so, it deprives knowledge of its apparent objectivity. It denounces the illusion of truth. Knowledge is not so much true or false as legitimate or illegitimate for a particular set of power relations.

Foucault frees us from the crushing power of a certain régime of truth. Against great truths, great syntheses, great systems, he practises a detailed analysis of the multiple mechanisms of power-knowledge. Foucault's genealogy, like Nietzsche's is 'grey' only in contrast with the 'blue skies' of 'great ideas'. Similarly, although he does not exclude 'great authors', he subjects them to the strict democracy that governs his sources. Indeed, they will usually serve his purposes less well than the franker, cruder statements of the less well known.

It is not in Hegel or Auguste Comte that the bourgeoisie speaks openly. Side by side with these sacralized texts, a quite conscious, organized strategy is to be read in a mass of unknown documents that constitute the effective discourse of a particular form of political action (B6).

Similarly, the interests of the oppressed are best expressed in their own words and these, too, are to be found in a submerged, invalidated mass of 'documents'. The Foucaldian genealogy is an unmasking of power for the use of those who suffer it. It is also directed against those who would seize power in their name. As François Ewald points out, there are three, not two, parties to every power struggle: not only those who exercise power and those who would exercise it in their place, but also those on whom it is exercised. Because one speaks against power, one does not necessarily speak with those who suffer it. Hence Foucault's concerted attack on all forms of interpretation and representation: on the use made of the linguistics of Saussure and Jakobson, on psychoanalysis, on Marxism. For the interpreter, things are never what they seem. People never say what they mean or mean what they say; they never know what they want or what they are doing. For Foucault interpretation is reduction, repression, obliteration of fact, discourse, and desire. It is a technique of knowledge; it is also a technique of power. Interpretation requires specially qualified interpreters, representatives. The dialectic is an interpreter's weapon for the seizure of power. The particular, detailed, shifting, even conflicting interests and demands of a multiplicity of groups are totalized and reduced to the single, eternal destiny of a class, the proletariat. But since the members of these groups are so thoroughly imbued with the ideology of the ruling class they cannot recognize their destiny, they need a Party to teach and guide them. The leaders of that Party were and still very largely are renegade bourgeois intellectuals—and lest the masses gain too large a voice even within the Party, things must be so arranged that this leadership perpetuates itself and imposes its discipline on the Party as a whole. Stalin and the Soviet State should be regarded not so much as aberrations of an otherwise correct system of theory and practice, but rather as its natural outcome. In an infinitely more benign way, the masses of our own 'capitalist democracies', or, rather, the heterogeneous mass of micro-powers that make up our societies, also have their systems of 'representation' in parliaments, trade unions, local government, and a mass of unelected experts in the social services.

Foucault's 'political anatomy' is the clearest and most fully developed version of a new political 'theory' and 'practice' that is just beginning to emerge from the discrediting of both Marxism and 'reformism'. In Gilles Deleuze's words, Foucault has operated.

> a theoretical revolution directed not only at bourgeois theories of the state, but at the Marxist conception of power and the relation to the state. It is as if, at last, something has emerged since Marx. It is as if a kind of complicity around the state had been broken. Foucault is not content to say that certain notions have to be rethought, he does not even say it, he does it, and thus proposes new co-ordinates for practice. . . The theoretical privilege that Marxism accords the state as an apparatus of power brings with it its own practical conception of the directing, centralizing Party, proceeding to the conquest of state power; but, conversely, this organizational conception of the party is justified by this theory of power. Another theory, another practice of struggle, another strategic organization are what emerge from Foucault's book (B10, 1212).

The régime of 'truth' gave the intellectual, whose business truth was, a certain 'universal' status. The 'disinterested' intellectual represented the conscience of society as a whole. But Foucault shows that truth does not exist outside power, still less in opposition to it. Each society has its own régime of truth: the types of discourse accepted as true, the mechanisms that make it possible to distinguish between truth and error. In place of the 'universal' intellectual, Foucault places the 'specific' intellectual who, like everyone else, is competent to speak only of what he knows and experiences. His task is not to enlighten, but to work upon the particular régime of truth in which he operates. He is called upon neither to reveal the truth nor to represent others. The will to the power of truth is a pitiless tyrant: it requires a singular and total devotion. It is a service that has tempted the European mind since Plato. Nietzsche gave the first signs of its possible end: he also provided a way out, which he called genealogy. Genealogy was a 'grey' activity, but it was also a gay science, a science of the hypothetical. That gaiety, that love of hypothesis, pervades all Foucault's work. He is the reverse of a guru, a teacher, a subject who is supposed to know, though he would, in all modesty, be flattered if, without excessive seriousness, he were compared to a Zen master, who also knows nothing. For him uncertainty causes no anguish: his prose is punctuated by such words and expressions as 'perhaps', 'no doubt', 'it may be', 'it is as if'. He advances hypotheses with the delight that others reserve for the revelation of truth. His last two books have been explorations of hypotheses. 'Can one draw up the genealogy of modern morality on the basis of a political history of the body?' he asks on the dust-jacket of *Surveiller et punir*. The whole of *Volonté de savoir* is a hypothesis, which irritates or angers those for whom a 'truth', however banal or ill-founded, is of more value than a hypothesis, however illuminating. As he remarks in an interview published in *Ornicar?*, the uncertainty is genuine, not a rhetorical device. He compares his last book to a Gruyère cheese, with holes in which the reader can install himself. In that interview, he confesses that he arrived at his hypothesis of the relation between 'sex' and 'sexuality' only after several versions of the book had been written and found unsatisfactory. At first he took 'sex' to be the initial given and 'sexuality' 'a sort of discursive and institutional formation that had battened on sex, covering it, even concealing it'—the usual, expected notion, in fact. So he decided to reverse the two concepts. 'It was a game. . . I wasn't at all sure where it would lead.' Perhaps sex, which seems a natural, biological given, possessing its own laws and constraints, is after all produced by the *machinery* of sexuality. Perhaps 'sex' is a relatively recent creation of that machinery, which, previously, had applied itself to the body, the sexual organs, pleasure, flesh, and so on.

A love of hypothesis, of invention, is unashamedly, a love of the beautiful. What drew Foucault to the case of Pierre Rivière was not the mass of official documentation, but 'the beauty of Rivière's memoir', a beauty that shamed the dreary prose of the educated experts who busied themselves around him. It was a daring, provocative remark, suggesting that beauty of expression is an indication that what is being said is worth listening to. The question of Foucault's own style is not insignificant. It is not so much that Foucault writes well—there are still academics who do that, though few contemporary writers of history, philosophy, or literary criticism give the pleasure of a Michelet, a Berkeley, or a Coleridge. It is rather that he writes with ostentatious brilliance: his writing betrays a quite shameless delight in its own skill that calls to mind the sumptuous prose of our own pre-Classical period, that of a John Donne or Thomas Browne. To write in this way is no affectation or self-indulgence. It is, if it requires justification, functional. Like all style, it is both natural and cultivated:

a natural mode of expression for a writer striving to renew contact with a pre-rationalist world of communicating Reason and Folly and a conscious rejection of the language of Reason that seeks by its grey, measured, monotonous tones to give an impression of authority, objectivity, and truth.

At the time of writing Foucault is still in his early fifties. *Histoire de la folie* was published eighteen years ago. The complete works may not even be half written. As it is, five more volumes of the History of Sexuality are promised and a footnote in *La volonté de savoir* refers to a certain *Pouvoir de la vérité*, an as yet unwritten work. In this or yet another book Foucault will undoubtedly return to the theme that has always exercised his mind, namely that 'will to truth' that has marked the whole of Western civilization over the last two and a half thousand years, a 'will to truth' in which Greek philosophy, Christian spirituality, and modern science are all partakers. For Foucault, the prospect of such labours ahead appalls, though he will find, no doubt, against so many other inclinations, that he 'must go on'. For he does not enjoy writing. In the essay, 'What is an Author?', he speaks eloquently of the kinship between writing and death. For the Ancients, writing was a means of cheating death through literary immortality. In *The Thousand and One Nights* the telling of stories is a strategy for postponing the death of the storyteller. For us, writing is a 'a sacrifice of life itself':

> It is a voluntary obliteration of the self that does not require representation in books because it takes place in the everyday existence of the writer. Where an *oeuvre* had the duty of creating immortality, it now attains the right to kill, to become the murderer of its author (B2, 80; LCP, 117).

The writer writes about 'life' by withdrawing from it: Foucault quotes Flaubert, Proust, and Kafka as examples of this reversal. Not that he considers himself to be of their number: 'I am shocked that anyone could call himself a writer. I'm a dealer in instruments, an inventor of recipes, a cartographer. . .' (B7). He had rather be any kind of thing than a writer. Yet Deleuze who quotes that remark in a review of *Surveiller et punir*, adds that Foucault is nevertheless 'one of the greatest writers living today'. Such a claim should not seem exorbitant. After all, no one would deny that Montaigne or Bacon, say, were to be counted among the greatest writers of *their* time—and they had a

great deal more competition than Foucault. But then an age whose
'creative writers' borrowed their plots from others—in contrast with
most of our own, who provide their own plots, but borrow everything
else—required more than information and opinions of its 'non-
creative' writers.

There is no 'Foucault system'. One cannot be a 'Foucaldian' in the
way one can be a Marxist or a Freudian: Marx and Freud left coherent
bodies of doctrine (or 'knowledge') and organizations which,
whether one likes it or not (for some that is the attraction), enjoy
uninterrupted apostolic succession from their founders. If Foucault is
to have an 'influence' it will no doubt be as a slayer of dragons, a
breaker of systems. Such a task should not be seen as negative;
indeed it is the system-building that is the real negation. Its positive
achievements may be measured by the range and variety of its effects,
not by some massive uniformity. Nietzsche's 'influence' has been of
this kind: Futurism, Dada, Surrealism; Freud, Mann, Hesse; Gide
and Malraux; Shaw, Yeats, Wells, the two Lawrences; Ibsen and
Strindberg—all acknowledge that influence. Nietzsche was felt,
instinctively, to be part of the new age that was ushered in by the
twentieth century—a new age that found its fullest expression,
perhaps, in the 'modernist' movements in the arts. During several
decades of total politics, Nietzsche suffered at the hands of his Fascist
admirers, his Communist revilers, and 'liberals' who saw his books as
a Pandora's box, better left unopened. Now that influence is once
more at work in our thought. If it seems strongest in France, it is due
in some measure to Foucault (and Deleuze). In England, where intellectual life so often appears to be in the grip of a narrow, smug,
mentally lazy (il)liberal consensus, threatened on its fringes by a small
band of Marxists, it is almost non-existent. Here, too, Foucault falls
on the stoniest of grounds. The English reviewers' evident inability to
read his books is seen, everywhere else, as a scandal. In America,
which benefits from a more pluralist culture and the devotion of
Walter Kaufmann, a German émigré, Nietzsche is widely read—so,
too, is Foucault. To assimilate one to the other would help neither.
Only those who know both can appreciate their profound kinship
and differences, but their destinies do seem, in some subterranean
way, to be entwined. It is difficult to conceive of any thinker having,
in the last quarter of our century, the influence that Nietzsche exercised over its first quarter. Yet Foucault's achievement so far makes

him a more likely candidate than any other. When one considers what is yet to come, one may well feel the ground stirring under one's feet.

◊

Bibliography

A. Works by Michel Foucault

I BOOKS

Maladie mentale et personnalité, Paris, P.U.F., 1954; 2nd revised edition, retitled *Maladie mentale et psychologie*, 1962.
  Mental Illness and Psychology, trans. A.S., New York, Harper and Row, 1976.
Folie et déraison, Histoire de la folie à l'âge classique, Paris, Plon, 1961; a considerably shortened version entitled *Histoire de la folie*, Paris, U.G.E., Collection 10/18, 1961; 2nd edition, *Histoire de la folie à l'âge classique*, Paris, Gallimard, 1972.
  Madness and Civilization, trans. Richard Howard, New York, Pantheon, 1965 and London, Tavistock, 1967 (trans. of shortened version, with additions from 1st edition).
Naissance de la clinique, Paris, P.U.F., 1963; 2nd revised edition, 1972.
  The Birth of the Clinic, trans. A.S., London, Tavistock and New York, Pantheon, 1973.
Raymond Roussel, Paris, Gallimard, 1963.
Les mots et les choses, Paris, Gallimard, 1966.
  The Order of Things, trans. A.S., London, Tavistock and New York, Pantheon, 1970 (with Foreword by M.F.).
L'archéologie du savoir, Paris, Gallimard, 1969.
  The Archaeology of Knowledge, trans. A.S., London, Tavistock and New York, Pantheon, 1972.
Hommage à Jean Hyppolite, Paris, P.U.F., 1971 (collective work, edited by M.F. and containing his 'Nietzsche, la généalogie, l'histoire'; Eng. trans., 'Nietzsche, Genealogy, History', in LCP).

L'ordre du discours, Paris, Gallimard, 1971.
  'The Discourse on Language', trans. Rupert Swyer, included as
  appendix to American edition of *The Archaeology of Knowledge*.
Ceci n'est pas une pipe, Montpellier, Fata Morgana, 1973 (on René
  Magritte).
Moi, Pierre Rivière, ayant égorgé ma mère, ma soeur et mon frère. . ., Paris,
  Gallimard/Julliard, 1973 (a collective work, edited by M.F., contain-
  ing an introduction and one essay by M.F.).
  *I, Pierre Rivière, having slaughtered my mother, my sister and my
  brother. . .*, trans. Frank Jellinek, New York, Pantheon, 1975 and
  London, Peregrine, 1978.
Surveiller et punir, Paris, Gallimard, 1975.
  Discipline and Punish, trans. A.S., New York, Pantheon and Lon-
  don, Allen Lane, 1977.
Les machines à guérir (aux origines de l'hôpital moderne). Dossiers et
  documents d'architecture, Paris, Institut de l'Environnement, 1976
  (collective work, edited by M.F., including his 'La politique de la
  santé au XVIIIᵉ').
La volonté de savoir, Paris, Gallimard, 1976 (vol. 1 of projected six-
  volume *Histoire de la sexualité*).
  The History of Sexuality, vol. 1: An Introduction, trans. Robert Hurley, New York, Pantheon, 1978 and London, Allen Lane, 1979.
Language, Counter-Memory, Practice, Selected Essays and Interviews,
  edited with an introduction by Donald F. Bouchard and trans. by
  Donald F. Bouchard and Sherry Simon, Cornell University Press
  and Oxford, Blackwell, 1977.

II TRANSLATIONS

Ludwig Binswanger, *Le rêve et l'existence*, Paris, Desclée de Brouwer,
  1954 (with introduction by M.F.).
Leo Spitzer, *Études de style*, Paris, Gallimard, 1962 (one article, 'Art du
  langage et linguistique', trans. by M.F.).
Emmanuel Kant, *Anthropologie du point de vue pragmatique*, Paris, Vrin,
  1964.

III PREFACES

J.-J. Rousseau, *Rousseau juge de Jean-Jacques*, Paris, Colin, 1962.
F. W. Nietzsche, *Le gai savoir. Fragments posthumes (1881–1882)*, Paris,
  Gallimard, 1967 (with Gilles Deleuze).
Arnauld et Lancelot, *Grammaire générale et raisonnée* (new facsimile
  edition of *Grammaire de Port-Royal*), Paris, Paulet, 1969.

Bibliography

Georges Bataille, *Oeuvres complètes*, Paris, Gallimard, 1970.

J. Brisset, *La grammaire logique*, Paris, Tchou, 1970.

Gustave Flaubert, *La Tentation de Saint Antoine*, Paris, Le Livre de Poche.

Serge Livrozet, *De la prison à la révolte*, Paris, Mercure de France, 1973.

IV SELECTED ARTICLES

'Le Non du père', *Critique*, no. 178, 1962, 195–209 (Eng. trans. 'The Father's "No" ', in LCP).

'Un si cruel savoir', *Critique*, no. 182, 1962, 597–611.

'Dire et voir chez Raymond Roussel', *Lettre ouverte*, no. 4, été 1962, 38–51.

1'Une Préface à la transgression', *Critique*, nos. 195–6, 1963, 751–69 (on Georges Bataille, Eng. trans., 'Preface to Transgression', in LCP).

'La métamorphose et le labyrinthe', *N.R.F.*, no. 124, 1–4–1963, 638–61 (on Raymond Roussel).

'Le langage à l'infini', *Tel Quel*, no. 15, août 1963, 44–53 (Eng. trans., 'Language to Infinity', in LCP).

'Guetter le jour qui vient', *N.R.F.*, no. 130, oct. 1963, 709–16.

'Distance, aspect, origine', *Critique*, no. 198, nov. 1963, 931–45 (on Robbe-Grillet, etc.)

'La prose d'Actéon', *N.R.F.*, no. 135, mars 1964, 444–59 (on Pierre Klossowski).

'Le langage de l'espace', *Critique*, no. 203, avril 1964, 378–82.

'Pourquoi réédite-t-on Raymond Roussel? Un précurseur de notre littérature moderne', *Le Monde*, 22–8–1964, 9.

'Le Mallarmé de J.-P. Richard', *Annales*, sept.–oct. 1964, 996–1004.

'L'Arrière-Fable', *L'Arc*, no. 29, 1966, 5–12 (on Jules Verne).

'La pensée du dehors', *Critique*, no. 229, juin 1966, 523–46 (on Maurice Blanchot).

'Nietzsche, Freud, Marx', *Cahiers du Royaumont*, Paris, Minuit, 1967.

'Un "fantastique" de bibliothèque', *Cahiers de la Compagnie Renaud-Barrault*, no. 59, mars 1967, 7–30 (Eng. trans., 'Fantasia of the Library', in LCP).

'Réponse à une question', *Esprit*, no. 371, mai 1968, 850–74.

'Réponse au Cercle d'épistémologie', *Cahiers pour l'analyse*, no. 9, été 1968.

'Ariane s'est pendue', *Le Nouvel Observateur*, no. 229, 31–3–1969, 36–7 (on Gilles Deleuze).

2'Qu'est-ce qu'un auteur?', *Bulletin de la Société française de philosophie*, t. LXIV, 1970, 73–104 (Eng. trans. 'What is an Author?', in LCP).

'Il y aura scandale, mais. . .', *Le Nouvel Observateur*, no. 304, 7–9–1970, 40 (on Pierre Guyotat).

'Theatrum Philosophicum', *Critique*, no. 282, nov. 1970, 885–908 (on Deleuze, Eng. trans. in LCP).

'Croître et multiplier', *Le Monde*, 15–11–1970 (on *La logique du vivant* by François Jacob).

3'Théories et institutions pénales', *Annuaire du Collège de France, 1971–72*, Paris 1971 (summary of M.F.'s course for the academic year 1971–2).

'Bachelard, le philosophe et son ombre . . .', *Le Figaro littéraire*, 30–9–1972.

'History, Discourse and Discontinuity', *Saligmundi*, no. 20, Summer/Fall 1972, 225–48.

V INTERVIEWS

Débat sur le roman (chaired by M.F.), *Tel Quel*, no. 17, printemps 1964.

'Nerval est-il le plus grand poète du XIXᵉ siècle?', *Arts*, 11–8–1964.

Entretien avec Raymond Bellour, *Les Lettres françaises*, no. 1125, 31–3–1966.

Entretien avec Madeleine Chapsal, *La Quinzaine littéraire*, 15–5–1966.

Entretien avec Claude Bonnefoy, 'L'Homme est-il mort?', *Arts et loisirs*, no. 38, 15–6–1966, 8–9.

4Deuxième entretien avec Raymond Bellour, *Les Lettres françaises*, no. 1187, 15–6–1967, 6–9 (republished in Raymond Bellour, *Le Livre des autres*, Paris, l'Herne, 1971).

Entretien, *Esprit*, avril 1968.

Entretien avec Jean-Jacques Brochier, *Magazine littéraire*, no. 28, avril–mai 1969, 23–5

'Foucault Responds', *Diacritics*, I, no. 2, Winter 1971, 60.

Entretien avec R. Mandrou, 'Histoire sociale et histoire des mentalités', *La nouvelle critique*, no. 49, janv. 1972.

5'Les Intellectuels et le pouvoir', *L'Arc*, no. 49, 1972 (with Gilles Deleuze; Eng. trans., 'Revolutionary Action: "Until Now" ', in LCP).

'Anti-rétro', entretien avec Pascal Bonitzer et Serge Toubidua, *Cahiers du Cinéma*, no. 251–2, juil.–août 1974.

6Entretien avec R. P. Droit, 'Des supplices aux cellules', *Le Monde*, 21–2–1975.

7Entretien, *Nouvelles littéraires*, 17–3–1975.

8'Entretien sur la prison: le livre et sa méthode' (with J.-L. Brochier),

Magazine littéraire, no. 101, juin 1975 (Eng. trans. by Colin Gordon, 'Prison Talk', *Radical Philosophy*, no. 16, Spring 1977).
Entretien avec K. S. Karol, *Le Nouvel Observateur*, 26–1–1976.
'Le Jeu de Michel Foucault', entrevue, *Ornicar?*, no. 10, 1977.
'Vérité et pouvoir', entretien avec M. Fontana, *L'Arc*, no. 70, 1977.
'La fonction politique de l'intellectuel', *Politique Hebdo*, no. 247, 29–11–1976 (Eng. trans. by Colin Gordon, 'The Political Function of the Intellectual', *Radical Philosophy*, no. 17, Summer 1977).

B. Works on Michel Foucault

I BOOKS

Annie Guédez, *Foucault*, Paris, Éditions Universitaires, 1972.
Angèle Kremer-Marietti, *Foucault*, Paris, Seghers, 1974.
Jean Baudrillard, *Oublier Foucault*, Paris, Galilée, 1977.

II BOOKS CONTAINING MATERIAL ON FOUCAULT

Jacques Derrida, *L'écriture et la différence*, Paris, Seuil, 1967. *Writing and Difference*, trans. Alan Bass, Evanston, Northwestern University Press and London, Routledge & Kegan Paul, 1978.
Mikel Dufrenne, *Pour l'Homme*, Paris, Seuil, 1968.
Jean Piaget, *Le Structuralisme*, Paris, P.U.F., 1968.
Michel Serres, *Hermès ou la communication*, Paris, P.U.F., 1968 (chap. 1 on HF and MC).
François Wahl, (ed.), *Qu'est-ce que le structuralisme?*, Paris, Seuil, 1968 (especially 299–441).
Roger Crémant, *Les matinées structuralistes*, Paris, Laffont, 1969.
Maurice Blanchot, *Entretien infini*, Paris, Gallimard, 1969 (on RR and HF).
Noël Mouloud, *Langage et structure*, Paris, Payot, 1969.
L. Millet and M. Varin d'Anvelle, *Le Structuralisme*, Paris, Éditions Universitaires, 1970.
Luc de Heusch, *Pourquoi l'épouser*, Paris, Gallimard, 1971.
Jean-Luc Chalumeau, *La pensée en France de Sartre à Foucault*, Paris, Nathan, 1971.
9Dominique Lecourt, *Pour une critique de l'épistémologie (Bachelard, Canguilhem, Foucault)*, Paris, Maspero, 1972 (on AS; Eng. trans. by Ben Brewster, *Marxism and Epistemology*, London, New Left Books, 1975).
David Robey, (ed), *Structuralism: An Introduction*, Oxford, Clarendon,

1973 (includes 'The Linguistic Basis of Structuralism' by Jonathan Culler).

Edward Said, *Beginnings: Methods and Intentions*, New York, Basic Books, 1975 (chap. 5 devoted largely to M.F.).

III ARTICLES

Roland Barthes, 'De part et d'autre', *Critique*, no. 174, nov. 1961, 915–22 (on HF, republished in *Essais Critiques*, Paris, Seuil, 1964, 167–74).

Jacques Derrida, 'Cogito et histoire de la folie', *Revue de métaphysique et de morale*, no. 4, 1963, 460–94 (on HF, republished in *L'écriture et la différence*, Paris, Seuil, 1967, 51–97).

Alain Robbe-Grillet, 'Énigmes et transparence chez Raymond Roussel', *Critique*, no. 199, déc. 1963, 1027–33 (on RR).

François Dagonet, 'Archéologie ou histoire de la médicine?', *Critique*, no. 216, mai 1965, 436–47 (on NC).

François Chatelet, 'L'Homme, ce narcisse incertain', *La Quinzaine littéraire*, 1–4–1966, 19–20 (on MC).

Gilles Deleuze, 'L'homme, une existence douteuse', *Le Nouvel Observateur*, 1–6–1966, 32–4 (on MC).

J.-M. Domenach, 'Une nouvelle passion', *Le Nouvel Observateur*, 20–7–1966, 26–7.

Michel Amiot, 'Le relativisme culturaliste de Michel Foucault', *Les Temps modernes*, no. 248, janv. 1967, 1271–98.

Sylvie Le Bon, 'Un positiviste désespéré', *Les Temps modernes*, no. 248, janv. 1967, 1299–1319 (on MC).

O. Revault d'Allone, 'Michel Foucault, les mots contre les choses', *Raison présente*, no. 2, fév.–mars 1967 (on MC).

Michel de Certeau, 'Les sciences humaines et la mort de l'homme', *Études*, t. 326, mars 1967, 344–60 (on MC).

Yves Bertherat, 'La pensée folle', *Esprit*, no. 5, mai 1967, 862–81.

Pierre Burgelin, 'L'archéologie du savoir', *Esprit*, no. 5, mai 1967, 843–61 (on MC).

R. D. Laing, 'Sanity and Madness—on the invention of Madness', *The New Statesman*, 16–6–1967 (on HF).

Gilles Deleuze, 'Un nouvel archéologue', *La Quinzaine littéraire*, 1–7–1967 (on MC).

Georges Canguilhem, 'Mort de l'homme ou épuisement du cogito', *Critique*, no. 242, juil. 1967, 599–618 (on MC).

François Chatelet, 'Où en est le structuralisme', *La Quinzaine littéraire*, 1–7–1967.

J.-C. Margolin, 'L'Homme de Michel Foucault', *Revue des sciences humaines*, t. 32, oct.–déc. 1967, fasc. 128 (on MC: 'Tribut d'un anti-humanisme aux études d'humanisme et de renaissance. Note sur l'oeuvre de Michel Foucault', *Bibliothèque d'humanisme et de renaissance*, t. 29, 1967, 701–11 (on MC).

B. Balan, G. Dulac, G. Marcy, J.-P. Ponthus, J. Proust, J. Stéfanini, and E. Verley, 'Entretiens sur Foucault', *La Pensée*, no. 137, jan.–fév. 1968, 3–37.

M. Corvez, 'Le Structuralisme de Michel Foucault', *Revue Thomiste*, t. 68, no. 1, janv.–mars 1968, 101–24.

P. Daix, 'Structure du structuralisme; II Althusser et Foucault', *Les Lettres françaises*, no. 1239, 3–9 juil. 1968, 7–11.

Maurice Cranston, 'Men and Ideas', *Encounter*, no. 30, 1968, 34–42.

J. Duvignaud, 'Ce qui parle en nous, pour nous, mais sans nous', *Le Nouvel Observateur*, 21–4–1969, 42–3.

Maurice Corvez, 'Les nouveaux structuralistes', *Revue philosophique de Louvain*, 67, no. 96, 1969, 582–605.

Roy McMullen, 'Michel Foucault', *Horizon*, 11–8–1969, 36–9.

Brice Parain, 'Michel Foucault: *L'archéologie du savoir*', *N.R.F.*, no. 203, 1–11–1969, 726–33.

David Paul Funt, 'The Structuralist Debate', *The Hudson Review*, 22, no. 4, 1969–70, 623–46.

Gilles Deleuze, 'Un nouvel archiviste', *Critique*, no. 274, mars 1970, 195–209 (on AS, republished as *Un Nouvel archiviste*, Montpellier, Fata Morgana, 1972).

N. Lacharite, 'Archéologie du savoir et structures du langage scientifique', *Dialogue*, t. 9, no. 1, juin 1970 (on AS).

Jean-Marc Pelorson, 'Michel Foucault et l'Espagne', *La Pensée*, no. 152, août 1970, 88–99.

Journées annuelles de l'évolution psychiatrique, Toulouse, déc. 1969, 'La conception idéologique de l'histoire de la folie de Michel Foucault', *Actes*, Toulouse, Privat, 1971.

Josette Hector, 'Michel Foucault et l'histoire', *Synthèses*, no. 309–10, mars–avril 1972.

Mark Seem, 'Liberation of Difference: Towards a theory of Antiliterature', *New Literary History*, no. 5, 1973, 121–34.

Hayden V. White, 'Foucault Decoded: Notes from Underground', *History and Theory*, 12, no. 1, 1973.

Marguerite Howe, 'Open Up a Few Corpses', *The Nation*, 26–1–1974, 117–19.

Christian Jambet, 'Une interrogation sur les prisons', *Le Monde*, 21–2–1975 (on SP).

Bernard-Henri Lévy, 'Le système Foucault', 7–9; Jacques Revel, 'Foucault et les historiens', 10–13; Marc Kravetz, 'Qu'est-ce que le

G.I.P.?', 13; Philippe Venault, 'Histoires de. . .', 14–19; Raymond Bellour, 'L'homme, les mots', *Magazine littéraire*, no. 101, juin 1975.

Jean-Marie Benoist, 'Le champ de la modernité,' *La Quinzaine Littéraire*, 16–31 oct. 1975, 21.

Jean Blot, 'Michel Foucault: *Surveiller et punir*', *N.R.F.*, no. 276, déc. 1975, 89–92.

10Gilles Deleuze, 'Écrivain non: un nouveau cartographe', 1207–27; François Ewald, 'Anatomie et corps politiques', 1228–65; Philippe Meyer, 'La correction paternelle ou l'état, domicile de la famille', 1266–76, *Critique*, no. 343, déc. 1975 (on SP).

Mark Seem, review of SP, *Telos*, no. 29, Fall 1976; 245–54.

Colin Gordon, 'Nasty Tales', *Radical Philosophy*, no. 15, Autumn 1976, 31–2 (on PR); 'Birth of the Subject', *Radical Philosophy*, no. 17, Summer 1977, 15–25.

François Chatelet, 'Récit', 3–15; Philippe Ariès, 'A propos de "La volonté de savoir" ', *L'Arc*, no. 70, 1977, 27–32.

Index

Index

Bosch, Hieronymus, 19–22
bourgeoisie, 71, 157, 167, 190–1, 220–2
Bouts, Thierry, 20
Brant, Sebastian, 20–1
Brecht, B., 201
Brueghel, Pieter, 19–20
Buffon, Georges, Comte de, 60, 102, 104–5

Canguilhem, Georges, 3, 6, 37, 91, 201, 232
capital, capitalism, 66, 157, 210
Castle of Otranto, 142
causality, 69, 92, 107, 129, 179, 185, 216
Ceci n'est pas une pipe, 88, 228
Cervantes, Miguel de: *Don Quixote*, 22, 52–3, 63–4
chance, notion of, 129
change, 107–9
character, 60, 66–7
Charcot, J.-M., 178, 189
children, 187; *see also* family; school
Christianity, 98, 115, 164–5, 173; *see also* confession; religion
chronology in historical analysis, 48
church, 98; *see also* Christianity; confession; religion
class, notion of, 139, 159–60
Classical age, 23, 25–6, 29, 32, 41, 44, 46–88, 91, 196, 212–14; *see also* Reason, Age of
classification, 49–50, 61, 66–7, 73; *see also* taxonomy
Collège de France, 21, 120, 131, 208
colonization, 161
commentary, 1, 124–6
communism, Communist parties, 5, 113, 197–8, 201–2, 204, 217, 221–2, 225; *see also* Leninism; Marxism; Stalinism
Comte, A., 220
Condillac, Etienne de, 54, 62, 66
confession, 140, 170–1, 177; *see also* Christianity; guilt

confinement, 23–39; *see also* penality; prison
conflict in economics, 83
continuity, notion of in history of ideas, 92, 103; *see also* discontinuity
contradictions, analysis of, 104
Cooper, David, 206
crime, 29, 142, 144, 158–60; *see also* penality; prison
criminal, 142–4; *see also* Rivière
cultural studies, 82
Cuvier, Georges, 54, 73–5, 104

Damiens, the 'regicide', 136
Darwin, Charles, 102
Daubenton, L. -J. -M., 57
death: of animality, 74; and individuality, 39, 43, 45, 69; in life, 42; and medicine, 36, 41–4, 74, 84–5, 192, 209; power of, 186; theme of, 19–20; and writing, 224–5
debauchery, 27, 173
Delacroix, E., 42
Deleuze, Gilles, 4, 47, 90, 114, 222, 224
delinquents, class of, 161
Descartes, René, 6, 23, 53, 57, 90, 149; Cartesian rationalism, 13, 57
desire, 84–5, 92, 180–1, 194
Destutt de Tracy, 54, 68
development, notion of, 71–2, 94
dialectic, 72–3
Dickens, Charles, 77
Diderot, Denis, 102, 105, 179
discipline, 135–6, 150–8, 219
Discipline and Punish, see Surveiller et punir
disciplines as principle of limitation in discourse, 126
discontinuity, notion of, 91–3, 109, 128–9, 205–6; *see also* continuity
discourse, 87–8, 210–11; access to, 127; analysis of, 115–31; as constituter of objects, 98–107; control of, 124–7; discourse

236

Index

God, 72–3, 81, 87, 118, 132–3, 159
Goldmann, L., 211
Goya, F. de, 23, 42
Grammaire de Port-Royal, 91, 104, 228
Gramsci, A., 201
Grimm, W. K., 75
Groupe d'Information sur les Prisons, 130, 132
Grünewald, Matthias, 20
Guibert, H. de, 152
guilt, organized, 34–5; *see also* confession

Hegel, Georg W. F., 3, 23, 66, 79–80, 116, 205, 220
Heidegger, Martin, 4, 204
Herkunft, 117–18, 138
Histoire de la folie, viii, 3, 8, 11–45, 47, 73, 80, 115, 164, 195, 204, 206–9, 213, 224, 227
historical *a priori*, 102
history: 67, 83, 85, 91–4, 109, 118, 195, 197, 201, 205, 208, 212–13, 218; and archaeology, 14; as arrangement of knowledge, 65; general history, 92; historicism, 204; historicity, 70, 74; *historie, wirkliche*, 119, 180, 205, 218; of ideas, 14, 91–110 *passim*, 208; and Marxism, 70–3; movement away from, 198–200; periodization in, 91; research into, 129–34; of science, 6, 48–9, 103, 201; of thought, 96; total history, 92
History of Sexuality, The, viii, 8, 12, 224, 228; *see also volonté de savoir, La*
Hölderlin, Johann C., 12, 36, 43–4, 46
Hommage à Jean Hyppolite, viii, 227; *see also* Hyppolite
homosexuality, 27–8, 174; *see also* sexuality
Hôpital général, founding of, 24, 28, 31
hospitals, 23; and discipline, 150–1,

153, 155; reorganization of, 40; *see also* medicine
Hôtel Dieu, 29
Human, All Too Human, 118
humanism, 71, 79
human sciences, 38–9, 43, 45, 48–9, 78–9, 82–4, 90, 157, 162–3, 177, 210
Husserl, Edmund, 3–4, 79, 204
Hyppolite, Jean, 3, 6, 115; *see also Hommage à Jean Hyppolite*
hystericization of female body, 187, 190

I, Pierre Rivière, see Moi, Pierre Rivière
Idealism, 210–11, 217, 220
ideas, *see* history of
Idéologues, 68, 145, 148
ideology and history, 40, 93, 106; ideology, Marxist concept, 210
incest prohibition, 188–9, 193
individual, 67; and knowledge, 43–4; and power, 155–6; as social being, 30; *see also* death
influence, notion of, 93–4
insanity, *see* folly; madness; unreason
intellectual, the, 222
interpositivity in discursive formations, 106
interpretation, 76, 101, 217, 221

Jackson, Hughlings, 5, 44
Jakobson, Roman, 37, 200, 221
Janet, Pierre, 5
Jones, William, 67
Jonston, 57–8
Joyce, James, 94, 124
Julius, N. H., 157
Jussieu, B. de, 66–7

Kafka, Franz, 224
Kant, Emmanuel, 68–9, 81, 228
Kaufmann, Walter, 225
Kierkegaard, Søren, 3
Klossowski, Pierre, 47
knowledge, 8, 48, 51, 56, 67, 71–2,

Index

75, 77–9, 84, 87, 121, 152, 206,
214–15; and discursive practices,
109; and history, 65; and the
individual, 44; language as, 77;
modern, 79–80; positive
unconscious of, 49; and power,
131, 138, 140, 161–3, 165, 172,
217, 220–1; scientific, 78–9; secret,
2–3; system of, 54; will to, 119,
123, 165, 170, 206; *see also*
archéologie du savoir, L'; *volonté de
savoir, La*
Kraepelin, Emil, 5

La Salle, J. B. de, 149, 151
labour, 24–5, 66–9
Lacan, J., 1, 38, 47, 86, 180,
199–200, 202, 204; *see also* Freud;
psychoanalysis
Laing, R. D., 206, 232
Lamarck, Jean Baptiste, 67, 73–4
Lamartine, A. de, 42
language, 48–55, 67–78, 82–3, 87,
92, 100, 127, 199–201; as act, 90;
as discourse, 56, 121; of
exclusion, 14–15; as freedom, 75;
as function, 55; as knowledge,
77; and literature, 86; and
medicine, 36–8, 40, 43; and
Nietzsche, 77–8; of psychiatry,
14–15; as representation, 49, 52,
55, 61; signification in, 83; *see also*
grammar; linguistics; structural
linguistics
Language, Counter-Memory, Practice,
viii, 47, 228
La Salpetrière, 178
Lautréamont, 50
law, 84–5, 165; as authority of
delimitation, 98; and death, 45;
and madness, 29–30, 33; and
rich, 159–60; and sexuality,
172–3, 180–1, 189–90
Law, John, 62
Lecourt, Dominique, 214–17, 231;
see also Althusser
Left, 71, 73, 114, 197; *see also*

communism; Leninism; Marxism;
Stalinism
legal systems, 137, 143–4
Lenin, Leninism, 201–2; *see also*
communism; Marxism;
Stalinism
leprosy, 17, 25, 42
Le Roy Ladurie, E., 128
Lévi-Strauss, Claude, 1, 38, 47, 86,
198, 200–2, 204; *see also*
ethnology, structuralism
libertinage, 27–8
life, 42, 68, 73–4, 190–2, 224–5; *see
also* biology
linguistics: 73, 84, 92–3, 199–203,
221; structural linguistics, 199–203;
see also language
Linnaeus, Carl, 30, 58–60, 102, 104;
see also natural history
literature, 21, 76–7, 82, 86, 94, 103,
123–5, 177, 200; and sexuality,
177
Lukàcs, G., 211
Lysenko, 11

macabre (and morbid), 42
machine, body as, 149
madness, 7–8, 12, 97–8, 207;
alchemy as, 27; as animality, 30;
discourse and, 21, 122; dreams
and, 21, 23; error and, 23; history
and, 15; as judgement, 13; in *King
Lear*, 16–17; and law, 29–30; and
libertinage, 27–8; and medicine,
29–30; literature and, 21; Medieval
idea of, 17, 19, 25; as natural
history, 30; and perversion, 174;
phenomenology and, 23; Reason,
Age of, and, 22–34; religion as, 34;
Renaissance idea of, 16–22; and
sexuality, 27; as substitute
for leprosy, 17, 25; treatment
of, 13–45; as undifferentiated
experience, 14; as unreason,
23–4, 27–9; water and, 18; *see
also* asylum; folly; reason;
Rivière

239

Index

Index

Reason, Age of, 22–34, 80–2; *see also* Classical age

reformatories, 147; *see also* prison

religion, 94; and asylum, 33–4; *see also* Christianity; confession

Renaissance, 16–22, 51, 55, 59, 61, 75, 79, 206, 210

repetition, 125; and Kierkegaard, 3

representation, 49–52, 54, 55, 61, 67–8, 72, 74–5, 77–9, 82–4, 114, 211, 221

repression, sexual (and 'tolerance'), 12, 166–7, 170–1

resemblance, 51, 53; *see also* similitude

Ricardo, David, 54, 61, 69–70, 73, 104, 212; *see also* economy

Rilke, R. M., 44

ritual, as system of restriction, 126–7

rituals of power, 155

Rivière, Pierre, 131–4, 223; *see also Moi, Pierre Rivière*

Robbe-Grillet, Alain, 47, 232

Romanticism, 39, 43, 77, 83

Rotrou, Jean de, 22

Rousseau, J. -J., 54

Roussel, Raymond, 12, 46–7, 86, 227, 229

Sade, Marquis de, 23, 27–8, 63–4, 74, 80, 171

sadism, 8

Same and the Other, 46, 49, 52, 80

Sartre, J. -P., 4, 90, 203–4

Saussure, F. de, 37, 91, 200, 221

Saxe, Marshall de, 149

Schlegel, F. von, 74

school, 2, 150–1, 153, 155, 172, 175–6; *see also* children; discipline

Schopenhauer, A., 79

science, 94, 103, 109–10, 220; history of, 48–9, 201; and language, 75; medicine as, 38–9; and reason, 78–81; of sexuality, 176–8; socialist, 11; *see also* human sciences

scientia sexualis, 176

Scudéry, G., 22

semiology, 203

sentence, 99–100; *see also* statements

Serres, Michel, 91, 231

Servan, J., 145

sex, 223; moralizing and, 190–1; and sexuality, 194

sexuality: 164–93, 223; and Christianity, 164–5, 173; and confession, 170, 176–7; defined, 223; in discourse, 122, 169–73, 177–8; evangelism of, 168; and family, 27, 186–90, 193; and law, 172–3, 181, 190; and liberation, 164; and literature, 177; machinery of, 187–90, 194, 223; and madness, 27, 97–8; and medicine, 172, 175–6; and micro-penality, 154; and moralizing, 190–1; multiple, 175–6; perversions in, 173–6, 187; and population problem, 171–2; and power, 165–7, 173–6, 180–6; and procreation, 166; and prohibition, 122; and psychoanalysis, 167, 179–80, 189–90, 193; and repression, 165–71, 179–81, 190; in school, 172, 175–6; science of, 176–8; and sex, 194; strategies of, 187–8; as surface of emergence, 97–8; and truth, 178–9; *see also* body; *History of Sexuality*; homosexuality

Shakespeare, W.: 6, 22, 211; *King Lear*, 16–17

Ship of Fools, 17–19, 23

sign, (signifier, signified), 37–8, 52–6, 61, 83, 91, 98–100, 106, 117, 128–9, 194, 200

similitude, 52–3; *see also* resemblance

Smith, Adam, 66–9, 212

social anthropology, *see* ethnology

Socialist Realism, 201

sociology, 82–3

sodomy, 174

Index

soul: and body, 140, 148, 219; as grid of specification, 98; punishment and, 137–8, 148
space, 36, 43, 51
spirit, notion of, 94, 105
Stalin, Stalinism, 114, 197–8, 221; *see also* communism; Leninism; Marxism
statements, 96, 99–102, 123; rarity of, 101; relations between, 96; site of, 99
status of speaker, 99
structuralism, 37–8, 89–91, 200–4, 210; *see also* linguistics
structure, 59–60, 67, 92, 105, 129, 208
style, literary, 1, 223–4
subject, 93, 100, 102, 119–20, 127, 198–9, 202–4
Surveiller et punir, viii–ix, 119, 135–63, 165, 192, 217–20, 223, 225
sympathy, 51, 142

table, *tabula*, 49, 71–2, 78; *see also* classification
tactics and discipline, 151
taxonomy, 49, 55, 73, 74; *see also* classification; order; table
teleology, 97, 117
text, 100–1, 104
thought, 80–1, 96
time, 65, 154
time-table, 151
Tolstoy, L., 77
torture, 136–7, 140–1, 144
totalization: notion of in history of ideas, 97, 103; of political struggle, 139–40
Tournefort, 57
tradition, notion of, 93
transformation, 104, 109

'transformism', 73
translation, 16, 37
treatment of madness, 13–45
Tristan L'Hermite, L., 22
Triumph of Death, 19
truth, 18–19, 40, 77, 109, 118, 123–4, 126, 204–6, 217, 220, 222–4; will to, 119, 123–5, 128, 179, 206, 224; *see also* confession; torture
Tuke, Samuel, 33–5
Turgot, A. R., 54

unconscious, 84–6, 164; *see also* Freud; psychoanalysis
unreason, 7, 23–4, 27, 36, 43, 73, 80; *see also* madness; reason
unthought, 79–80
Ursprung, 117–18; *see also* origin
utopias, 72

value, 62, 66, 69, 73
Van Gogh, Vincent, 12
Velázquez, Diego: *Las Meninas*, 50–1
Vermeil, F. M., 146
Victorians, 166–7, 171
Vincennes campus, 114–15
Viq d'Azyr, 67
volonté de savoir, La, ix, 119–24, 164–94, 217, 223–4, 228; *see also* knowledge

war, 192
water and madness, 18
wealth, *see* analysis of
Will to Knowledge, The, see volonté de savoir, La
Wittgenstein, Ludwig, 95
writing, 52–3; and death, 224–5

243